W9-CHS-470

$\mathcal{F}$ar and Wide

ESSAYS FROM CANADA

REFLECTIONS IN NON-FICTION

EDITED BY SEAN ARMSTRONG

▛ Nelson Canada

I(T)P   An International Thomson Publishing Company

Toronto • Albany • Bonn • Boston • Cincinnati • Detroit • London
Madrid • Melbourne • Mexico City • New York • Pacific Grove
Paris • San Francisco • Singapore • Tokyo • Washington

I(T)P™

International Thomson Publishing
The trademark ITP is used under licence

© Nelson Canada,
A Division of Thomson Canada Limited, 1995

Published in Canada by
Nelson Canada,
A Division of Thomson Canada Limited
1120 Birchmount Road
Scarborough, Ontario
M1K 5G4

ISBN 0-17-604705-0

Project Editor: Tara Steele
Production Editor: Bob Kohlmeier
Art Director: Liz Nyman
Series Design: Tracy Walker
Cover Design: Hania Fil
Cover Illustration: Simon Ng
Typesetting: Alicja Jamorski

Printed and bound in Canada by
Best Book Manufacturers

234567890 / BGBM / 109876

Canadian Cataloguing in Publication Data

Main entry under title:

Far and wide: essays from Canada

Includes index.
ISBN 0-17-604705-0

1. Canadian essays (English)–20th century.*
2. Canada–Literary collections. I. Armstrong,
Sean.

PS8365.F37 1995 C814' .540803271 C94-931200-2
PR9197.7.F37 1995

Reviewers

The publishers thank the following
people, who contributed their
valuable expertise during the
development of this book:

Terry Benbow, Collingwood, Ont.
Bob Bilan, Winnipeg, Man.
Anne Carrier, Toronto, Ont.
Gordon Francis, Bay Roberts, Nfld.
Dave Kelly, Calgary, Alta.
Joanne LeBlanc-Haley, Fredericton,
    N.B.
Regina Maher, Saskatoon, Sask.
Nazira Mawji, Whitby, Ont.
Greg Ponsart, Burnaby, B.C.
Stefan Sierakowski, Agincourt, Ont.
Sylvia Unkovich, Vancouver, B.C.

↶ CONTENTS

ℰ INDEX OF GENRES

ℰ INDEX OF ALTERNATE THEMES

Canada with its division of races presents no common denominator in those profundities which normally unite, in race, language, religion, history and culture. If a common focus is to be found, it must come out of the common homeland itself. If the Canadian people are to find their soul, they must seek for it not in the English language, or the French, but in the little ports of the Atlantic provinces, in the flaming autumn maples of the St. Lawrence Valley, in the portages and lakes of the Canadian Shield, in the sunsets and relentless cold of the prairies, in the foothill, mountain and sea of the west and in the unconquerable vastness of the north. From the land, Canada, must come the soul of Canada.

— A.R.M. Lower
from *Colony to Nation*

FOREWORD

Non-fiction writing surrounds us, but there is something that sets an essay apart. Perhaps it is the element of reflection, the perspective arrived at by thinking something over and assembling an understanding of it.

The essays in this collection come from Canadians whose traditions are as varied as those represented by the ancestors of Carol Geddes, David Suzuki, and Rohinton Mistry. As a country, we have never been able to agree on our definition of who we are. But our common awareness of the land ties us together and dominates our history, as Robert Fulford points out in "The Lesson of Canadian Geography."

While a memoir by Janice McCurdy Banigan reminds us of unpleasant aspects of our past, and Drew Hayden Taylor takes an amused look at one of our many culture clashes, esssays by Michael Ignatieff and Janice Kulyk Keefer remind us that many people came to Canada to escape conditions far worse. Josh Freed pokes fun at our national character, W.O. Mitchell and Ray Guy remember childhoods in different parts of the country, and Roch Carrier wonders whether we can keep the kind of Canada we grew up with.

Today, we all carry apprehensions about the future of our natural environment and about the tremendous power of our technology. Adrian Forsyth cautions us about the interaction of the two, Margaret Atwood offers a grim satirical view of our worst possible future, Ursula Franklin talks about how technology changes our ways of seeing the world, and Dan Strickland comments on how we take the natural world for granted.

People write about issues, but they also write for pleasure. We hear the voices of those who enjoy writing, as when Moira Farr tells us what she learned from a popular magazine, when Mordecai Richler remembers how he was changed by a novel, or when Rudy Wiebe describes coming to the end of a long search.

The word "essay" comes from the French *essayer*, meaning "to attempt." At bottom, then, an essay is an attempt to express a personal understanding. In these essays, all recent, many by familiar authors, you will hear a variety of personal voices attempting to express who they are and what they value.

Pretty like a White Boy: The Adventures of a Blue-Eyed Ojibway

BY DREW HAYDEN TAYLOR

"I once was described as a slightly chubby beach boy. But even beach boys have tans... "

In this big world, with all its billions and billions of people, it's safe to say that everybody will eventually come across personalities and individuals that will touch them in some peculiar yet poignant way. Individuals that in some way represent and help define who you are. I'm no different; mine was Kermit the Frog. Not just because natives have a long tradition of savouring frogs' legs, but because of his music. As you may remember, Kermit is quite famous for his rendition of "It's Not Easy Being Green." I can relate. If I could sing, my song would be "It's Not Easy Having Blue Eyes in a Brown-Eyed Village."

Yes, I'm afraid it's true. The author happens to be a card-carrying Indian. Once you get past the aforementioned eyes, the fair skin, light brown hair and noticeable lack of cheekbones, there lies the heart and spirit of an Ojibway storyteller. Honest Injun, or as the more politically correct term may be, honest aboriginal.

You see, I'm the product of a white father I never knew and an Ojibway woman with poor judgment. As a kid I knew I looked a bit different. But, then again, all kids are paranoid when it comes to their peers. I had a fairly happy childhood, frolicking through the bullrushes. But there were certain things that, even then, made me notice my unusual appearance. Whenever we played cowboys and Indians, guess who had to be the bad guy, the cowboy.

It wasn't until I left the reserve for the big bad city that I became more aware of the role people expected me to play and the fact that physically I didn't fit in. Everybody seemed to have this preconceived idea of how an Indian looked and acted. One guy, on my first day of college, asked me what kind of horse I preferred. I didn't have the heart to tell him "hobby."

I've often tried to be philosophical about the whole thing. I have both white and red blood in me; I guess that makes me pink. I am a "pink" man. Try to imagine this, I'm walking around on any typical reserve in Canada, my head held high, proudly announcing to everyone, "I am a pink man." It's a good thing I ran track in school.

My pinkness is constantly being pointed out to me. "You don't look Indian." "You're not Indian, are you?" "Really?!?" I get questions like that from both white and native people; for a while I debated having my status card tattooed on my forehead.

And like most insecure people—and especially as a blue-eyed native writer—I went through a particularly severe identity crisis at one point. In fact, I admit it, one depressing spring evening I dyed my hair black. Pitch black.

What was the reason for such a dramatic act, you may ask? Show Business. You see, for the last eight years or so, I've worked in various capacities in the performing arts and as a result I would get calls to be an extra or even to try out for an important role in some native-oriented movie. This anonymous person would phone, having been given my number, and ask if I would be interested in trying out for a movie. Being a naturally ambitious, curious and greedy young man, I would always readily agree, stardom flashing in my eyes and hunger pangs from my wallet.

A few days later I would show up for the audition. That was always an experience. What kind of experience, you may ask? Picture this: the film requires seventeenth-century Mohawk warriors living in a traditional long-house. The casting director calls the name "Drew Hayden Taylor" and I enter.

The casting director, the producer and the film's director would look up from the table and see my face, blue eyes flashing in anticipation. I once was described as a slightly chubby beach boy. But even beach boys have tans. Anyway, there would be a quick flush of confusion, a check of the papers and a hesitant "Mister Taylor?" Then they would ask if I was at the right audition. It was always the same. I never got any part I tried for, except in a few anonymous crowd shots. Politics tells me it's because of the way I look; reality tells me it's probably because I can't act. I'm not sure which is better.

It's not just film people either. Recently I've become quite involved in theatre—native theatre, to be exact. One cold October day I was happily attending the Toronto leg of a provincewide tour of my first play, *Toronto at Dreamer's Rock*. The place was sold out, the audience very receptive and the performance was wonderful. One of the actors was also half white.

The director later told me he had been talking with that actor's father, an older non-native chap. Evidently he had asked a few questions about me and how I did my research. This made the director curious and he asked about the man's interest. The father replied, "He's got an amazing grasp of the native situation for a white person."

Not all these incidents are work-related either. One time a friend and I were coming out of a rather upscale bar (we were out yuppie-watching) and managed to catch a cab. We thanked the cab driver for being so comfortably close on such a cold night. He shrugged and nonchalantly talked about knowing what bars to drive around. "If you're not careful, all you'll get is drunk Indians." I hiccupped.

Another time, a cab driver droned on and on about the government. He started out by criticizing Mulroney and eventually to his handling of the Oka crisis. This perked up my ears, until he said, "If it were me, I'd have tear-gassed the place by the second day. No more problem." He got a dime for a tip. A few incidents like this and I'm convinced I'd make a great undercover agent for one of the native political organizations.

But then again, even native people have been known to look at me with a fair amount of suspicion. Many years ago when I was a young man, I was working on a documentary on native culture up in the woods of northern Ontario. We were at an isolated cabin filming a trapper woman and her kids. This one particular nine-year-old girl seemed to take a shine to me. She followed me around for two days, both annoying me and endearing herself to me. But she absolutely refused to believe that I was Indian. The whole film crew tried to tell her, but to no avail. She was certain I was white.

Then one day as I was loading up the car with film equipment, she asked me if I wanted some tea. As I was in a hurry, I declined. She immediately smiled in victory, crying out, "See, you're not Indian, all Indians drink tea!"

Frustrated and a little hurt I whipped out my status card and thrust it at her. There I was, standing in a northern Ontario winter, showing my status card to a nine-year-old nonstatus Indian girl who had no idea what one was. Looking back, this may not have been one of my brighter moves.

But I must admit, it was a native woman that boiled everything down into one simple sentence. You may know of that woman—Marianne Jones from *The Beachcombers* television series. We were working on a film together out west and we got to gossiping. Eventually, we started to talk about our respective villages—hers on the Queen Charlotte Islands, or Haida Gwaii as the Haida call them, and mine in central Ontario.

Eventually, childhood on the reserve was discussed and I made a comment about the way I look. She studied me for a moment, smiled and said, "Do you know what the old women in my village would call you?" Hesitant but curious, I shook my head. "They'd say you were pretty like a white boy." To this day, I'm still not sure if I like that.

Now some may argue that I am simply a Métis with a status card. I disagree; I failed French in grade 11. And the Métis, as everyone knows, have their own separate and honourable culture, particularly in western Canada. And of course I am well aware that I am not the only person with my physical characteristics.

I remember once looking at a videotape of a drum group, shot on a reserve up near Manitoulin Island. I noticed one of the drummers seemed quite fair-haired, almost blond. I mentioned this to my girlfriend of the time. She shrugged, saying, "Well, that's to be expected. The highway runs right through the reserve."

Perhaps I'm being too critical. There's a lot to be said for both cultures. For example, on the left hand, you have the native respect for elders. They understand the concept of wisdom and insight coming with age.

On the white hand, there's Italian food. I mean, I really love my mother and family, but seriously, does anything really beat good veal scaloppine? Most of my aboriginal friends share my fondness for this particular kind of food. Wasn't there a warrior at Oka named Lasagna? I found it ironic, though curiously logical, that Columbus was Italian. A connection, I wonder?

Native people also have this wonderful respect and love for the land. They believe they are part of it, a mere link in the cycle of existence. Now as many of you know, this conflicts with the accepted Judaeo-Christian— i.e., Western—view of land management. I even believe somewhere in the first chapters of the Bible it says something about God giving man dominion over nature. Check it out, Genesis 4:?: "Thou shalt clearcut." So I grew up understanding that everything around me is important and alive. My native heritage gave me that.

And again, on the white hand, there's breast implants. Darn clever, them white people. That's something Indians would never have invented, seriously. We're not ambitious enough. We just take what the Creator decides to give us; but no, not the white man. Just imagine it, some serious-looking white man—and let's face it, people, we know it was a man who invented them, don't we—some serious-looking white doctor sitting around in his laboratory muttering to himself, "Big tits, big tits, hmm, how do I make big tits?"

So where does that leave me on the big philosophical scoreboard? What exactly are my choices again? Indians: respect for elders, love of the land. White people: food and big breasts.

In order to live in both cultures I guess I'd have to find an Indian woman with big breasts who lives with her grandmother in a cabin out in the woods and can make fettucini alfredo on a wood stove.

Now let me make this clear. I'm not writing this for sympathy or out of anger or even some need for self-glorification. I am just setting the facts straight. For as you read this, a new nation is born. This is a declaration of independence—my declaration of independence.

I've spent too many years explaining who and what I am repeatedly, so as of this moment I officially secede from both races. I plan to start my own separate nation. Because I am half Ojibway and half Caucasian, we will be called the Ocasians. And since I'm founding the new nation, I will be a Special Ocasian.

Prairie Summer

BY W.O. MITCHELL

A well-known writer describes the effect of growing up on the prairie.

e The first 12 years of my life were spent on the Saskatchewan billiard table south of Regina, and this childhood geography has had a great deal to do with the rest of my life. The late novelist and historian Wallace Stegner, who was a prairie boy from East End, Sask., said in *Wolf Willow* that the prairie should create poets. I agree with him; all that land and all that sky has done so, whether the prairie of mid-America, the moors of England, the steppes of Russia, teaching early in life that to be human means to be conscious of self, separate from all the rest of the living whole. Human, therefore, equals lonely. The cost of being aware of an inner self that can mirror the outer remainder of the whole has an outrageously high price in loneliness. It is impossible to rejoin the living whole to ease the pain of human loneliness except by dying. That works in the end.

I wonder that being a prairie human we do not have to pay a higher loneliness price because we have such a shallow and recent past, whether we realize it or not—that our part of the earth's skin is really still both wild and tame. We have no medieval cathedrals with soaring Gothic arches to awe and to comfort us with ancestor echo; we do not unearth Roman baths and walls and roads. Here in Canada, really, we are the newest of the New World. My own generation was newest of all. We were the first whites to be born and stained in childhood by the prairie west. It is difficult to be much newer than that and, therefore, historically lonelier.

As a child, I wandered over the prairie a great deal, with the prairie wind dirging for me on the great prairie harp of telephone wires; they hummed and they twanged and seemed to adjust themselves endlessly against the prairie stillness. I can remember barbed-wire fences, hung with butterflies, grasshoppers, perhaps field mice, impaled there, the shrike's supermarket. In winter, bird prints in the snow, the alternating tracks of a coyote, the domino ones of jack-rabbits, all signalled animal life to me, not human. Very young I felt the total thrust of the prairie sun upon my vulnerable and mortal head. I looked down to the dry husks of dead gophers, crawling with ants and flies and undertaker beetles, worked over by black-and-white surpliced magpies. Again and again the skipping lift of a prairie meadowlark's song surprised me.

In my new world, at a very young age, I learned I was mortal: I could die—the end of Billy Mitchell. The humming, living prairie of old did not give one good goddamn about that. My mother, brothers and friends did, and my grandmother and Auntie Josie perhaps. When you learn you are going to die you truly understand that you are human. You have been then given a perspective that is very helpful in deciding what is important and what is unimportant, valuable and not valuable.

For all of us, summer was our favourite season. Ours always began, logically, on May 24, when we would walk out past the fairgrounds and Miss Hart's three little cottages on the eastern edge of town. Miss Hart seemed to have an awful lot of nieces living out there with her. She pulled out of Weyburn in 1925 and moved to Calgary. I'm almost certain that she changed her name to Pearl White and opened her famous Mount Royal bordello.

But enough of houses of ill repute; let's get back to prairie summer. We were all headed for the Little Souris for our first swim of the year. Naked, of course, and watched by several outpatients from the provincial mental hospital just upstream from our swimming hole. Several are vivid in my memory: Buffalo Billy in 10-gallon hat and hairy chaps, with his two toy six-shooters in hip holsters; and Blind Jesus, not in the usual green hospital-gown uniform but in pure white, his arms outstretched in the crucified position as he stared upward, always directly into the sun. That was how he had blinded himself.

For me, the best part of the summer was July and August, when in the McLaughlin touring car we drove the 80 miles east to our cottage at Carlyle Lake on an Assiniboine and Saulteaux Indian reserve. Here, the Black Hills of the Dakotas trickled out. We welcomed the sight of cottonwood and birch trees we hadn't seen since the summer before, the smell of leaf mould and the perfume of wolf willow. The vivid orange of hillside tiger lilies with their freckled throats and all those horses grazing with a new crop of stilting colts.

Every year old Sheepskin would be across the road in front of our cottage, seated in the lotus position like a Buddha under the cottonwood and saskatoon, smoking his clay pipe. My brother Bobbie and I and Sheepskin bonded to one another. Very early we managed to establish communication even though Sheepskin spoke virtually no English and we couldn't handle Saulteaux.

Sheepskin did know a few monosyllabic words in English. Words like *you*, *him* and *me*. He communicated with us in other ways too: a back toss of his head and a curved thumb thrown back over a shoulder followed by palms, down and flattened out, spreading wide, meant "all them others." A sharp chop at the elbow certainly meant "Shut up!"

There was another signal the old man used often. It was a long drawn-out "Shhhhhhhhh... ," which ended with a short, sharp and punctuating "Tuh!"

The old man broke wind. The wild smell lingered long, overpowering the campfire and buckskin smell that always breathed up from him. It was just a natural event, like the squeak of a gopher, the quick skipping notes of a meadowlark, the cawing of a crow.

I guessed the old man to be in his very late seventies or perhaps early eighties. So he would have hunted hundreds of buffalo as an adolescent, most likely far to the west in the Cypress Hills, where the dwindling herds sought refuge from "civilized" hunters. He had missed smallpox and tuberculosis and venereal disease to survive most of his life on wild game.

Sheepskin would show up daily in his democrat with a young woman and her baby. His granddaughter and his great-granddaughter, we guessed. The woman would unsling the baby and prop her up against a birch tree trunk, unhitch and hobble the team to graze in a new spot, spread out a blanket, load it with beaded jackets and moccasins for sale. She would rim the blanket with Maple Leaf lard pails filled with saskatoon berries, pin- or chokecherries or wild raspberries. This location in front of our cottage was a good business spot for them, for our road was the main access route to the beach and the hotel, and sooner or later cottagers and weekenders would pass and stop and buy.

I did business with Sheepskin. Each year I would gather a supply of discarded boots from McCormick's Harness and Shoe Repair in Weyburn. Bobbie and I and Sheepskin traded: one pair of boots for a bow and arrows fletched with wild goose feathers; three pairs of boots for one boy's-size fringed and beaded buckskin jacket. Most important of all: four pairs of boots for one shaganappi pony to ride for one week bareback with Bobbie, taking turns at who would have the lines and who would sit with his arms around his brother's middle. We were the only mounted whites at Carlyle Lake all those summers.

Actually, in retrospect, I think the young woman with the baby might have been Sheepskin's wife.

Bobbie and I were the only people at Carlyle Lake who prayed for wind. Without rain. We ached for whitecaps, listened for the tapping of leaves and sighs through the birches. I may even have considered asking Sheepskin if there was a wind dance as well as a rain dance he could do for us.

We had a 16-foot Peterborough canoe and, given wind, would step a short mast in the bow and hang it with a lateen sail, lower the leeboards and take off over the lake. I was always the skipper in the stern with a paddle for a rudder and the sheet line in my teeth. Bobbie crouched midship, gripping the gunwales with both hands, ready to lift his butt up and out on the canoe rim so when the sail bellied he could hang out to contradict the wind. Again and again there would be a fear thrill as we tried to marry the wind gusts in our thirsty shell, tipping and gulping water over the sides.

Our mother had an understanding with Mr. Diamond, the hotel owner, that if we capsized, the hotel launch would come to our rescue. It did so a couple of times each summer.

I was ten and Bobbie was eight the first summer we sailed the length and breadth of Carlyle Lake, our broad Atlantic. When we would beach on the far side we were the only humans over there. We would strip and play Tarzan of the Apes, climb a giant cottonwood to swing from branch to branch, then drop from the big bough that hung out over the water. This was truly dangerous, for in the tree's main crotch was a grey paper wasps' nest. One Sunday afternoon when my foot slipped, the wasps got to *my* crotch. They stung my genitals, both cheeks, chest and arms before I could drop into the water. There was no way I could skip the canoe back over the lake, so I had to turn the sheet and the paddle-rudder over to Bobbie. A hundred yards offshore we turtled. We managed to unstep the mast and lateen and get the leeboards off, but the canoe resisted all our efforts to right it. We decided to rest awhile, and as we did I realized that the cool lake water had softened my wasp stings some.

We decided we'd better dive and come up under the canoe and check out if the clothes we should have put on before disembarking were still there. They were. We stayed under. Very early in our canoe life, Bobbie and I had discovered the green luminous bubble under a capsized canoe with the water's slap, tap and gurgle amplified. It was a magic place of wandering shadow and the glimmer of reflected light on the shell above our heads. Our voices became resonant and importantly hollow sounding, solemn and grown-up.

Bobbie was the first to duck his face below the water surface, to suck and gargle, then squirt me. Our usual water fight followed. I heard a ticking sound faint and far off. I wasn't sure I was hearing it, but the tightening of Bobbie's face told me I *was*. We both came out from under, and there it was, a hundred yards away: the hotel launch with a dozen passengers under the fringed canopy taking their Sunday afternoon sightseeing cruise. And us knacker-naked! We dived back under the canoe.

Hanging on to our thwarts, our worst fears were realized as the launch stopped, then circled our canoe for almost half an hour. Thank God neither the pilot nor the passengers knew about our magic air bubble. They gave up and took off to tell our mother about another Mitchell boys' tip-over and that, alas, there had been no sign of either of them or their drowned bodies.

When they'd left, Bobbie and I swam to shore, shoving the canoe ahead of us. We righted her and bailed her out. This time, we put on our clothes, wet as they were, but we didn't step the mast or lower the lee-boards; we paddled all the way back to the opposite side. Often in recall dreams I have been under that magic bubble, and I've apologized for what we put our mother through. She strapped us both, grounded us for a week and made us haul the canoe out for the rest of the summer.

Here was the least common denominator of nature, the skeleton requirements simply of land and sky—Saskatchewan prairie. It lay wide around the town, stretching tan to the far line of the sky, clumped with low back brush and wild rose bushes shimmering under the late June sun and waiting for the unfailing visitation of wind, gentle at first, barely stroking the long grasses and giving them life; later, a long, hot gusting that would lift the black top-soil and pile it in barrow pits along the roads or in deep banks against the fences.

That's the opening of a book I once wrote—my first novel, *Who Has Seen the Wind*.

I was born in 1914, too soon for universal pasteurization of milk, so that I picked up bovine tuberculosis and for a whole year I was taken out of Haig School. I was the only kid alive in Weyburn or Saskatchewan, or Canada for that matter, between the hours of nine and four. I used to wander up Sixth Street to the prairie beyond, and because of all those hours alone out there—talking to myself, smelling, seeing, hearing—I ended up a writer.

Prairie distance between neighbours probably makes us try harder than others to bridge that distance. It explains why, perhaps, I became a writer, seeking creative partners in print.

I agree with Wallace Stegner. The prairie, with all that sky and all that horizon, does produce creative people. Look at Dostoevsky, Pushkin, Tolstoy—not much difference, I suppose, between the steppes of Russia and the steppes of Saskatchewan.

All Quiet on the Northern Front

BY JOSH FREED

"Put a Yankee and a Canuck at a hotel fire, and they describe different events."

In the American film *True Believer*, actor James Woods, playing a lawyer, asks his assistant to track down two witnesses. She tells him that one is dead, and the other has moved to Canada.

"Same thing," Woods says laconically, then tells her to forget it.

Only days after seeing the film, I was reading Britain's *Manchester Guardian* and noticed a story about Wellington, the capital city of New Zealand. It was described as: "A place so boring even the Canadians seem interesting."

Neither remark was really unusual. They were just routine spears flung into the tattered hide of the Canadian, a maligned, insulted and allegedly dull creature said to be only slightly more interesting than the mollusk.

An Ottawa columnist reports being told that "one Canadian is as boring as three Swiss or five Belgians."

A British survey asks people what comes to mind when they hear the word "Canada." The answer: "rocks."

The respected *Economist* magazine pronounces us "more boring than all other nations, except Singapore."

What is going on? Am I just sensitive or are we really a nation of limp flapjacks—the polyester of the international set. Whither this image of the dull Canadian?

Personally I think it's a bum rap—the result of living next to the most opinionated, loudmouthed nation on earth. I noticed the difference again recently on a trip to Costa Rica, where most tourists are from the U.S. or Canada. The two groups look identical, but you can locate the Americans the moment you walk into a room—by their sound.

"The skiing in my state is absolutely *unreal*," a young American will be saying, as if through a megaphone. "I mean we are talking *mega*-skiing here, totally merciless... AWESOME."

He is describing an obscure hill in Idaho, barely larger than Montreal's Mount Royal. Yet ask the Canadians at the next table about skiing the Rockies and they'll reply:

"Well, it depends on the season. It can be quite impressive in winter—if it's not too crowded, or too foggy, or too wet."

Canadians are a nation of qualifiers, ever cautious, obsessed with accuracy and truth. Our national image pays heavily for this trait, especially when compared to our larger-than-life neighbours. Unlike us, Americans talk to entertain, with little concern for truth. Chicago is "the greatest town on earth." The Philadelphia Flyers are the "world champions." Their corner restaurant makes "the best French food you'll ever taste."

Who can possibly keep up? As a journalist I'm aware of the difference between us every time I cross the border to cover a story.

Whether I interview a U.S. senator or a gas station attendant, Americans reply in colourful "clips"—punchy made-for-television anecdotes fired out in machine-gun-like bursts.

Not us. Put a Yankee and a Canuck at a hotel fire, and they describe different events.

REPORTER: What happened?
AMERICAN: It was awesome. I heard a rumble, then KAPOW!!—there was this incredible explosion—flames everywhere! It was like hell, only worse.
CANADIAN: I heard the sound of the explosion... well actually, I didn't know it was an explosion at the time. It was more like... a... *thumping* sound.
REPORTER *(eager for dramatic clip for news)*: What then?
CANADIAN: Well, I put on my bathrobe to investigate... I went downstairs, and there was... well I couldn't actually *see* the fire... but I certainly saw a good deal of smoke.

REPORTER *(desperate)*: How did you *feel?* Weren't you scared?

CANADIAN: Ah... it's not really fair for me to answer. I wasn't in the best place to see the fire... My wife had a better angle, didn't you, dear?

WIFE *(in bathrobe, popping awake)*: Oh no, not really dear. You were in a better position than me... Really, I was looking after Nathan.

CANADIAN: No, no dear... I'm almost sure you were closer than I wa—

(Reporter rushes off to find more Americans staying at hotel.)

After several years of cross-continent reporting I've come to the conclusion that finding clips, like growing grapes, has a lot to do with the sun. The further north you go the leaner the harvest. Take the American South. People there talk in a slow drawl, but invariably deliver pearls, like:

"Son, your reasoning is about as bumpy as a moose's rump."

Hit New York and it's all hype. People's hands wave about like a conductor's and superlatives are the only form of adjective.

Everything is "stupendous... unique... divine."

As you approach the border, good clip fades as fast as sunshine. Even in northern Maine you can already hear the earnest Canadian tones of an Edmund Muskie; by the time you reach Montreal or Toronto, lively clips must be extracted like molars, unwilling to leave the mouth.

The hands have stopped moving. Hyperbole has vanished. Adjectives are scarce—replaced by qualifiers like "somewhat" and "possibly."

The linguistic modesty is most visible in the heart of Canada—the far north—where people ration words like wood for a fire. Typical is a Whitehorse musher I interviewed during a dogsled race several years ago. He was about to leave for three weeks alone in the bush and I tried vainly to get a dramatic quote out of him.

— Are you worried about the weather? I asked.

— Nope.

— But storms can be dangerous when you're alone? You could die.

— Yep.

— What about your dogs? Isn't it tough on them?

— I haven't asked 'em.

This northern silence may have meaning. On one icy journey in the north, I pestered my Inuit guide David with a litany of questions: Why did he seem so comfortable in the cold? How come his fingers didn't freeze when he took his gloves off to work? Why wasn't he shivering—like me?

After a series of patient, laconic replies, he offered some unexpected advice: "Words take energy, Josh... They burn up heat. If you talk less, you'll be more warm."

It was the last thing he said to me for hours. Reluctantly, I was forced to take his advice, and the quieter I became, the warmer I got.

Perhaps it is from here—this Darwinian need for silence—that Canadians have evolved. And developed our undeserved reputation as dull.

Wrapped in thick parkas, toques pulled over our ears, brains busily thinking about how to start the car, we are less generous of breath, less quick to expound than our southern neighbours.

It's not that we're boring. We've just got better things to do than talk about the weather. Like survive it.

When Jannies Visited: Remembering an Outport Christmas

BY RAY GUY

Scenes from childhood in a Newfoundland outport village, when the fearsome "jannies" came knocking in the dark of midwinter.

Jannies didn't spoil Christmas for me but they surely put a crimp in it. I was terrified of them. Even when I was old enough to be one myself there was still something dreadful about jannies.

On Boxing Day after supper at about eight there would come a heavy rapping at the door. Nobody else ever knocked, they just stamped snow off their boots in the porch in winter or cleared their throats in the summer. Nobody ever knocked except strangers... and jannies!

Christmas 1947 stands out more than any before or since, perhaps because I was eight that year. When you get to be eight a good many things clang into focus, the pieces of the great jigsaw seem to have grown larger, you can count past 10 without taking off your socks. So I knew, by then, that jannies, or mummers, were really only people.

Still, there was that gut-flopping dread. Someone went out into the dark porch and opened the door and you heard the King Jannie speak in a harsh, gabbling rasp of words made while sucking the breath in: "Any jannies in tonight?"

"Yes. O.K. But... " There'd be a feeble attempt to set conditions. Not too much noise, granny wasn't well. Not too rowdy, the youngsters were scared. But nothing short of a deathbed constrained them.

Out of the dark and the frosty air they blundered and bumped and bundled, into the heat of the kitchen and the soft light of the kerosene lamp, roistering, hulking, tripping, stomping, lurching. They were big and bloated and mostly mute.

They had grotesque humps on their backs or obscenely protruding bellies, sometimes both at once. Their faces were mummified with scraps of old lace curtains or masked blank with cardboard that had torn-out holes for eyes. They stank, they reeked.

A raw sheepskin hung over this one's deformed back, cow's horns attached to a piece of bloody skull were lashed to that one's head. Another wore a jouncing girdle of fox pelts, two or three were in oilskins turned inside out, putrid with bilge water and week-old fish.

They danced a lumpish dance, shuddering the floorboards, trembling the teapot atop the stove, flaring the lamp in its wall bracket, led in their floundering by a mouth organ crudely played by one of their number through its soggy mouth cloth.

The only game to it was to guess who they were. If a jannie was guessed he had to unmask on the spot, which drained the dread away and destroyed the whole mob of them. But although there were fewer than 200 people in the whole village of Arnold's Cove, Nfld., jannies were seldom guessed.

They carried staves or hook-tipped gaffs and if you tugged at their disguises they hit, not with raps or taps, but with bruising, bone-deadening clouts. Even your father, gamely smiling, gave off a fear of them.

They might lunge and seize anyone and drag them into their ogreish dance, prodding and fumbling them in a most improper way. Or they might spitefully smash a bowl or upset a water bucket. At some unseen signal they all moved to leave, were offered a shot of rum or a tumbler of water, and blundered and reeled off into the night.

Two or three other gangs of jannies might show up before the night was over, or on any night of the twelve days of Christmas, between December 26 and Old Christmas Day on January 6.

There seemed little reason to tolerate this mummering except that it was the "done thing" and had been since time out of mind. Later when I was old enough to join in the jannying I glimpsed a dark attraction—the power of being that capricious Unknown, and feared.

*   *   *

Compared to jannies, most else about Christmas then was bright and beautiful. For instance, snotty var. It was the very essence of the season and still is the most powerful trigger of memory.

At school in the first week of Advent, the teacher began shoring up our spiritual foundations. We were catechized after morning prayer with questions like: "What is the first thing that must come to our minds when we think of Christmas?"

She asked again, this time ending the word "Christmas" with a definite hiss. "Please Miss," said one of the Bigger Boys, Leonard, I'd guess, "Snotty var, Miss." She twisted both his ears until they stayed red for an hour.

He'd been guilty of insolence, blasphemy and lapsing into the local dialect, his mother tongue. Teachers strove to knock all three out of you, especially the latter. There was a whole dictionary full of punishment words and on top of that a tireless knuckle-rapping campaign against wrong pronunciation of right words.

In 30 years, had he lived that long, Leonard might have said that the first thing that came to his mind when he thought of Christmas was the pungent tang of balsam fir sap. Not snotty var. By then he might have learned the new language in which emmets were ants, dumbledores were bees, piss-a-beds were dandelions and a merrybegot was an illegitimate child.

But schooling then was like that. Now that I was eight I knew that the green light said "go" and how to spell "squirrel" although there was neither one nor the other within 150 kilometres. I could draw a soldier of the Roman legions and we sent coded notes to each other in the Phoenician alphabet. But it was long after I'd finished 17 years of schooling that I learned that John Guy, merchant adventurer out of Bristol, had met the Beothuks on a beach just over the hill. In 1612.

Or that my mother's people lived across the harbour at a place known as "Burdle," but which was once a French plantation called Bordeaux.

My hometown of Arnold's Cove (nobody named "Arnold" lived there) lies on the eastern shore of Placentia Bay, Newfoundland's largest bay, a great triangle 130 kilometres long and 100 kilometres across at its southern base. Its three main landmarks are Cape St. Mary's, Chapeau Rouge and, at its northern point, Pipers Hole. Arnold's Cove is about 16 kilometres south of Pipers Hole.

The village was on a low, treeless peninsula about three kilometres long and half a kilometre wide, and the wind roared across it from every direction. It was like a monstrous raft at sea. But at its western end the peninsula rose up to become the High Head with cliffs that dropped straight down 75 metres to the ocean.

One day in June when I was eight the Bigger Girls came to borrow me. While you were still in short pants the Bigger Girls seemed to like minding you. After that you were allowed to hang around in places where the men worked.

They were taking me, they said, to pick crowberries behind the old graveyard, but we went much farther than that. We went along the goat path through the bogs and by the low cliffs to the Otter Rub where the Americans had watched for submarines. Beyond that we went, on and on.... Then, scrambling up through the scrubby spruce and the dusty rockslides, we came out at the top of the High Head. Here was my sudden enlightenment of a lifetime. Down in the village, the line of sight of an eight-year-old extended from the cat in the shade of the dooryard rhubarb to a glimpse of blue hills an improbable distance away. But now I could see where I was in the world.

There were the islands of the bay, Long Island, Red Island, Iona, Merasheen. On them were villages like Jean de Gaunt and Peaches Cove, Harbour Buffett and Tacks Beach, Rose au Rue and Haystack. The islets of Bread and Cheese, the cove next north from us called Come By Chance. And Bay Bulls Arm across the narrow Isthmus of Avalon in Trinity Bay where John Guy first met "ye savages of ye clime."

I could see now where the fishing boats went after they thumped away around the point in the early morning to the fishing grounds, as well known to them as the fertile patches of a farmer's field: the Jerseyman, called "Jasmin," Burdle Banks, Goose Island Ground, the Pancake, the Big Neverfail and the Little Neverfail.

That was all full and plenty, but then one of the Bigger Girls said: "There's only one salt water in the world, you know, and it goes on and on and on. To China and to where the King lives. To where the cowboys is in the States, even!" I wanted to run headlong down from the High Head to the beach away below and throw so big a rock in the water as would make waves that might go to China. To where the palm trees were. I reserved doubts about the cowboys.

*   *   *

This great enlightenment from the top of the High Head all went to make me especially remember 1947 and the Christmas of it.

Christmas then seemed like a test or a statement of readiness; all was as ready as could or would be to face the winter to come. In the weeks before Christmas the stacked firewood in the back porch rose toward the ceiling, enough to last those 12 work-free days of the season. Most of it was dry, had seasoned for a few years, but some was raw green fir, oozing sap and covered with turpentine blisters, and used to damp the kitchen stove when a winter's gale drew the fire like a blacksmith's forge and the stovepipe glowed dangerously hot. Potatoes gathered in mid-October were heaped in earthen root cellars, and by the end of November all the animals for killing had been killed and their carcasses hung at the back of fish sheds built on stilts over the water.

Each family had a dozen or more sheep, nearly everyone had a pony to plough the potato fields in May and to haul firewood throughout the winter. There were hens, ducks, and occasionally geese. And there was a pig or two to rend the still fall air on its fatal day.

You knew it was pig day when the advisory went around for women and children to stay indoors. A monstrous cauldron used for tanning nets was lugged up from the beach, set over a fire by the pig pen and set steaming. Soon, the loud and prolonged squeals of the pig arose. I was eight and convinced they were boiling it to death. Granny reassured me: "That's only the way pigs are, 'tis a pig's nature to make a great fuss over every sort of little thing."

The Bigger Boys claimed the pig's bladder, which was inflated and covered in sail canvas and used in great formless games of football played during Christmas before the heavy snows of January set in.

A few people kept cows so there might be a calf or two for slaughter and the larder was further stocked with game: moose, caribou, rabbits, ducks and ptarmigan. In December there was a secure feeling of sufficiency and just a tinge of trepidation about "the long and hungry month of March." The basic, rock-bottom ration against a shortfall in that lean time at the end of the winter was the setting aside of one barrel of potatoes and one barrel of salted herring for each family member.

A Newfoundland fishing village at that time had a subsistence economy in which broody hens, spavined ponies and haystacks had as important a part as salt cod, dories and a following sea. Which is probably why a

Quebec farm journal, *The Family Herald and Weekly Star*, was the journal of choice all over the island.

A mini-ritual sometime in mid-December was "the Opening of the Gaps." Gaps in the maze of fences which enclosed potato fields, hay meadows and cabbage patches were opened up to create a new road cutting through them all—the winter road, the slide path.

As soon as the ice on the ponds was thick enough, a caravan of ponies in jingling harness set out in the morning for the firewood places beyond the railway tracks—stands of spruce and fir that were hereditary and had names like Whiffen's Droke, the Level Brook, the Place Where Poor Bill Lost the Pocketknife or the Pond Where Uncle Steve Caught the Otter.

They filed back in the early winter dusk, slides loaded with firewood for the insatiable kitchen stoves, a boat knee (the rib of a boat) or a stem of larchwood on top that might have been noticed 10 or 15 years before for its unusual shape, a brace or two of partridge or rabbits swinging from the slide, harness bells jingling, steam wafting from the pot-bellied ponies, sparks from the runners where the winter road was bare.

Sometimes at Christmas a dozen or more men were missing. The herring fishery was the last of the year. The boats went out 15 kilometres or more to a reach between islands in the bay where the shoals of herring appeared. They stayed away for a fortnight… and hoped for "light nights" (nights when the moon shone clear and bright) at Christmas.

If the nights were moonless or stormy, the herring couldn't see the nets, the catch was abundant, and even Christmas was no excuse to leave such bounty and come home. But if it chanced that there were light nights, the boats came back for a day or two.

That Christmas of 1947 when I was eight there was a full moon but dark and heavy clouds night after night. On December 23 the sky cleared and the moon and stars glared down. As the church bell rang near midnight on Christmas Eve, the boats were heard coming far off and they rounded the point into the cove, their masts hung with lanterns and green boughs. As they came they made a trail of stars on the black glass of the water.

Not only had the herring men brought themselves back in good time, they'd met a moonshiner among the islands who was freshly back from St. Peter's—as they called the French island of Saint-Pierre. So there was tobacco and a better-quality spirit to enliven that Christmas.

What other rum there was for Christmas, Easter, weddings and wakes was called swish. Fishermen were entitled to the thick-staved puncheons that brought undiluted rum from the West Indies. These were sawed in two and used as tubs for salting fish.

But if 10 or 15 litres of water were poured into these empty casks and let stand for a week and the casks rolled back and forth to swish it around, it was the Wedding in Cana all over again. The staves gave up their essence and you had 10 or 15 litres of the best Demerara rum.

So then it was Christmas. The church decorated all up and down the lampposts with balsam fir and tissue-paper roses. Socials, dances, soup suppers, "meat teas," concerts in the school every other night. Card games and signing and stories and midnight "scoffs" in the houses and… jannies.

That year I got an orange, a fifty-cent piece, an American chocolate bar, a prayer book and a new pair of mitts in my stocking, but the big thing was my father had made me a slide out of a salt pork barrel and it went like billy-be-damned down the hill in our meadow along the icy winter road.

Since there were 12 days of Yuletide—and all the baking done as well as the firewood laid in—there seemed to be no frantic festive pace, just that assured and designated time in the darkest part of the year when people came to your house every night or you went to theirs.

It was an obvious portion of the year. Between pig-killing time and Candlemas Day, February 2, when the lamps were not lit until after supper. Then to the middle of February when the bleating of new lambs was added to the evening's sounds and on to early March when the hammering to repair the boats on the beaches began.

Thirty-five years later I was living in a St. John's suburb with cable TV and a microwave oven. One evening in early January two station wagons stopped out front. A mob of mummers debouched.

By now, jannies like much else had gone full circle and beyond, from being a base embarrassment, a low practice from the past to being folkloric and historic and a piece of precious heritage. The two-faced Roman god, Janus, had been brought into the picture, an actual script of the mummer's play had been reconstituted, there were elaborate costumes and the university crowd delighted in floating a revival.

They banged on the door. They said, "Any jannies in tonight?"

No, I said. I was a big boy, now.

The Mothers of Confederation

BY SYDELL WAXMAN

Life was a story of unending toil for many women in pioneer Canada.

Canadian history alludes to women of the last century only incidentally, yet our country owes an enormous debt to those not immortalized with the "Founding Fathers." Our "Founding Mothers" led lives filled with endless toil, too numerous pregnancies, cumbersome dress and second-class citizenship, but by the end of the nineteenth century a dramatic, courageous tale of "women's sphere" began to unfold.

The story began before Confederation when there was a great demand for female labour. Newspapers, promoting the planned mass immigration, praised women as "invaluable as a sympathetic companion, an economical manager, an actual helpmate in the farm work, as a mother of future citizens and as a standard-bearer of civilization."

Our Founding Fathers, not oblivious to the importance of the female role in the future of Canada, were very cautious about the quality of women immigrants. Although the Election Act of the Dominion of Canada stated that "No woman, idiot, lunatic or child shall vote," there was a steadfast belief that women were the cornerstone of family and nation. The values they would pass on to the young, it was unanimously agreed, should be British values, since Canada "would be a nation that was British in outlook and character."

Long before this search for the ideal Canadian mother began, colonial women had cleared land, worked as loggers, owned and operated mines, hunted for meat and trapped for fur. They did this while raising families and they often kept journals about their pioneering lives. The 1820s saw a significant number of women working in "nontraditional jobs" such as silversmith, woodworker, coachmaker, lumberjack and mortician. "A short-handed country," wrote one observer, "could not disdain womanpower."

Despite this past history of woman's work, Canada's late-nineteenth-century servant-recruitment campaign began looking for the "best classes" of British women. Applicants were scrutinized to determine their moral character, respectability, job performance, attitudes, intelligence and physical health. These women were assured that as servants their work would not be difficult, since Canada boasted labour-saving machines and varnished woodwork. In fact, the life of work left little leisure time. "It was nearly five o'clock before I had done my room, changed my working dress and was ready to enjoy my one hour 'off' during the day," recalled one woman who had been a domestic servant in pioneer Alberta.

Most female immigrants embarked on the voyage to Canada with the belief, as one expressed it, that "they would lead not unpleasant lives at starting and speedily rise to better things." When they arrived, the women were sorted into groups by destination and taken to temporary shelters or hostels. Other women usually supervised the grouping of these new servants onto trains headed for distribution centers in Montreal, Calgary, Regina, Edmonton and Vancouver. The uncomfortable and overcrowded trip from Montreal to Vancouver took five days, and rumours spread that women disappeared from the trains, no doubt into "white slavery."

Most found their way to be placed as servants in Canadian homes. For their services they often received as little as five dollars per month, with room and board.

Motherhood was thought to be the goal and primary social function of every Canadian woman. This socialization process, moulding Canadian girls into potential wives and mothers, began early. They were encouraged to play with dolls until they were teenagers. According to *The Young Lady's Book* of 1876, games such as chess were not allowed because "Chess is not a game much played by ladies as it requires rather more thought and calculation than women possess." The author of this book was a woman.

Many children were not allowed card games, since card playing resembled gambling, but reading was encouraged. *The Young Lady's Book*, subtitled "A Manual of Amusements, Exercises, Studies and Pursuits," was meant to fill girls' leisure time. *The Holiday Album for Girls* of the same period contained moral stories of "ideal" little girls—thoughtful Maggie who helped an old lady off the train, Eva who was crippled but still managed to be happy, and naughty Esther who would come to no good because she stayed in bed after she had been wakened by her mother. Meanwhile boys were reading about the glorious adventures of other lads in gold mines, on whaling ships, sailing the seven seas and mountaineering.

When children grew up and married the household cradle was rarely unoccupied, even though infant and maternal mortality was alarmingly high. The situation was not helped by primitive obstetric practices.

Once babies were delivered they were bathed and their umbilical cords rubbed with tallow and a light dusting of nutmeg. Babies were then dressed in layers of clothing, since swaddling had gone out of fashion in Canada by the nineteenth century. One last item was sometimes added if superstitious parents could afford it—a coral bead which was hung around the baby's neck. This was a charm to ward off the evil eye.

Gynecology had developed into a medical specialty by the late 1800s. These "experts" considered themselves knowledgeable, not only in the medical realm of the female body, but related their unfounded expertise to female sexuality, female social roles and "female spheres."

Who would argue with the male experts? So women devoted their lives to children and found that motherhood led them from the cradle to the kitchen. Cooking became women's duty by birth and this formidable job included making all staples such as bread, butter, pickles, catsup and preserves. Fruits and vegetables were inconveniently canned on the hottest August days when the produce reached suitable ripeness.

Bread was made from wheat flour, with corn, rye and buckwheat being used occasionally. Pumpkins were an important mainstay, used for soups, pies and "pumpkin sass"—a type of molasses. Later, apples replaced pumpkins as a major pie material, and by the end of the century plants imported from England produced gooseberries, raspberries, strawberries and currants.

Cooking and canning did not stop at the family's needs, for meals often included farm hands, especially at harvesting time.

Ella Sykes, a visiting English journalist, recorded this story of a prairie woman: "In shearing time, I had to cook for fifteen men... they needed five meals a day... I just got into the way of thinking nothing but how to get through the day's work."

Besides cooking, every housewife had her family formula for making ink, floor polish, silver cleaner, whitewash, rat poison, boot spray, shampoo,

Reaping oats in Beynon, Alberta, ca. 1909.

cold cream, tooth powder, hair tonic, soap and candles. Roots and herbs were stored for sickness, because mother was often the family "doctor" with traditional remedies for most minor ailments.

Family life centered on the kitchen and the fireplace. The kitchen was at the back of the house so that the smell travelled outside. Not only were kitchen smells thought unpleasant, but it was believed they carried disease. Hot roasted coffee beans were carried around the house to kill the odours.

The front doors were reserved for strangers and special visitors, while all other traffic flowed through the kitchen. The floors were usually plain wood until the late 1800s when linoleum was invented. Tables were covered with oilcloth. The zinc sinks, home-helps and wives soon discovered, were difficult to clean.

Cooking was done traditionally on the fireplace and the poor continued to use this method long after the rich could afford huge iron ranges that burned coal and wood. These ranges, kept going all day and night, were a prized household possession. Fireplaces were not readily replaced by central heating and many saw the new heating discovery as the potential cause of family breakdowns. Fireplaces had not only been the cooking area, but the place where families gathered to keep warm, discuss the day's happenings, and share time together.

Almost everyone agreed on the favourite household treat—ice cream. It took a long time to prepare, since a hot custard of milk, sugar, egg and vanilla had to be made first and then churned and cooled. Cream was put into a tin pail that was set in a large wooden pot packed with ice and salt. Willing helpers turned the handle for hours, adding new ice and salt from time to time.

It would seem that the cult of domesticity had enmeshed Canadian women in never-ceasing household chores. Ladies' magazines, edited and published by men, romanticized the role of the farmer's wife. In actuality, loneliness, alienation and despair were repeatedly expressed in written records kept by farming women. Statistics show disproportionate incidents of mental breakdown among that era's women.

The story of "Women in the 1800s," amazingly, does not end in domestic detail and despair. The great changes occurring in Canada by the end of the century affected women profoundly. Inventions such as the sewing machine and the bicycle brought not only labour-saving devices but acceptable sport and leisure. Cities provided the important opportunity for women to meet and organize.

The first generation of Canadian social feminists appeared as early as 1860. As women moved from being predominantly household servants into factories, schoolrooms and nursing homes, organizations began to develop. Local church groups and benevolent societies grew with the towns and gave women the chance to move beyond their homes.

Motherhood and cooking, however, were still considered "women's sphere" and the groups proceeded with great caution and assurances that family balance would be upheld. Lady Aberdeen, wife of the Governor General, an experienced diplomat, pointed out that Canadians needed "careful handling" on the "woman question." The National Council of Women of Canada, formed in 1893, could advance only after repeated guarantees of its loyalty to the ideal of a domesticated and conciliatory womanhood.

So these women, anxious to take an active part in society, concerned themselves with "acceptable" projects such as working girls, urban housing, children's recreation, and cultural improvement.

Medical care was another cause to which the National Council of Women of Canada directed its efforts. Lack of medical attention inflated the infant and maternal mortality rates. The Victorian Order of Home Helpers, a forerunner of the Victorian Order of Nurses, was founded in 1897. Having been taught techniques of household sanitation, the nurses set out for remote Canadian dwellings, bringing much-needed medical knowledge of sanitation and infant care. Still, they had to justify their jobs as nurses in the light of the ideal of domestic Canadian womanhood. This was accomplished by signing a contract denying independence. The contract stated that "a respectable and acceptable nurse was an ideal lady who showed wifely obedience to the doctor, motherly self-devotion to the patient and a firm mistress/servant discipline to those below the rung of nurse."

Women's groups knew they were treading on dangerous ground and facing hardened ideas about women, the family and the Canadian nation. They moved out of their homes into groups and activities with continuous caution and verbal justifications that their actions would in no way impede what they knew was their role and position in life. They even reassured the Canadian public with contrasts between "feminine" Canadian women and "argumentative, mannish, ill-mannered, fast" Americans.

Change had begun, as this editorial in the *Victoria Times* of 1893 verifies: "Ten years ago people were much more content to lead a vegetable life, troubling their heads but little over what are now considered to be the burning questions of the day. There was a stifling air of *laissez-faire* in those times, and a strong tendency towards the suppression and ridiculing of all women's higher aims and ambitions; but in this *fin-de-siècle* much of that is changed, and the ability of the gentler sex to cope with and successfully master many of the deeper problems of life is becoming an established and recognized fact."

These courageous women's groups succeeded in opening not only the eyes of many Canadians, but eventually the doors of the universities and professions. Confederation women are not in the famous "Founding Fathers" picture, but without their endless physical toil the country could not have developed. Against great social pressure, they did the groundwork for the suffrage movement as well as for other profound social changes, the effects of which are still being felt today. To forget the details of their lives is to forget an important part of Canadian history.

Life and Death in Ontario County

BY HUGH GRAHAM

"Unmarked in death, John Beedon, his wife, and son left almost no impression either among those who knew them or had hired the old man." An essay written as a mark of respect for some forgotten lives.

I was seven in the winter of 1959 when my parents and I went to look at a farmhouse near Greenbank, about forty kilometres north of Whitby, Ontario. It was occupied by a ferretish old man with faded blue eyes, and his wife, and their sixty-year-old son. They lived in one large room and my mother discovered that they slept under coats upstairs. Everything they had was old and worn out. The ceiling was low and buckled, the blistered wall-paper was from the twenties, and the air thick and dry with stove heat. Puzzles of Scottish castles had been framed and hung on the wall. Everything that could be saved was stacked in another room behind a door closed and stuffed with rags.

We returned several times that winter, sometimes after dark, and entering that house was to cross into a warm and dim place that was other-worldly and unsettling. The son, a lumbering giant of a man, shaved in front of us beside the stove in his undervest and suspenders using a cracked mirror, a straight razor, and a basin with steaming water from a blackened kettle. The old man sat idly in a rocking chair among other chairs around the stove with flattened torn cushions. The old woman was the only one who was moving, large and birdlike, giving me and my friends candy and pictures. Out in the back, on the unfinished planks of the woodshed wall there was a tattered collage of pasted-up magazine illustrations that included a painted thirties advertisement of an old countryman in a suit playing the violin. The evening light in the picture seemed to be like the light in their house, the night sky was the colour of his suit, and for a long time I was certain that the fictional fiddler was the old man. Beyond the woodshed a track through the snow led to a hand pump. In the depths of that hard winter when they were snowbound, food had to be brought them from the village. I had never seen such people. My mother explained to me that it was poverty. They maintained the land for a beef farmer, their name was Beedon, and I later realized they were the forgotten; tenants of a type commonly associated with the American South.

When we took possession and began work on the farmhouse, they had moved down two concession lines to a solid ancient fieldstone house on high and bald melancholy farmland. The old man, John Beedon, and his son, Alf, put in our garden, built livestock fencing, and taught us how to manage our woodlot and twenty-five hectares of pasture. And now we seemed to be visiting in the new place, where they had brought the same heavy smell of mildew and stove heat, just as we had visited the old. Mrs. Beedon still had a miniature museum she had created in an aquarium that displayed a growing and changing collection of postcards, dolls, doll furniture, miniature flags, and buttons, which she called her "funny box."

I had been afraid of them at first. They were crude, spoke with "don't" and "ain't." Beedon was slight, bantamlike, testy, and irascible, and the son, haunted and moronic, towered over his parents. The three looked alike, with sharp eyes and big noses and thin flat mouths and the two men had abscess scars in the right cheek, which gave them a look of wild inhaling. One winter Mrs. Beedon was talking to my mother, when, in a moment of womanly confidence, steadying her thick glasses, she pulled down a black stocking and then pulled up a leg of long underwear and showed a faint blue mark where the old man had given her a kick.

The son, Alf, as Beedon told us outright, was dim, subnormal, while Alf himself, with his monumental craggy face and deep-set grey eyes, seemed to agree with equanimity. All his life he had held menial jobs and worked with his father in labouring or picking up highway tree-trimmings in a horse and wagon for Ontario Hydro. Alf spoke with a solemn nodding expertise about cutting post tops to a slant to keep out rot and expounded with an air of grave foreboding on the common details of maintaining the property. He had a high hearselike black '48 Dodge and at every opportunity he opened the hood to display the engine with my father listening and nodding politely while trying to get on with things. But when his father was discussing the plans for the day with mine, and Alf attempted to add a detail, the old man snapped, "There, we heard enough from you," with a swift kick in the shin.

On weekends Alf drove home from a cleaning job in Milton and spent the time with a case of twenty-four in front of the television mildly sloshed; the program, which he highly recommended, was *Popeye*. "I've courted every girl in Reach Township," he told us, with the implication he'd turned them all down, but it was when my mother hired him to drive her into Port Perry to do shopping that he talked. My mother, who was easily bored, was impressed with his skill as a raconteur as he told his stories with reverence and amazement, saying he'd been overseas during the war and that an English girl had slapped him for proposing they go to Petticoat Lane. His father told us flatly that Alf had never been out of the country and had been turned down for the service "because of bad nerves." My mother later gathered that Alf had taken stories he'd heard from braggarts, farmers, and servicemen, and honed them into his own imaginary past.

In the summers when I got to know the old man, he was eighty and cycling about ten kilometres a day to our place over hilly gravel concession roads. I recall him always in indigo twill trousers with suspenders, a light-coloured fedora he never took off, hawklike without teeth, and with alert pale eyes that never seemed to change; an expression of amused, open-mouthed, almost delectable outrage, as if he had caught you doing something he had predicted you would do. In those summers I was a city kid with no friends in the country and I spent my days with the old man. He taught me how to build livestock fencing, to use an axe and a scythe, to cut and trim timber and till a garden. He worked slowly and with certainty and economy. He used an axe gently and perfectly, everything he had was immaculate and shopworn, his tools white with wear, fastidiously sharp and clean. He had nothing new, but rather items that seemed to be part of the derelict inside of our barn: rags, pegs, bottles, wire, and a jealously guarded enamel drinking ladle. For stretches of summers running, my only life was his, as we replaced rods of fencing in hot dry pasture ringing with crickets. He stretched fence wire by hand, strand by strand with a crowbar, set posts in straight, dug out stones a metre and a half in the ground, planted solid anchor posts, and cut exact and tightly notching brace poles. With a pale wild eye he could line up posts so that lengthwise they appeared as one from here to the horizon. I stayed with him while he ate his gum-soft lunch out of the same old Wonderbread bag and drank Pepsi (Coca-Cola was "poison") in the noon shade of the driving shed.

He and his family had lived dirt poor with no plumbing in the same kinds of houses for close to sixty years. He had visited no city since he'd been to Toronto in 1908. He had gone to see the Exhibition, then a celebrated agricultural fair, disliked the city, condemned the fair, which was nowhere near as good as the one in Lindsay, and went home quickly, never to return. His time was that of teams and traces; he operated no machinery, would not even touch a tractor. He had no use for television, found football ridiculous, could just read headlines and sign his name, and kept their money in cash at the post office. But all his life seemed to have been lived in a struggle to prove he was, or had been, right. He argued tooth and nail with my mother about putting in the garden and was always vindicated; when my father's car arrived on weekends, Beedon looked up with a smile, ready to show him his errors. The old man's tales were of cleverness and cheating, triumphant accounts of meanness and dishonesty, and in these he seemed to stand alone in a world of rural propriety. Where the conversation of the farm wives and close-mouthed farmers that we knew was filled with righteous anodynes, tact, and caution, Beedon's eyes lit up at recollections of incompetence and shabbiness. Perhaps he had nothing to lose by such stories; he seemed to have fought with every employer he had ever had; he walked out on fence-building jobs because the farmer insisted on hanging the wire upside down. His suspicions of malice were often senseless and extravagant—for example, that a shovel of ours found in the pond had been thrown there by a man we hardly knew, for spite.

We on the other hand were city middle-class, devoid of the natural suspicion of farmers, and since we had the money to pay him what he wanted without welshing, he seemed, for that practical reason, to respect us—even if he always told us we were wrong, or was amused by our ignorance and capriciousness. After my father hung a stark contemporary conceptual piece over the mantel, the old man smiled toothlessly and said, "What you doing with a picture of a shovel?" His affections were indeed practical and determined his loyalty, and yet when local painters accidentally set our house on fire, he ran in alone through dense smoke and tried to drag out the furniture before he was pulled out by firemen.

He had lived and worked longer in the county than almost anyone and yet for all his stories almost no one seemed to know him. In turn, the world he described seemed to have passed, a spectral place devoid of witnesses where he fought two men to court a woman, where he had been able single-handedly to lift a full-grown heifer into the back of a wagon. When he'd dart in laughing and jab at the tail of my pony just to make him kick, he seemed very much of another age. Likewise, his entertainment was in talking: in denials, claims, and tales; the brush with death riding the famous long slope at Sandy Hook after his bicycle chain broke; a renowned giant elm near Goodwood, which he said had yielded seventy-odd cords of wood in its death, and then regretted, "I never did get down to see that tree."

The stories he told were redolent of the abandoned farmhouses that were scattered around Greenbank, of suicide, fraud, and arson, of vandal-ized, trashed, melancholy places where frozen overalls still hung by the door over boots ghosted with dust and among the mites and mildew of a medicine cabinet where you could find a dusky tin of brilliantine, still vis-cous and marked by the scoop of fingers; where the son of a man whose farm had a broken dam decorated with a cow skull had died drinking strychnine. Those very places that smelled of mildew and damp plaster but hadn't fallen to dereliction were the places lived in by Beedon and his fam-ily. In a house rented in Uxbridge the attic had been closed and several nights running he heard a heavy chain dragged the length of the house across the floor above. In the daytime he investigated and found nothing; it was bare and completely sealed, but a few days later he learned that two years before the butcher who lived there had hanged himself. There was a story of the thirties that began with a column of smoke he had seen over near Uxbridge and ended with the owner of a blazing house tearing out of the front door with a baby carriage draped for protection with heavy blan-kets. And what made Beedon look at you as if he dared you to believe any-one could be courageous or honest was the fact that the carriage had concealed no baby but four expensive folded suits. The implication, of course, was insurance fraud.

After five years I could scarcely remember the time when I had been afraid of him and now he was the first person the prospect of whose death made me sad. By then I knew he didn't mind me, and his gone world, which seemed to live on in the stillness before thunderstorms and the dry decay of barns, had become mine as well, a ghost world of Reach Township that followed me back to the city and to school. He had become a major figure in my life and in my imagination.

When my father hired an old farm couple from Quebec to live and run a mechanized operation on our place, it now seems we were pushing Beedon on as the world was pushing him. While he was still working for us, I remember the two old men talking in lawn chairs and my mother's remark that they were rivals and fundamentally disliked each other. Indeed, he moved on but even the riot of the sixties and what appeared to be relentless and ineluctable change were well on their way before I saw the last of him, and one spring when he didn't come round to the farm, it seemed only inevitable. We visited him and I saw him pale as parchment, small and hatless in his rocker. Then they were gone from that house too; the world seemed determined to move them on.

About eighty-five years ago, John Beedon, the eleventh or twelfth son of a Wiltshire game warden, came to Canada as a Barnardo Boy: one of the thousands of orphans sponsored by the Barnardo homes in England to populate the Empire from a pool of unskilled labour that Great Britain couldn't feed. This was how he had made his way to his first job turning over vegetable gardens with a horse and plough in Uxbridge, Ontario, in 1906. He also did the ornamental flower bed that spelled CNR at the Uxbridge railway station. But it was in the network of walking and wagon-hopping itinerant farm labour that he met and courted and married a hawk-faced woman, his female doppelgänger, a farmer's daughter from a remote hamlet at the end of the Marsh Hill road. Even when Beedon was old, you could see from his arms and hands, elongated and burly for his small frame, that his life had been the eternity of ploughing, pitching hay, managing horses and cattle, and all the other endless and thankless work of a time now unknown to us.

Two daughters who had disappeared seemed to us long gone and mythical. "Oh, she was wayward," they had spoken in gruff euphemism of one who had run off with a variety of men, perhaps in the twenties or thirties, and whom they had never seen since. Cannier, perhaps more worldly than the first, the other had married a lawyer in Whitby and, apart from meager financial help, refused to acknowledge her parents, having risen into a middle-class town world where such people as her parents supposedly didn't exist. So the Beedons and their son lived on in a world without clan or extension, where the old woman noted, remembered, and honoured every birthday in every neighbourhood they moved to. With the mechanization of farms and the reduction of country labour after the war, the old man took to his bicycle and travelled the same circuits tending gardens, and in that quiet time when we first went to Port Perry, many of the handsome gardens around the commodious Victorian villas would have been his work.

In the summer of 1970 I was nineteen, they were long gone, and with education and travel, childhood had become remote, when I heard somewhere that they were still alive and living on in another old house, inevitably in Ontario County—this time in the village of Kinsale. It would be their last. I went down with a couple of friends and we found a listing frame peaked Victorian farmhouse covered in Insulbrick and we knocked. The old woman, vague and almost blind now, told us to come in and again there was the hot odour of old plaster and stove heat I had smelled twelve years before. She had no idea who any of us were and told us to sit down and began without comment to give us tea. I asked her where Beedon was, and she waved a massive work-hardened hand dismissively in front of her face and croaked, "They killed him. He's gone. They took him away two months ago." She couldn't explain more than that. She couldn't remember either of the farms where we had known them, and apologized and directly began to recall her youth in Marsh Hill at the turn of the century. We spoke to a neighbour who confirmed that Beedon had died in hospital two years before, and not two months, and if we wanted to know more we should wait till Alf came home.

Alf came by and Mrs. Beedon offered us dinner with her son. Close to seventy, he was just as massive, still a bachelor but had whitened and was a different man. He jobbed at country fairs and came home irregularly with money for his mother. He ate a corncob with giant forearms on the oilcloth and spoke with a sober hardness as if finally wakened by the death of his father. "We always lived in the houses like this, old houses, every damn one built the same way, foursquare, mortise and tenon joints, the same roof joists." But he remembered me and even my best friend who was with me: "the little yellow-haired fella." Our place, which had remained in my mind their original place, he remembered tersely as "the place with the pond"— turning out to be but one of myriad tenancies. I asked him about his father and he said, "They said he died, but they took him in the hospital and cut off his leg, they killed him." As we left, I saw him watching us leave, shadowed and headless behind a drawn blind.

In a year I came back to that house in the winter, the Insulbrick had been half stripped off and the door was answered by downtrodden people I had never seen. A young and toothless woman told me the old woman and her son were gone. Mrs. Beedon had died, and he had been committed to a mental hospital, but they believed the gravestone of Beedon and his wife had been erected in the cemetery at the next concession road. In blowing snow that formed wells around the monuments I found no stone, not even an unmarked plot.

When they disappeared, the Beedons had lived in twenty-two houses in a single county since he had arrived in 1906. Unmarked in death, John Beedon, his wife, and son left almost no impression either among those who knew them or had hired the old man; few could recall them well, fewer could really distinguish him in their memories of the gone world into which he had dissolved like a footprint in pasture.

The Misery Index

BY ARTHUR BLACK

Where would you rather spend the winter—Winnipeg, Regina, or Chicoutimi-Jonquière?

E dmonton's bad, but not as bad as Regina. Newfoundland's capital, St. John's, is pretty crummy too, but Chicoutimi-Jonquière is crummier. Victoria and Vancouver? Leave those two wimps out of this. They don't even rate. We're talking *real* Canadian cities. Cities like, well, Winnipeg. Now *there's* a Canuck burg for ya! Winnipeg's the absolute top of the list.

Misery is what we're measuring here. As in urban winter misery, and it's official: when it comes to Canadian cities, Winnipeg is the worst one to spend the winter in.

The trouble with Canadian winters is that there really is no such animal. Winters here are very different, depending on where in the Great White North you choose to plant your mukluks. A Prairie winter is not like a Maritime winter, just as a winter in Prince Rupert would seem a little weird to a Mennonite farmer from Elmira, Ontario.

Except for one thing. There is one commodity that virtually all Canadian winters have in common.

Misery. It is safe to say that a Canadian winter is a miserable winter, one way or another.

Which is where David Phillips comes in. Mr. Phillips is a climatologist who toils for the Atmospheric Environment Service in Toronto. Looking out his office window one winter morning, across a scabby snowscape of dirty, salt-encrusted banks interspersed with ice patches, Mr. Phillips had a revelation. "What this country needs," he realized, "is a good Winter Misery Index."

So David Phillips designed one. He came up with a list of eleven pointed questions that he could ask about any city's winter experience, questions like: how much snow do you get, how many sunny days, how many times does the thermometer dip under 20 below, how much wind—questions like that. By assigning a numerical value to each answer, Phillips had a method of plotting any Canadian city's position on the Misery Map.

Winnipeg won, mittens down. On a scale of 100, Manitoba's capital copped a frosty 62. Regina wasn't far behind with a 61, and Chicoutimi-Jonquière was nipping at both their heels with a rating of 60. That was Win, Place, and Show for David Phillips's Misery Sweepstakes. You'll be happy to learn that all other Canadian cities were way back in the pack.

Edmonton for instance, which I thought would rate pretty rotten, pulled a respectable 49. Toronto, which has never been my first choice for a January tryst, got a 34. A little farther south, Windsor scored a semitropical 29. As for equatorial hangouts like Vancouver and Victoria? Ten and eight on the scale, respectively. (I know, I know—I said I wouldn't talk about them, but I thought you should know just how bizarre things get in this country, winter-weatherwise.)

I'm glad we have David Phillips's Winter Misery Index. It's a stroke of genius that was long overdue. Especially when our only alternatives were the Druidic pronouncements emanating from Environment Canada—what in the name of heaven is an average mortal to make of a wind chill that is measured in *watts per square metre?*

And yet... the existence of David Phillips's Misery Index begs one unignorable question: Now that we know how miserable our winters are, what are we going to do about it?

Most of us would have trouble finding permanent work in the Greek islands, and retsina is an inferior substitute for Canadian lager.

Victoria's not big enough to take us all in. Besides, trading snowshoes for swim flippers is a dubious bargain at best.

Given the climate of economic restraint, I doubt that Ottawa will seriously consider financing a retractable dome stretching from the Queen Charlottes to Conception Bay.

And anyway, just think of the bill for windshield solvent.

Nope, let's face it. Dave Phillips's Misery Index only illustrates something that every Canadian knows in his permafrosted soul—we have lousy winters.

The thing is not to whine about it. Just accept it. If it makes you feel better, you can go around reciting the words of the English poet Shelley: "If winter comes, can spring be far behind?"

Easy for Shelley to say, of course.

He'd never visited Winnipeg.

The Lesson of Canadian Geography

BY ROBERT FULFORD

"History strives earnestly to teach us its enduring lessons, but in Canada geography is our real teacher, the one to which we must listen with the greatest care."

Every Canadian is conscious of the hugeness of our country. Perhaps this awareness is the one thing we all share.

History strives earnestly to teach us its enduring lessons, but in Canada geography is our real teacher, the one to which we must listen with the greatest care. It is geography which sets the tone of Canadian life just as it sets the rules of our working lives and governs our economic relations with other countries. Perhaps the Japanese can mostly ignore their own terrain; possibly Austrians can shove the geography of Austria to the margin of their national consciousness. But Canadians have no such choice. The history of our culture is the history of our attempt to come to terms imaginatively with the variety and vastness of the Canadian landscape—a process which even now may be only in its preliminary stages. In Canada it is of course possible to live a mainly urban life, and in this generation most of us do so. It is also possible to ignore, in one's daily work and recreation, the size of Canada. But inside the unconscious of even the most citified Canadian sits the vast and almost unimaginable empire that we govern. Its presence colours all that we do and feel; it shapes our politics, our public philosophy, our poetry, our very selves. In 1946 Wyndham Lewis, the English novelist and painter, wrote: "Canada will always be so infinitely bigger physically than the small nation that lives in it, even if its population is doubled, that this monstrous, empty habitat must continue to dominate this nation psychologically, and so culturally." A visitor with the sensitive nerve-ends of an artist, Lewis grasped the central point of the country in which he spent the Second World War. But few foreigners ever quite understand the force of Canadian geography. Canadians, for our part, have it in our bones, yet find difficulty articulating our feelings about it.

The most impressive work of Canadian art I have ever seen is an official map of Canada I once encountered in a government boardroom in Ottawa. It was about nine feet high and thirty or so feet across. As I stood before it at midpoint, with my nose almost touching it, my eyes met what most of us would call "the North"—indeed, a place much farther north than most Canadians have ever been. But the real north still went on and on, above my head, toward the ceiling of the room. Southern Ontario, where I have spent most of my life, was a tiny corner at my right foot; the heavily settled part of British Columbia was another tiny corner far to my left. The cities in which most Canadians live, right up to Edmonton, made only a small strip near the floor.

The map had no specific relationship to the purposes of the room in which I found it, and I assume it was put there simply to remind the bureaucrats who used the room of the lengths to which their imaginations must stretch to encompass the reality of Canada. Try as we may, Canadians cannot ignore this reality, but so far we have reached only a dim understanding of how it conditions us.

For generations the study of Canadian history consisted mainly of showing how our country was shaped from the outside—how France and Britain and then the United States manipulated the conditions of our existence. The story of that historical dependency, and of our glacial movement toward independence, is important, but as we told and retold it we failed to understand the internal reality, the mythic power of the land itself. We came to believe (as many of us believe yet) that if only we could understand the foreigners dominating us, and perhaps understand our own failure to resist them, we would somehow come to a realization of our own identity. We made the common mistake of believing that we could define ourselves exclusively by our relation to others. Only a handful of white Canadians— some explorers, later some entrepreneurs, later still some artists—understood what the natives knew all along, that we were at the mercy of our geography and for good or ill we would be moulded by it. A.R.M. Lower stated the conventional theme of his classic history of Canada in the political terms of his title, *Colony to Nation;* but he concluded by pointing toward a future in which Canadians would come to terms with the Canadian landmass:

> Canada with its division of races presents no common denominator in those profundities which normally unite, in race, language, religion, history and culture. If a common focus is to be found, it must come out of the common homeland itself. If the Canadian people are to find their soul, they must seek for it not in the English language, or the French, but in the little ports of the Atlantic provinces, in the flaming autumn maples of the St. Lawrence Valley, in the portages and lakes of the Canadian Shield, in the sunsets and relentless cold of the prairies, in the foothill, mountain and sea of the west and in the unconquerable vastness of the north. From the land, Canada, must come the soul of Canada.

If that was true when Lower wrote it in 1946, it is far more true today. Canada has developed in the last three decades perhaps the most liberal immigration policies in the world. Unlike other democracies of the West, Canada does not temporarily import "guest workers," use their talents, and then send them home when they are not wanted. Instead it offers the gift of full citizenship—and many, from all over the world, eagerly accept that gift. The result is that the growing population lacks a shared pre-Canadian background; all that Canadians have in common (and it is, I argue, a great deal) is the physical fact of Canada and the opportunities that fact offers.

Since Lower wrote, Canadians have spent some considerable time in search of the soul he imagined; what we have found has so far surprised us, and in some cases alarmed us. Slowly we are beginning to understand what a Canadian is, but that turns out to be different from what we expected. We are a "nation," but not in the sense that history (mostly European history) taught us to use that word. Conditioned by our experience of and our reading about nineteenth-century nations, we expected that a mature Canada would resemble those earlier nations in certain essential ways. Canadians would, for instance, develop a patriotism more or less binding on all citizens; we would develop a point of view, perhaps an ideology. We would have an identity. But maturity for Canada has turned out to be something new under the sun, something for which the history of others could not prepare us.

Public policy, in everything from railway construction to broadcasting regulation, has urged us in the direction of unity; instead we have grown more diverse. Public policy has tried to elicit agreement on methods of national development; instead we have tended to disagree more and more, and to make our disagreements more vocal. Public policy in Ottawa has pushed for centralization of power; instead the regions of Canada have become more self-consciously separate. Our most characteristic public forum is the First Ministers Conference, at which provincial premiers become television stars, each with a performance to give, each with a set of regional or provincial grievances to state, each with an audience back home to please. And the focus of our national public life is not the improvement of our general condition but rather the appropriate method of dividing the revenues from our natural resources. The issues dictated by geography overcome all other issues, moving back and forth across party lines, so that socialists and conservatives from one region, while disagreeing on all else, find themselves in agreement on their region's entitlement to the fruits of the earth. All the calculations of political scientists and historians are defeated by the brute facts of the Canadian terrain. Michael Bliss, the historian, recognized this when he described the federal Geological Survey as "that little band of explorers who have done as much to map our national identity as all our writers and artists combined." The identity the geologists map is the same identity we see displayed at the First Ministers Conference.

What is at work here is not the frustration of a benign national purpose by fractious regionalists; it is the inevitable development of a pluralistic society coming to terms with the proprietorship of an empire. The force of our geography has not been diminished by modern communications, as many once thought it would be. Mass communications have instead made us all more conscious of our rights and our separate identities; they have reinforced rather than dissolved our demands by providing us with the means to express our feelings. At the same time, they have helped us to find pleasure in our diversity. In an earlier time many a theorist of mass media guessed that television would smooth out regional differences and create a bland sameness across society. But something like the opposite has happened. While television has taught us to know one another better, it has heightened our awareness of one another. And jet aircraft, while they take us swiftly from place to place, don't make us want to eliminate the distinctions between regions. A Torontonian and a Newfoundlander can now visit each other with some ease, but each in the end will probably decide that what makes the other valuable is his separate and different existence. It is only in the age of mass communications that genuine pluralism can flourish, because it is only in this age that we have the means to learn about one another.

The size of our country and its physical variety, combined with democratic traditions, have created a unique political and social atmosphere. A dozen years ago, when I was counselling American draft dodgers on their future in this country, I caught a glimpse of Canada as it must seem to outsiders who have personal reasons to be concerned about the openness of Canadian life. The draft dodgers were escaping from forced military service, of course, but I discovered among them a good many who had other concerns; there were even some who were physically ineligible for the army but who had declared themselves "draft dodgers" anyway and had crossed the border. What they were fleeing, no matter their politics (and some were far more conservative than I had expected), was the pressure of American political opinion. In the United States they had felt called upon to commit themselves to political factions, whether they wanted to or not, because American public life demanded commitment to this or that point of view. What they noticed first about Canada was the absence of a compulsion to conform. They discovered to their surprise that patriotism is not a prerequisite of Canadian citizenship. What the draft dodgers found in Canada was a unique kind of psychic freedom, a rather different matter from political freedom. It is this freedom, expressed in ethnic, linguistic, and regional terms, that forms the real basis of Canadian life.

The curious fact is that in order to qualify as Canadians we are not required to be loyal, even in theory, to the idea of Canada. At an editorial meeting at *Maclean's* early in the 1960s, the then-new subject of Quebec separatism was introduced. One editor declared firmly that separatists should be prosecuted for treason. He was an English immigrant, still innocent in Canadian ways, and his suggestion was greeted with derisive laughter, but it occurred to me at the time that if one looked at his views from a global perspective they were not altogether preposterous. In a very few countries would the idea of national dismemberment be greeted with such insouciance. But in fact, by unspoken agreement, Canadian citizenship carries the ultimate freedom: the freedom to declare that one doesn't want to be a Canadian, to urge that one's region should cease to be part of Canada, and yet to go on being a Canadian and receiving the appropriate benefits. No Quebec or Alberta separatist, so far as I know, has been denied a federal welfare payment or even a Canada Council grant because of his or her desire to separate.

This is the openness which the draft dodgers found at first rather baffling and then engaging. It is an openness which some Canadians find vexing, and which makes our public life unpredictable. It even makes it possible for the leader of the allegedly federalist party in Quebec, the provincial Liberals, to explain constantly that his loyalty to Canada is contingent and may be withdrawn at any moment. This relaxed and almost casual style of public discourse has always created difficulties and always will. Nevertheless, we should cherish it: nothing is closer to the essence of Canada, and nothing makes a greater contribution to the freedom of the Canadian citizen.

Out of the immense problems created by our geography, we have made a political system based on severely limiting the power of each level of government. It is commonly assumed in Canada that the individual is more important than the state, no matter how powerful the state becomes, and that one's private life is more important than one's public life. These assumptions flow directly from the troublesome but finally beneficial contest between the centralizing force of Ottawa and the disparate forces which stubbornly resist the central government. We understand, without having to articulate it, that it is as Canadian to resist Ottawa as to support it. This struggle is so all-encompassing that it touches every aspect of our lives: it affects the individual because it cripples the psychological power of government. When a country's government is so clearly split, so obviously at war with itself, it is unable to impose conformity on the citizens. In these terms, federal–provincial conflict can be seen as one of the keys to individual liberty. To a foreigner it may seem odd—even perverse—that Canadians so often vote for one party provincially and another party federally, but this is no more than the Canadian way of keeping government in its place.

The vastness of Canada has made this federal–provincial balance both possible and necessary: Canada as a unitary state would be a nightmare of bureaucracy. But while our size effectively brakes most of the excesses of government, it has an even more striking effect on political ideas. When they arrive in Canada, political ideas change. The harsh demand and the urgent appeal are dissipated by the size of the country; radicalism of left or right turns up in one region or another from time to time, but no truly radical idea has ever seized the country as a whole. Neither of the two great malevolent myths of the twentieth century, communism and fascism, has developed a sizeable following in Canada. Political movements which set out to swallow the country are instead swallowed up themselves, lost somewhere over the prairies. A neat, compact European country can generate among its citizens enough agreement to bring even the most terrifyingly brutal idea to power, but in Canada too many countervailing forces are at work. In this, as in so many other ways, Canadians are more fortunate than most of their fellow citizens of the globe.

This is true even of specific and apparently manageable issues, and even among people one might expect to agree easily. In Vancouver today liberal, enlightened opinion believes that the Newfoundland harp seal hunt is barbarous and should be outlawed; in St. John's, liberal, enlightened opinion believes precisely the opposite. What the people of one area regard as wise, the people of another may see as ridiculous. Once, when I tried to explain Canadian cultural nationalism of the 1970s to an art college seminar in Halifax, I found that the whole nationalist movement—developed by dozens of artists across the country over several years—was dismissed as "Ontario politics." A political generality which seems strikingly true in Prince George may appear shaky when it reaches Thunder Bay, rather dubious when it gets to Chicoutimi, and outlandish when it is heard in Cornerbrook.

This means that in Canada no proposition can be finally binding, no argument settled, no plan totally agreed upon. For that reason Canada offers an especially frustrating life to intellectuals, whose training is usually based on European or American models. At some point in their careers, having absorbed foreign experience, they turn to their own country and attempt to impose on it patterns and ideologies developed elsewhere.

They almost always break their swords. They discover that Canadians can't or won't make hard decisions; that every idea approved in one part of Canada is cancelled out by another part. Canada, because of its size and diversity, is not a country of *either/or* but a country of *maybe* and *I hope perhaps*. This is a basic fact of our nature, but to intellectuals it appears as nothing more than a form of spinelessness. Intellectuals want clear definitions, and Canada can't provide them. Leslie Armour, professor of philosophy at the University of Ottawa, is just such an intellectual. Armed with his Ph.D. from the University of London, he brings the full weight of the western philosophical tradition to bear on the problems currently besetting

Canadian life. In his *The Idea of Canada and the Crisis of Community* (1981), he examines our life as a nation and (no surprise!) finds us wanting. Canada is disintegrating, he says, because we haven't evolved a common view of ourselves and our future. He notes that we come together—sometimes— when faced with a threat from outside, but "this is not enough to make a nation. To have a nation there must be a tendency toward a common strategy." Intellectuals adopt this theme when commenting on every area of our national life, from secondary manufacturing to mass culture. An economist seeking to revive our sickly manufacturing sector will talk endlessly of "industrial strategy" (which means emphasizing one industry at the expense of another, and usually one region at the expense of another). A cultural bureaucrat trying to make sense of, say, Canadian television will write papers about long-range planning and the political will required to support it. Canadians will hear these views, nod in apparent agreement, then ignore what has been said—and the politicians, sensing the national attitude, will do the same. In place of the central planning and ruthless decision-making favoured by the Japanese and the West Germans, Canadians put their faith in luck and improvisation. A common strategy—even a tendency toward a common strategy—is precisely what Canadians, collectively, do not want and never have wanted, except perhaps in wartime. This has been the case for so long that it must be a part of our national character, and to ignore it when considering the fate of Canada is to miss the essence.

On the last page of his rather melancholy book, Leslie Armour declares: "We must, indeed, eventually decide what we want." *Au contraire*, it is just by declining to make that sort of decision that we have so far survived. Even those institutions which have endured in Canada for centuries—the Crown, for example—have rarely been subjected to careful examination or defined with care. No one can say what the Crown means to Canadians in 1982, any more than anyone could say what it meant in 1922; we avoid deciding upon that definition precisely because to do so would be divisive. Were we to make a national decision (abolish the monarchy, say, or, on the other hand, place it squarely at the symbolic core of the country), we would require assent from all the regions of Canada, and not all the regions would be able to give assent. Ergo, the Crown is allowed to float free above Canada, neither quite rejected nor quite embraced; every Canadian is thus permitted his own view of the Crown, as of so many other things.

One of the few intellectuals who understood this, almost from the beginning of his career, was Mackenzie King. He drove the most thoughtful of his fellow citizens almost mad with rage by adamantly refusing to make the decisions that they thought needed to be made. When King died, the socialist poet F.R. Scott wrote a bitter memorial tribute:

> He blunted us.
>
> We had no shape
> Because he never took sides,
> And no sides
> Because he never allowed them to take shape.

A cruel indictment, and not altogether inaccurate, yet King governed Canada during some of its most painful years, and left it intact. It was King's party, not Scott's CCF, that successfully (if rather surreptitiously) brought the welfare state to Canada. And King's most persistent and brilliant critic during his career, the historian Frank H. Underhill, acknowledged at the end of the day that it was King, not Underhill, who understood how to govern Canada.

That aspect of life that intellectuals most enjoy and admire—the sharp clash of ideas, the articulation of fully developed ideologies—was precisely what King laboured to avoid. No wonder we hated him, and hate his memory still. Someday a thorough search of King's diaries—that vast ocean of insight, gossip, and malice, cumulatively the most important work of literature in our history—may finally reveal his secret. How did he see so deeply into the nature of his country? Perhaps he himself never consciously grasped the quality of his own genius. Perhaps King's ascension to power and his ability to hold it were produced by the fortuitous conjunction—so rare in history—of an unshaped, inarticulate people and a leader who perfectly embodied his nation's character.

Plutarch says of the geographers of the ancient world that they would "crowd into the edges of their maps parts of the world which they do not know about, adding notes in the margin to the effect that beyond this lies nothing but sandy deserts full of wild beasts, and unapproachable bogs." In the mind of the modern Canadian, the map of his own country has many such edges, each of them filled with images (accumulated since childhood) of vast empty wastelands beyond the horizon, uninhabited and therefore uninhabitable. The maps prepared by our cartographers are accurate and detailed, but our spiritual maps have much in common with those of

Plutarch's time. Now and then word comes back to us—from an artist or an explorer—that some empty space on our map is in fact filled with life, and mentally we adjust our conception of that one place. But the process is necessarily slow. A Canadian comes into the world with a spatial imagination no larger than that of a Belgian or a Greek, but to understand his own country he must stretch that imagination to its limits. He may find it easier simply to ignore or belittle most of the country, and in this the Europeans long ago set an example for us: it was Voltaire in *Candide* (1759) who had a shrewd, cynical character describe Canada as "a few acres of snow." But those of us who have inherited those acres of snow, or who have adopted them by moving here from somewhere else, cannot so casually dismiss our surroundings. If we wish truly to inhabit Canada, rather than simply to live in some circumscribed area of it, then we need to fill those empty acres imaginatively. We can do this only through art, and art of a particular kind. Landscape painting and photography, nature poetry, novels like W.O. Mitchell's that set down on paper the style of a terrain—these are the means by which human beings take spiritual possession of territory. Before we can finally take Canada into our minds we need to experience it through art; in effect, artists must invent it for us.

This was the central insight of the Group of Seven, who made it their business to display the landscape of Canada to the people who controlled it. In this the Group was not entirely original: there had been landscape painters in Canada for centuries, and one artist after another had tried to set down with oil paint or watercolour the essence of the country. In most cases they had brought to Canada the manners of European art; the Canadian landscape as they recorded it had a gentle, romantic air. While the members of the Group of Seven also drew a great deal from the European tradition, they set for themselves a sterner artistic task. They shaped their style to fit the material, producing a rugged and even (by the standards of their time) brutal art. Working together, exchanging ideas constantly, they moved forward like mountain climbers linked by rope, developing what would become almost a religion. In their view, the Canadian landscape deserved no less. Tom Thomson (who died in 1917, three years before the Group was officially formed), Lawren Harris, A.Y. Jackson, and the others eventually produced a challenging visual account of the physical fact of Canada. In their hands, central and northern Ontario, the Rockies, and the Arctic became the setting for a great and vigorous artistic drama.

Hills, Killarney, Ontario (Nellie Lake), by A.Y. Jackson, ca. 1933.

Their paintings shocked some of the first to see them, but before many years had passed the Group received an astonishing reward for their labours. Though they never achieved more than fleeting recognition outside Canada, within it they became the most remarkable success in the history of our culture. No other artists—in music or literature or any other medium—have had such an impact. No others have appealed simultaneously to rich patrons, schoolchildren, their fellow artists, and the public in general. No others have maintained their status over the decades. The Group of Seven captured the imagination of Canada in a way that it has never otherwise been captured, before or since.

This success was not an accident produced by publicity or the machinations of art dealers; had it been, it would have slipped away when the early Group of Seven paintings grew old and the painters, one by one, died. But the popularity of the Group has instead grown with every passing decade; by the time Harris and Jackson died, in the 1970s, they were treated as national heroes, their obituaries running as long as those of generals or statesmen. The Group had become part of the cultural myth of a whole people.

When Canadians looked at the Group of Seven's paintings they experienced a rare moment of self-recognition, and they continued to have this experience whenever they returned to the art. They saw in those hundreds of paintings and sketches a vision of the Canadian spirit as formed by the Canadian landscape. As a result, the Group has inspired generations of artists—not only painters but also filmmakers, photographers, and illustrators. It is even arguable that their influence has moved into literature; certainly Canadian literature continues to exhibit an exceptionally close relationship with Canadian geography. "Everything that is central in Canadian writing," Northrop Frye tells us, "seems to be marked by the imminence of the natural world." Even though Canada in the twentieth century became more and more a country of city-dwellers, art and literature continued to find their focus in natural settings. This was not nostalgia for the audience's or the artists' rural backgrounds; it was part of a continuing attempt to come to terms with the country.

From the beginning, Canadian artists have at the same time reacted against the use of the landscape in Canadian art. "Every damned tree in the country has now been painted," a young rebel on the Toronto art scene commented in the 1950s, and in doing so spoke for a whole generation that at first had found the Group of Seven oppressive. For these artists the Group's tradition, far from opening up new frontiers to art, seemed on the contrary to foreclose possibilities by dictating a narrow view of artistic possibilities in Canada. In the 1950s and 1960s, abstractionism was fuelled by international sources of inspiration and reflected mainly the newer urban reality—or seemed to do so for a time. But even the most urbanized of artists ended up by returning in his or her own fashion to the landscape and its continuing impact on Canadians. The generation that started out by reacting against the Group ended up by embracing it. In Toronto an artist like Gordon Rayner, after drawing on all the techniques of abstraction developed in New York, and using them brilliantly, returned—just like the Group of Seven—to the central Ontario bush for the background to his most impressive canvases. Michael Snow is above all other things an urban intellectual, but when he took a major exhibition to Paris he included in it a re-interpretation of the Group of Seven's insights. Harold Town, who in his early career saw little value in the Group's heritage, eventually wrote a compelling and important book on Tom Thomson. Joyce Wieland, whose first canvases were as far from the Group as it was possible for them to be, later turned to filmmaking and used the myth of Tom Thomson—as well as his physical surroundings—as the basis for her feature film, *The Far Shore.*

Meanwhile, the painters who consistently appealed to a large public—for instance, Toni Onley in Vancouver and the late William Kurelek in Toronto—were those who found fresh ways to interpret the Canadian landscape; Onley through the lovely haze of a gentle, English-influenced manner, Kurelek in the rough but expressive terms of the self-taught primitive.

Each of these artists encountered the land in personal terms. Kurelek, who grew up in deprived circumstances on a prairie farm in the Depression, was telling the public his own story as much as the land's; in the process he became perhaps the most universally admired artist of his generation as well as the most successful book illustrator in Canada. Kurelek reflected in his work a quality that eastern city-dwellers have often noted in westerners: they are closer to the land, not so much in space as in time. Even that majority which has no direct experience of rural life carries a folk memory of breaking the plains: an accountant in Calgary, say, is the grandson of a pioneer, and his childhood memories include stories of the heroic age of western development. Even in the 1980s, the remembered vision of the prairie as virginal and untouched—menacing in its way, and yet conveying enormous promise—is always just on the edge of the conversation.

For an artist like Joyce Wieland, who grew up in Toronto, the experience is different but no less profound. In her case the encounter with the landscape is a matter of consciously seeking out the background to Canadian life. Her work may in some ways reflect a more romantic view of the landscape, but it remains a view that places the natural world at the core of Canadian consciousness.

The function of art is to make life comprehensible and bearable, but the function of these particular artists is to resolve the tension within us between the enormity of Canada and our urgent need to encompass it. The size of Canada, and the emptiness of it, George Woodcock has noted, are two facts that are often present in the mind of every Canadian. To make art out of that emptiness, to humanize nature—to deny, in fact, that the country is empty—is a supremely human act, an act which is required of the Canadian imagination if the country is to realize its own artistic possibilities.

In the end the need to know Canada's physical nature is crucial to our future because it is in the land that we can find the grounds for genuine optimism. Native mythology, to which few of us pay sufficient attention, has always insisted that life will be governed by the natural world; it has always drawn its symbols from the immediate landscape, and carried the powerful implication that an understanding of human conduct can be drawn from that landscape. And from the moment when the earliest explorers were swallowed up by the apparently endless St. Lawrence River, the land has been the basis for hope. In later generations it was always the astonishing gift of our geography that stimulated the ambitions of Canadians—in one era the abundance of fish in the waters, in another the opening of the west to agriculture, in another John Diefenbaker's northern vision, in still another the slow unfolding of the Arctic's infinite promises of resource development.

The incredible space on earth which history absent-mindedly gave us has laid down the rules of Canada's existence: it determines the content of parliamentary debates as much as it determines the content of our art galleries; it has protected our freedom and made us, in comparison with almost any other peoples in the world, enviably wealthy. It is our heritage and our problem and the source of our future happiness. Perhaps we shall never come to terms with it intimately; but it is the task and privilege of the present generation, in the midst of our self-generated tensions and conflicts, to move still closer to an understanding of what this geographic empire means to us and to our descendants. James Reaney, that remarkable poet who has written so often and so well on Canada, has given us a brief account of a childhood memory; it might be called The Birth of a Canadian Imagination:

> I can remember as a child looking at a map of Canada at school and wolfing down the whole thing as *my* country. The shape of Hudson Bay, the Northern Arctic islands, the coast of Labrador and the shapes of the Great Lakes were particularly lovable. Quebec always seemed like the profile of—someone—the Duchess in *Alice in Wonderland* with the Ottawa River defining her chin and jaws, Cape Jones as her nose, Labrador as her headdress and some unknown river (the Nottaway) as the outline of her rather pursed mouth. Ontario seems like someone in a rather grotesque rocking chair. The Arctic Islands had the fascinating fretted shapes of mackerel clouds in a sunset. Naturally I have never since known Canada as well as I did then.

ARGUMENTS 2

Shoot That Puck, Grab That Briefcase

BY HARRY BRUCE

Who was it who said, "Winning isn't the main thing, it's the only thing"? Have we become too stuck on winning? Whatever happened to playing games for the fun of it?

The real function of organized kid hockey is to teach corporate values to tykes, to mould their little personalities so that when they grow up they'll fit smoothly into the solemn machinery of Big Business. Today's peewee is tomorrow's vice-president of management services. Mom and dad—even as they rise at 4 a.m. to drive peewee through a blizzard to a rink where he skates hard with other tiny, apple-cheeked potential vice-presidents—are only vaguely aware that the outfit in which they've enrolled their kid is not only a hockey team but also the kindergarten of corporate life. Not that they'd mind. But dad secretly dreams his boy is bound for the NHL, and mom just thinks it's good for him to enjoy himself when he's young, have nice chums and help beat the piss out of a team coached by the husband of a woman she detests.

"Kill 'em," the moms screech at their boys. "Kill 'em, kill 'em!" This was when things got rough along the boards during kid hockey in a small town I once knew. The hockey moms had a bloodthirsty streak that made the hockey dads look like flower children. Wearing curlers and kerchiefs, bundled up in duffle coats in the unheated rink, sucking on coffee and cigs, they'd perch near centre ice and shriek at small boys. One mom was already turning her kid into a semi-pro. She gave him two bucks for each goal he scored, and since her husband coached the team, the kid got lots of ice time.

I don't know what she gave him when he missed the open net, but he was as tense an urchin as you're ever likely to meet. One night, a goalie allowed eight goals in one period. He wept in the dressing room. No one consoled him. No one would even talk to him. I wondered if anyone would talk to his mother.

Though teams from other communities played against the locals, the town itself had only two teams, and as everyone and his dog well knew, the coaches had hated each other's guts for years. During games between the town teams, the rink's mood was therefore nasty but zesty. Both coaches were poor winners. They were gloating needlers, and the boys played their hearts out to save those fat, steaming, puffy-cheeked and red-faced middle-aged men from the violent humiliation of defeat. Such games were "a learning experience." You see, company presidents sometimes hate other company presidents, and it's just as well that the little fellows learn about such unpleasantries early on. After all, as someone once said, "The road to the boardroom leads through the locker room."

Others make the same point. Some argue that the reason why women haven't gained their rightful place in the corporate world is that as little girls no one tore them from their dollies and shoved them into team sports. "The traditional boy's games are far from pointless, childish pursuits," Betty Harragan wrote in *Games Mother Never Taught You: Corporate Gamesmanship for Women*. "They are training grounds for life, preparation for adult imperatives of working with others, practical education for the discipline of business.... Baseball, football, and basketball are all team sports, and a structured, organized team is a well-defined social unit.... Each player knows exactly what his duties are and how they dovetail into operations of the rest of the team... and each player knows that he has to perform smoothly and cooperatively with the others if he wants to retain his place on the team."

Fathers, when they face the fact that junior will never be a Gretzky, recognize that team sports do teach boys useful business attitudes. Gai Ingham Berlage of Iona College, New Rochelle, N.Y., described a recent survey of 222 fathers of boy hockey players and soccer players in Connecticut and New York. Most fathers thought the most important values that hockey and soccer taught their boys were teamwork and self-discipline. Now hear Michael Maccoby, author of *The Gamesman: The New Corporate Leaders*. He describes "the new corporate top executive" as "a team player whose centre is the corporation.... Thus he thinks in terms of what is good for the company, hardly separating that from what is good for himself.... He has succeeded in submerging his ego and gaining strength from this exercise in self-control." Moreover, he's the organizer of a team, and, like any good coach, he's not interested in stars, prima donnas, locker-room loudmouths or guys who think they're so good they can skip practice. What he wants is total dedication from everyone on the team. If you can't give that, you're out on your ear.

An eight-year-old first-string player for a hockey team that travels already has much in common with, say, the 45-year-old marketing chief of an outfit that manufactures internationally known photocopying machines. As company obligations dominate the man's life, hockey obligations dominate the boy's. Wives and children know daddy's job comes first, and must inevitably clash with dinner hours, vacations and other family pursuits. But in the Berlage survey, 80 percent of the *fathers* said their *boy's* hockey career messed up dinner hours, 44 percent said it disrupted vacations, 72 percent said it threw family activities out of gear, and 28 percent said it even interfered with the kid's schooling.

Why do parents put up with this? "The reasons," Berlage states, "are similar to why company men let the corporation interfere with their family life.... As social prestige for the father revolves around his work, for the child social prestige at school and in the community often is a product of his sports participation. As families bask in the reflected status of the corporate husband, parents bask in the reflected status of having an athletic son." Moreover, as the boss calls the shots not only for the marketing manager but also, to some extent, for his family, so the coach calls the shots not only for the eight-year-old but also, to some extent, for the boy's family. Parents plan family trips to accommodate their little left winger's schedule. Among all 222 hockey and soccer fathers, Berlage reported, "No one expressed the idea that family trips, even at Thanksgiving or Christmas, took precedence over travel games."

If parents refuse to arrange their lives to suit the coach, there are always more cooperative parents waiting in line. In hockey, as in business, there's always another boy on the way up. No one is indispensable. Bosses fire fractious adults. Coaches fire fractious tykes. Those who work for bosses or coaches quickly learn to obey commands or get out.

A sad sidelight on kid hockey as a prep school for corporate life is that it teaches children that winning justifies cheating, if you can get away with it. In organized sports for the young, sociologists Lewis Yablonsky and

Jonathan Brower argue, it's now O.K. to use "all 'reasonable' tactics to win. Getting away with undetected rule infractions… and taking advantage of an umpire or referee's mistakes has become institutionalized as 'all part of the game.'" Some day these pint-sized sharpies on skates may be able to arrange secret price-fixing deals, collaborate on rigging construction bids or bribe politicians. It'll make the bribing go especially smoothly if the politicians, too, are graduates of boys' hockey teams, where they first absorbed the fine old lessons about teamwork, obedience, sacrifice, dedication to a corporate cause and spearing a guy when the ref's not looking.

Finally, Berlage's report on the New York and Connecticut fathers revealed that "favoritism sometimes exists, whether it be for the coach's child or that of a large contributor…. The expression, 'It's not what you know, but who you know,' although not the case most of the time, has some basis in reality." The boys, in short, were already learning a bitter truth of corporate life: The best man does not always get the job. One father told an interviewer, "We think that instead of providing a focus for development and happiness during the important years between eight and twelve, youth hockey quickly becomes a harbinger of events that probably would occur in adult life." Actually, most kid hockey players start at six or seven. Too bad their childhood couldn't last a bit longer. But what the hell, it's a tough old world out there, and they might as well learn to pitch in like everyone else. After all, as no less a figure than ex-president Gerald Ford has said, "Few things are more important to a country's growth and well-being than competitive athletics." Shoot that puck, kid. Grab that briefcase.

Hi-Tech Conception Ignores Kids' Rights

BY JIL McINTOSH

It is time to examine some of the long-term consequences of in vitro fertilization.

Over the last four years, using $28 million, a royal commission came to its conclusions on what Canadians need to know about reproductive technologies.

They didn't go far enough. They considered the people trying to conceive, and the doctors and researchers trying to help them. They considered the technologies themselves, and the taxpayers who help to pay for them. The one thing they forgot was the final product.

Very few people do think about the children produced by such space-age solutions as artificial insemination and surrogate motherhood other than as bouncing, blue-eyed babies presented to grateful parents. If only it was as simple as that.

But bouncing babies grow up into adults who can think for themselves, and one of their most compelling questions is "Who am I?" Reproductive technologies can answer what they are, but any procedure involving anyone other than the child's biological parents can never successfully answer "who."

The need to know is stronger than many people imagine. It is evident in the booming business of genealogy and family crests. It is evident in multicultural programs and in immigrants who ensure that the language and foods of their homelands are passed along. For the adopted, there is a complete network of associations, lawyers and private investigators who have made a business of "seeking out" relatives, and a huge number of adoptees who are perfectly happy among their adoptive family still have a hunger to learn more about their origins.

Couples who adopt, or who use artificial insemination, generally want an infant who looks like them, and will often perpetrate the story by concealing the truth from the child as it grows older. People who successfully adopt often continue to try to produce a child of their own. There is no doubt that people need to be able to find their proper place in a long, unbroken line of descent.

Reproductive technologies utilizing third parties seldom allow for this. Children produced by artificial insemination or ovum donations will never be able to know about themselves if the donor is allowed to remain anonymous. And even if surrogate mothers are impregnated with the sperm and ovum of the child's biological parents, how does anyone know how an adult mind will react to the knowledge that three people were involved in his birth?

The arguments over reproductive technologies must go beyond the actual birth, and concentrate on what will happen 20, 30, 40 years in the future. These people are not producing lab rats, but human beings who will have questions.

It would not be easy for some to accept, but there can be no justification for intentionally creating a child outside of its biological family. In my perfect world, couples would have to live with their infertility if technology could not produce a child using only their own sperm and ovum. No matter how painful their situation, it does not give them the right to make a child who would have to live with the consequences all of its life.

Realistically, I know that the "me-first" attitude will always prevail, and couples will demand donor insemination and surrogate motherhood. That being the case, information on sperm and egg donors must be taken, and made available freely should the child ever ask.

Undoubtedly, the fear of this knowledge would prevent a few from donating, and many would argue that men and women would live in fear that children created from their donations would one day knock on their door. This must be one of the possibilities. It is criminal for people to think that they can blithely give away their genetic makeup without having to answer to the consequences, and irresponsible that people could then use these donations to create life under a cloak of secrecy.

If we were talking about puppies or rats, the ethics would be much simpler. Unfortunately, we are talking about children who will grow up with a need to know, a need which is often undermined by those who don't understand it, or disregarded by people who believe that their right to conceive, by any means possible, outweighs the rights of their offspring.

There need to be controls: mandatory donor records available to all concerned, and an end to any procedure which intentionally creates children using secrecy or third parties, and they are needed now. One child who can never answer "Who am I?" is one too many.

Our Home and Racist Land

BY JANICE McCURDY BANIGAN

What one woman remembers about growing up in Canada makes us re-examine our past.

Thirty-five years ago, my dad answered the telephone after a meeting of the town council in Amherstburg, Ontario. The caller, a Ku Klux Klan member, threatened my father's life because of his civil-rights activities. Dad was the first of many to be threatened.

Back then, Canadian blacks had few rights. Although the Windsor area had been a terminus of the Underground Railway, most of southwestern Ontario was segregated. Blacks couldn't eat in restaurants, for instance. A travelling barber cut our men's hair. Women did their own hair.

My family unwillingly accepted the barriers; we avoided them as best we could. Our lives revolved around the church, our cultural, social and religious centre, the one institution in which we were all equal. The church actually spawned our civil-rights movement. Until then, blacks in Canada had no collective voice.

When the KKK surfaced, I was terrified. I knew of the KKK in the U.S., but was wary of black Americans because of my own racism. As far as I was concerned, their struggles weren't mine.

That phone call began an inevitable process that changed the old system of segregation. Many whites, sharing an abhorrence of racism and intimidation, joined blacks in this process of change that led to the accomplishments of my dad's generation in the late fifties and early sixties. My father died last December. In writing about the past, I hope to pay tribute to him, and play a part in my generation's continued struggles.

In the thirties, jobs were scarce, especially for blacks. Many black men, including my dad, cooked on the Great Lakes freighters, enduring loneliness, low pay and long hours.

After that job, my father spent five years working for a white family, as their "all-around" man. His employers had several homes in Canada and the U.S., so we saw him infrequently. But segregation in the States was strict and nerve-wracking, causing Dad to quit his job and return to Amherstburg. Although a high-school graduate, he was restless, and unchallenged.

In 1942, he began working at the Ford Motor Company's transportation centre in Windsor. He was thrilled—and finally with us every day. His chemistry skills, obtained through night courses and correspondence, were recognized by his white supervisor. He moved to the foundry lab, later progressing to laboratory supervisor, the first black to hold such a position there. His promotion meant he had two things to celebrate that day: the arrival of a baby girl (me), and a job with a future.

In 1946, when supervisors were reduced, he was offered a job as a furnace man. He refused the demotion; management *had* told him he was an excellent foreman. He persevered as supervisor of the lab and water-treatment systems. For seven years, he worked days and attended night school, earning a B.Sc. in chemistry. I remember his graduation, and my pride.

Dad later developed a procedure to treat oily wastes, saving the company millions of dollars. In 1973, he joined Ford's World Headquarters and travelled to Ford installations over the globe, instructing foreign chemists on his process.

Yes, we were proud of my father. Yet I remember one night when I woke up and came downstairs. It was dark. My mother was silhouetted by the street lights, at the window, alone. Snowflakes hit the glass. I was intruding. I withdrew. Now I am sure that she was lonely and worrying about raising us, for my dad's education had meant great sacrifice. He was a part-time father and husband during those years, putting his cherished relationship with us on the back burner, choosing to study toward a fulfilling career rather than accept a mediocre job and the more stable life it could bring.

* * *

In Amherstburg, blacks lived in an area named "backa town." There was a clear demarcation line. In 1949, my parents bought and renovated a larger house, hurdling barriers by moving into the previously all-white area. Initially, we were ostracized. Later, we were accepted by some neighbours, but felt like strangers in a foreign land.

There were definitely economic strata among blacks in our community: middle-class, working poor, and a large contingent of the desperately poor. Once when I was very young, my mother took me to visit a sick friend who lived in a shack with a dirt floor. Several ragged, dead-eyed children huddled in the cold there. Even at that age, I understood our differences. Because of such disparities, the black community lacked cohesiveness.

Some churches tolerated discrimination. Black ultrafundamentalist groups believed that we would be rewarded in Heaven for our sufferings on Earth. Others encouraged members to better their earthly lives. Despite their differences, all of our churches preached nonviolence—even before Martin Luther King's teachings—and all had a burning vision of equality.

Whenever I smell lilies of the valley, I am pulled back to our side garden, where I played alone. Mom advised us to avoid the house across the street. It was immaculate, framed by two snowball bushes and a manicured lawn. One day, I heard laughter, and a child's voice say, "Oh, Grampa!" I don't recall how, but I struck up a fast friendship with that little girl. Later, we were playing by the garden. Suddenly, her grandfather's booming voice: "What are you doing with these people?"

My new friend and I were dumbstruck. Her grandfather towered over us, grabbing her arm. I watched her arm whiten in his grip. He dragged her inside, scolding her, slamming the door. I was standing alone on the steps of the white house. The door opened again, and the man spat. "Go home! Niggers aren't allowed!" I was crushed, and must have blocked out the rest.

But I vividly recall my first civil-rights demonstration. It happened in music class, where Stephen Foster's songs were routinely taught. We sang "Ol' Black Joe" as Mrs. Pierce played the piano. Our white classmates sang and jeered at us black students. Mrs Pierce never noticed. So, one day, on a pre-arranged signal, we carefully tore "Ol' Black Joe" out of our music books. It was painful for us, as we'd been taught to respect books. Mrs. Pierce was mystified at this pint-sized rebellion. She eventually cut Foster's songs from our repertoire, but she never understood our daily humiliation, or racism's scope.

Then, when I was eleven, while at a church convention in Dresden, Ontario, I participated in a sit-in to desegregate a diner in that town. Our terrified group (my aunt, two other young friends, and myself) was ignored for an hour, except to be given smouldering looks. Finally, the owner appeared. His eyes were hard, like the sun's glint on the silver Ford that was parked outside. He towered above us, spitting, "Niggers ain't allowed! Get out!" It was that same voice: the grandfather in the white house, towering, spitting.

There were many, varied gains. My grandfather was one of the first black councillors in Amherstburg, and in 1953 he became deputy reeve, a first for a black man in Canada. Later, in the sixties, when diabetes took his legs, he called his four sons together and said that one of them must take his place, must maintain his accumulated power. My father decided to run, and was elected in 1965. He remained on council throughout the ensuing battles, as blacks in the area toughened up and demanded more.

Across from Amherstburg is Bob-Lo Island, an amusement park on the Detroit River. Owned by Americans, for years it was closed to blacks, except on Sundays—when the amusements were shut down for the day. Blacks had long been employed there, though, working behind the confections or doing custodial jobs, like cleaning toilets.

When I finished high school with honours, I got a "good" job in the souvenir shop at Bob-Lo, which was co-managed by a black woman, Barbara Hurst. Barb warned me that I must stay hidden, just like her. I unpacked stock, kept up supplies, was the janitor. I stayed out of sight, deeply hurt. I was smarter and better educated than those white front employees!

Anger and frustration were building. Threatening calls from the KKK continued, and their acts of intimidation escalated. In 1969, my uncle, George McCurdy, drew Dad's attention to vandalized signs on Amherstburg's outskirts. Both held crudely painted messages: "Niggers beware. The Klan is here."

A cross was burned on the main street. Two attempts were made to torch our church. Curses defaced the siding of this building that was the centre of our lives. Our modest church *stood* for something—it had been renovated; it had been revitalized by our American minister, Reverend Payne, who had helped break down prejudices we unknowingly harboured against American blacks. The congregation felt a deep violation.

Many civil-rights groups emerged that decade. Windsor's Guardian Club was begun by Howard McCurdy, now a Member of Parliament. His group tested hiring discrimination by using white volunteers. They got jobs, while black and Jewish applicants did not.

Dad was dynamite on council, and Mayor Murray Smith was a doer. In 1969, a civil-rights group, "The Mayor's Committee," was created, which included Dan Hill of the Ontario Human Rights Commission. The committee targeted institutional racism and unemployment. My cousin, Alvin McCurdy, worked with the local Catholic youth group to physically desegregate facilities.

In June, at a Bob-Lo Chrysler picnic, blacks were beaten. Paranoia was rampant; if the phone rang just as Dad came home after a council meeting, then surely it was another threat. It seemed his movements were being monitored. Perhaps by a friend. Who could be trusted?

In 1966, my first husband and I bought a house in all-white suburban Windsor. Most neighbours refused to speak to us or our children. Things got so bad that the local Catholic priest called, ashamed of his flock. During mass, he reminded them of Christ's admonition to "love your neighbour." Four white families befriended us. Our lives settled down. We integrated a nearby, previously all-white church, and drew in other blacks, including my parents and my younger brother, Norm.

My handsome brother! The young white girls in the church swooned, but their parents began to stiffen. Male friendships between blacks and whites were accepted, but interracial dating was frowned on. When it turned out that the minister supported this position, I became very disillusioned with our so-called integration.

Incredibly, there was still one segregated school in Essex County. Another school for white children was nearby and modern, so the South Essex Citizen's Advancement Association pressured the Essex County Board to bus black children to the white school. In a demonstration of solidarity, protestors met in a packed church and then drove to the new school. Behind and ahead, lights were shining like beacons: blacks were united. The school board gave in, and the segregated school was closed.

Activists worked to sensitize teachers to the traumatic experiences of black children in such an educational system. There *were* good white teachers, who respected bright children no matter what their colour. Unfortunately, black kids frequently dropped out.

* * *

My life was changed forever by the Panel of Concerned Women, a civil-rights group that was started by Elaine Crowell. Crowell, an American, had been told there was no racism here. When the truth hit, she modelled a panel after the Panel of American Women, whose founder, a Jewish woman, Esther Brown, was the first American to legally challenge busing, in *Brown v. Kansas.*

The panel, comprised of blacks, Jews, Catholics and WASPs, was the most challenging, exciting thing I'd ever encountered. It took months to forge a united group, ferreting out and dealing with bigotry. Meetings ran from white-hot rages to tears of discovery and love. I met women I'll call "friend" for life.

Finally ready, we presented panels in southwestern Ontario, sharing experiences and offering solutions. A symbiotic group, the Black Heritage Club, was formed. Blacks fielded the most panel questions: the U.S. civil-rights movement was exploding, spilling into Canada. We studied our heritages; I was enraged, and then uplifted. Why had I been proud of my other racial mixtures and not about my black part? I hadn't known much about black achievements, and the educational system had not informed me.

For example, the discoverer of blood plasma, Dr. Charles Drew, was a black man. My ancestors had been amazingly resilient and intelligent blacks. Why didn't I know that Cleopatra was black; that Christ, a Semitic man, couldn't have been blond and blue-eyed?

Eventually, panel members burned out. Some, like me, went to university. We ended bad marriages, or changed careers. The Mayor's Committee in Amherstburg also disbanded.

In 1972, I met Richard Banigan, a college teacher, who changed my life once again. Our races and religions were different, but we fell in love. Richard was a civil-rights advocate, extraordinarily aware of black history. He celebrated our differences, and was well accepted by my four young children from a previous marriage.

In 1973, I bought a home in Colchester, near Windsor. Our agent confessed that the mechanic next door said he would "fix her car good" if she sold to blacks. There had been race riots in Colchester years earlier, and the town had always been volatile. Our lawyer discovered an old by-law, excluding home ownership from non-white non-Christians. In my father's time, these attitudes were exemplified by public signs reading "No Jews, Niggers or Dogs Allowed!" (That same old voice.)

After my mother's death, my father married a lovely white Catholic widow. A petition emerged, and rumours abounded. Was it true that they had ten children? Well, in reality, she had six teenagers, and dad's four children were all grown and independent.

My family and I moved to Oakville in 1981, hoping that prejudice would be more moderate in a larger urban area. The next day, a "For Sale" sign appeared on the lawn next door to ours.

There had been few East Indians in Windsor, and we were appalled to encounter the term "Paki." The large West Indian community was also fending off racism.

The local school was called White Oaks High—we renamed it "White Folks High."

Civil-rights accomplishments have greatly deteriorated. There's a general dehumanization and polarization in our society. Minorities are ready targets. Institutional racism has worsened. Police relations are at an all-time low. Unemployment is rife, especially among visible minorities. Neo-Nazi groups are emerging. Multicultural funding has been reduced. Many minority parents are terrified that the hopelessness of their children will result in more deaths. The phones are still ringing with threats, yet there are still fires in our bellies. Rational, dedicated civil-rights advocates, working together, must continue to ferret out bigotry.

Mine is only a partial picture of our journey for acceptance. May our journey end soon. May we arrive triumphant.

Hoard Money and Food, but Never Joy

BY ANNA NIELSEN

Joy cannot be saved.

Like thousands of other Canadians, we are living on the edge. My husband hasn't worked for almost two years, and soon his unemployment insurance benefits will run out. I am still working, but the future looks bleak.

Yet for dinner last Friday we lingered over lobster, a small bottle of Chardonnay, imported raspberries and a pot of premium coffee. For the next two weeks we'll have cheese on toast or eggs and chips or hamburger stretched to the breaking point.

I can hear the gasps of nutritionists and the disapproving murmurs from friends and acquaintances—all of them wonderful, sensible people who, like Lear's daughters, would have us knuckle down to the reality of our situation. "Eat sensibly and prudently," they say. "Forget such luxuries. What need have you of lobster and wine and raspberrries?"

If I had Lear's courage, I would rage with him, "O, reason not the need." Instead, because I am civilized and they are civilized, I will flippantly toss off the words of a very wise lady: "A bit o' what you fancy does you good."

You see, some days despair hangs over us like a sodden blanket. Our generation doesn't take kindly to reversed roles—the woman bringing home the bacon and the man cooking it. Some days we carp at each other, let our resentments loose, rail at the unfairness of it all, lose our sense of humour.

We know we are more fortunate than some. One of us at least still works. We are neither homeless nor hungry. We can even manage an occasional luxury. Yet some days it seems we could count our blessings with only two fingers.

So let me try to explain why we occasionally eat beyond our means, or buy a book, or take in a movie.

It was shortly after the Second World War. The fighting had ended but the shortages and rationing continued. The day-in, day-out scrimping and saving and hoarding ensured the survival of our bodies, but it put our hearts and spirits at risk.

Gran had survived the First World War, though it took her husband. She had raised six children on a war widow's pension and then adopted an orphaned niece. She made it through the Depression and through the five years of a second world war, and still the hardships continued. When my mother died, she took me in too, though at her age she shouldn't have been worrying about a six-year-old child.

We would sit together in the evenings by firelight, because there were no shillings left for the electric meter. She'd tell me stories, or sing me songs. Sometimes I would sit right on the hearth where the light from the coals was just enough for young, strong eyes to make out the words in a book or magazine, and I would read to her.

But sometimes, when the night seemed especially long and especially dark, Gran would rise stiffly from her chair and shuffle into the kitchen. She'd cut two huge slabs of bread (doorsteps we called them) and spread them with a whole week's butter ration. We'd sit by the fire and eat them and I'd marvel at the tooth marks in the thick butter. We'd sit in silence and in joy and eat our bread and give no thought to tomorrow and tomorrow and tomorrow when dry bread would wad in our mouths and catch in our throats.

Some nights, when Gran sensed that the light of joy flickered low, she'd make her way over to the massive Welsh dresser, find the wide, cut-glass sugar bowl (part of her Sunday-best set), scoop up a great mountain of the precious, rationed crystals and, with a wind-up worthy of Cy Young, toss the whole lot onto the dying coals.

For an instant the room would blaze with light and colour. We'd laugh demonically. Then the darkness would return and we'd stare once more into the grey ashes. But we knew we'd make it through another week of scrimping and hoarding and saving.

You see, Gran knew that you can hoard money and food, but that hoarded joy festers into bitterness. She'd seen the evidence. Even some of her daughters, in their zeal to save for a rainy day, had a "lean and hungry look" about them. The rainy day might never come, but for certain they'd be blind to any rainbows it might bring.

So, some time in late March, when winter hangs around like a stray dog and spring seems as unlikely to arrive as a cheque from Ed McMahon, we'll visit the fish market or the butcher, order some lobster or filet mignon and spend a few dollars on a bottle of wine, and for an evening the recession will fade into oblivion.

Once in a while we'll throw a handful of sugar onto the fire, marvel at the colours and the light, laugh demonically and stay sane for a few more months.

On Being Creatively Homeless

BY PAT STEPHENS

What would you do if you had to find somewhere to live and you didn't have any money?

*E*ver wonder what you'd do if your parachute didn't open?

Lately I have, because that's how I feel as I watch my bank balance dwindling to two figures and no job in sight.

Free fall, it's called.

I figure I have two choices—I can give way to hysteria or I can enjoy the view on the way down.

I've already gone through the hysteria stage, the sleepless nights. Then a kind of numbness sets in. I expect it's similar to freezing to death. Toasty warm, you lie there in the snow, drifting off.

After a while, I kicked myself out of that stage, and by then the question "What am I going to do?" had answered itself. I could no longer expect to maintain my existence as a single person in a pleasant apartment.

"*What* am I going to do?" gave way to "*How* am I going to do it—exist as a homeless person?"

There's still time, whispers a voice. Enjoy the view. I spend a lot of time walking around appreciating the trees against the sky.

And another little voice in my mind keeps intruding with desperate Pollyanna-like stabs at optimism: At least you're not in Sarajevo…

From the coffee shop I watch the parade of people along the street. A man walks by wearing thong sandals. It is 20 below. I see homeless people, wrapped in blankets, huddled in doorways—these are the ones who've crashed to earth. It's a nightmare I don't want to face. It may not be Sarajevo, but trees against the sky offer little comfort.

There has to be a way and I've come up with a disaster plan. Welfare is a temporary respite, but it won't pay the rent. And if I find a cheaper apartment, I still won't be able to come up with first and last month's rent. Landlords are reluctant to consider unemployed tenants with no money in the bank and who can blame them?

Better to take the plunge and go for creative homelessness.

For the price of a month's rent I can buy a year's membership in a health club, complete with locker. And I can rent a post office box. That means I'll always be able to take a hot shower and receive mail. I could even work out and get fit. Hey, I'll have the time.

Imagine the freedom, the lottery ad says. Without that crushing anxiety about paying the rent every month, life could be incredibly stress-free.

I can do volunteer work in hospitals. As a volunteer, your meals are usually free, and I'd be out of the cold, contributing to society. Most important, volunteer work provides that sense of a place to belong—a social context to relax into, people who know you and say hello.

Then I could keep track of gallery openings. Wine, cheese, pâté, joie de vivre—culture, too. And then there are libraries with cozy armchairs where I can read and expand my mind.

There remains the problem of where to sleep. I could find seven friends who'd put me up one night a week in exchange for house-cleaning. Maybe I could do house-sitting and pet-sitting.

Homelessness might not necessarily mean becoming a ragged, stinking denizen of alleyways and fleabag shelters. It could be seen as a liberated state. Not homelessness but rent-free-ness. Backpacking through the city. Fit, warm, cultured, informed.

It could work. But there's still a little bit of time. Maybe a miracle will happen. And anyway, the trees arch gracefully against the winter sky.

Free fall. Exhilarating, terrifying—a lot of us are in it these days. Enjoy the ride, guys. Happy landings.

The Poverty of Affluence

BY JACINTA GOVEAS

A young woman describes the restrictiveness of looking at who we are based on what we have.

എ**B**efore I immigrated to Canada from Pakistan, I had often been warned about "culture shock."

I had already experienced culture shock when I spent three years working as a community development worker in a village in India, more than 2400 kilometres away from my middle-class home.

Most of the people were landless farmers whose whole families, including the children, worked on land owned by absentee feudal landlords. They were paid with a share of the crop, selling most in the neighbouring towns and keeping the rest for themselves.

They were very poor and had very little of what we consider the necessities of life—a choice of food products, clothes, entertainment. Even the real necessities—drinking water, staple foods, medical assistance, education—were hard to come by and people often died as a result. The injustices they suffered as a result of the system of landless farming made it impossible for them to escape their way of life.

Since coming to this world, my mind has often been transported back to that village. For people such as myself who come from very restrictive cultures, North America offers the possibility of realizing so many of our hopes and ambitions.

Couples being able to demonstrate their affection on the streets, people being allowed to express different opinions and freely criticize the government, a choice of sexual preferences, the right to pursue whatever career path you want regardless of sex or class—this is what I thought made the difference between a free society and a restricted one.

I was not at all bothered by these differences.

What was a real shock to me was the abundance of material goods here, from food to clothes to gadgets that we are seemingly unable to live without.

Advertising campaigns make sure that we really need these things. We end up feeling apologetic because we don't have as much as our neighbours.

The sense of not being acceptable was strong—and confusing. Many of us had never before experienced ourselves as different because of our accent or the colour of our skin.

We may not recognize racism in our everyday lives, but we do know that what we are, who we are, is not enough. Our qualifications, our culture, our language, our food—we sense that all of this is not acceptable to the dominant community.

And so we resort to compensating for the things we feel we are not by accumulating material possessions. We need to feel accepted into the new society, so we get what they have. We decorate our houses like theirs; we use the same cosmetics, clothes, cars—whatever it takes. Rather than share the values we bring with us we bow to the obvious material values.

And in the end, we promote the myth that immigrants all come to this country for economic prosperity.

It is sad to listen to newcomers, particularly refugees, who have risked a lot to come here to join a friend, relative or even acquaintance from their home community. It is hard for the people here to find time for the new-comer. They are busy with their jobs—sometimes two jobs—paying off mortgages and loans, saving for the new car or for next year's vacation or to start a family.

I realize that all this is important, but are we losing sight of our priorities? Are we playing into the hands of the corporations by accepting their ideas of what we need? Are we agreeing to live our lives as others think we should?

My first job here was in an office. I was one of the hundreds of nine-to-fivers, but with a difference—I was the new kid. My colleagues were kind, and so decided to take my education in hand. It was interesting to listen to the things they felt I simply had to know: The kinds of clothes I should wear, the need to develop an image, an interest in makeup, all the places I simply had to go to, and how important it was to have a man in my life.

What struck me most was that they seemed to have no sense of who they were as people. All of the talk was of shopping and credit card limits. People who had worked together for years had developed very superficial relationships with one another.

There was little awareness of Canada, never mind the rest of the world.

Poverty was not an alien experience to many of this group, but it was poverty within a local, narrow frame of reference: It meant not being able to afford a particular dress, feeling intimidated by the prices of electrical gadgets, having to wear the same coat for a third winter in a row. Christmas was the saddest time of all, because there was so much that they wanted to get for their children and friends but could not afford.

Before I came to Canada, I used to envy Western women for their political awareness and freedom to fight for a different way of life. I took it for granted that they were all as aware as I of the possibilities available to us if we were free enough to explore them. This was one of the main reasons I wanted to make this country my home. We were socialized to think that almost every woman in the West is a disciple of women's liberation.

Imagine the disillusionment when I found that women here were "liberated" only to the extent of having accepted a different set of rules, instead of having the freedom to question what was being offered.

Very few, for example, questioned the way management was using women's liberation slogans to encourage women to accept exploitation. Few had questioned the codes that made women feel they had to struggle to be more decorative rather than rise within the company by pursuing professional development that would help them to get ahead. Women, like immigrants, had accepted and integrated the values of the dominant culture.

A friend of mine, a new arrival, was talking to me about how appreciative he was of his new country. He was especially grateful to the advertising on television. "At least we know what to buy," he said.

Nobody ever said a truer word. The advertising not only tells us what to buy, it gives new meaning to old words, like "freedom for a dollar." The Lotto 6/49 advertisement proudly proclaims "freedom for a dollar" and flashes images of dreams fulfilled—fancy cars, boats, vacations to exotic places. Freedom becomes synonymous with the acquisition of possessions.

Where I came from, material possessions were few. But what we did have, and were rich in, was a deep sense of what was right and what was important. We always had time for our families and for our children. There was no need for Hallmark cards to tell our children how much we cared, because we expressed it to them every day in so many ways.

Relationships there were real. People invited you into their hearts and into their families very quickly.

There was no pressure to rush around trying to meet mortgage payments or beat credit card debts, and so there was time to be present for people in a very deep way.

No need to worry about counselling bills, because there were people right there to talk to, people who would be ready to walk many miles with you in your struggles.

I often think of the obvious poverty of the people in that faraway village, and of their wealth, and of the obvious wealth of people in this society. Here, there is not much you could wish for that is not obtainable—if you have the money. So we spend a lot of time and energy getting the money that is going to make getting that particular thing possible.

But are we not losing sight of something very basic in this rush for collecting material wealth? What about our relationships with one another?

I am continually struck by the loneliness and pain in this society. We feel the need to legitimize our friendships, so we have programs like Big Brothers/Big Sisters. Special committees are appointed to welcome new people into the neighbourhood.

What does it say about us that we need others to organize us to do things that should come naturally to us—and have come naturally to us before?

When I made the transition from my home to this country, I came looking for personal freedom. I appreciate this above all else in this society.

But faced with consumerism and the need to fill in the empty spaces with things, I think we are all called upon to choose alternative lifestyles and make choices that will enable us to leave something other than our possessions to the ones who come after us.

My Body Is My Own Business

BY NAHEED MUSTAFA

A Canadian-born Muslim woman, a journalism student, believes wearing the traditional hijab garments liberates her. (Her point of view contrasts with the one expressed by Catherine Meckes in the essay that follows this one.)

I often wonder whether people see me as a radical, fundamentalist Muslim terrorist packing an AK-47 assault rifle inside my jean jacket. Or maybe they see me as the poster girl for oppressed womanhood everywhere. I'm not sure which it is.

I get the whole gamut of strange looks, stares and covert glances. You see, I wear the *hijab*, a scarf that covers my head, neck and throat. I do this because I am a Muslim woman who believes her body is her own private concern.

Young Muslim women are reclaiming the *hijab*, reinterpreting it in light of its original purpose—to give back to women ultimate control of their own bodies.

The Koran teaches us that men and women are equal, that individuals should not be judged according to gender, beauty, wealth or privilege. The only thing that makes one person better than another is her or his character.

Nonetheless, people have a difficult time relating to me. After all, I'm young, Canadian born and raised, university-educated—why would I do this to myself? they ask.

Strangers speak to me in loud, slow English and often appear to be playing charades. They politely inquire how I like living in Canada and whether or not the cold bothers me. If I'm in the right mood, it can be very amusing.

But why would I, a woman with all the advantages of a North American upbringing, suddenly, at 21, want to cover myself so that with the *hijab* and the other clothes I choose to wear, only my face and hands show?

Because it gives me freedom.

Women are taught from early childhood that their worth is proportional to their attractiveness. We feel compelled to pursue abstract notions of beauty, half realizing that such a pursuit is futile.

When women reject this form of oppression, they face ridicule and contempt. Whether it's women who refuse to wear makeup or to shave their legs or to expose their bodies, society, both men and women, have trouble dealing with them.

In the Western world, the *hijab* has come to symbolize either forced silence or radical, unconscionable militancy. Actually, it's neither. It is simply a woman's assertion that judgment of her physical person is to play no role whatsoever in social interaction.

Wearing the *hijab* has given me freedom from constant attention to my physical self. Because my appearance is not subjected to public scrutiny, my beauty, or perhaps lack of it, has been removed from the realm of what can legitimately be discussed.

No one knows whether my hair looks as if I just stepped out of a salon, whether or not I can pinch an inch, or even if I have unsightly stretch marks. And because no one knows, no one cares.

Feeling that one has to meet the impossible male standards of beauty is tiring and often humiliating. I should know, I spent my entire teenage years trying to do it. I was a borderline bulimic and spent a lot of money I didn't have on potions and lotions in hopes of becoming the next Cindy Crawford.

The definition of beauty is ever changing; waifish is good, waifish is bad; athletic is good—sorry, athletic is bad. Narrow hips? Great. Narrow hips? Too bad.

Women are not going to achieve equality with the right to bear their breasts in public, as some people would like to have you believe. That would only make us party to our own objectification. True equality will be had only when women don't need to display themselves to get attention and won't need to defend their decision to keep their bodies to themselves.

Wearing a Uniform of Oppression

BY CATHERINE MECKES

A Canadian journalist who has lived in Muslim countries offers a response to the Naheed Mustafa essay that appears ahead of this one. Catherine Meckes sees the traditional hijab garments not as a means of liberation but as badge of oppression.

It takes some pretty twisted logic to call wearing *hijab*, the head-to-toe covering for women prescribed by the Koran, liberating. It's like saying an animal in a cage is free because it doesn't have to deal with the realities of its natural habitat.

Choosing to wear *hijab*—which leaves only the face, hands and feet showing—is a form of hiding, of crying uncle, of saying to men who leer and gape, "You win, it's my fault you are staring, assaulting, raping. You guys can't control your sexual urges, so it's up to me to make sure there isn't even a suggestion of a body under my clothes to tempt you. My fault. Sorry."

Naheed Mustafa, who wrote "My Body Is My Own Business," justifies wearing *hijab* as a way that Muslim women can take control of their own bodies. But the covering of Muslim women has its origins in the need men felt to protect their women, considered to be their property, from the sexual predations of other men, not because these advances were an aggression against another person but because they were an afront to the honour of her male relatives. The result of such sexual tampering was severe punishment for the perpetrator—and also for the woman, who, having lost her value with her virtue, was cast out or killed, regardless of her innocence.

Look at the profound shame and self-loathing Muslim women who were raped in Bosnia are suffering because they believe their communities will no longer accept them.

How ironic and sad that Ms. Mustafa should claim that wearing *hijab*, so symbolic of women's subjugation, is evidence of her freedom. Surely it's just the opposite.

Ms. Mustafa is right, or course, in her indictment of a society that objectifies women, using their bodies to sell products and assigning them value based on physical attributes. There's no doubt it's a struggle for women to live in the West with the lie that they are free and equal. The world, the West included, is still emerging from the tradition that has existed during most of its history, that of woman as man's possession. We in the West have chosen to go in a different direction from the Muslim world in this evolution. And Middle Eastern countries themselves vary in how much they take part in this tradition, from the recent crackdown on improper covering by women by the reactionary regime in Iran to more liberalized customs in Lebanon and parts of Turkey.

The kind of attitudes that produce, for example, the Miss CHIN Bikini contest, an annual Toronto parade of female flesh before throngs of ogling, hooting males, or the Sunshine Girl daily offering of bulging breasts and bums in *The Toronto Sun*, are odious and offensive. But there are other ways of dealing with them than sticking your head, ostrichlike, into a veil.

Having lived in a Muslim country and studied Islam, I have some understanding of, and sympathy with, Muslims and their culture. There's a great deal of unjustified fear and ignorance in the West about Islam. Fortunately for Muslim immigrants, Canadian society is committed to pluralism, and most Canadians believe in that principle, if the practice is sometimes trickier to accomplish.

For example, we longtime residents of a west-end Toronto neighbourhood have adapted to new and sometimes strange sights as each new influx of immigrants transforms our streets. There are many women in our area— Indians, Middle Easterners, Africans—wearing all sorts of traditional dress, from strict *hijab* to filmy scarves flowing from head to shoulders. They are now as much a part of my neighbourhood as the modern dress most of us wear.

But recently I encountered a Muslim woman in the supermarket, shopping with her family. She was wearing *hijab*, but she also wore a veil across her face, hiding it from the eyes down. With a head scarf covering her forehead, there was just a slit left for her to look through. A few days later, I saw another woman, similarly veiled, walking on the street.

I found the sight of these women with their hidden faces disturbing. It's one thing to see covered faces as the exotic and mysterious product of another culture you can leave behind when you return home. But finding them on my home turf, I have to confront my fears about what this kind of dress represents for me, and for all women: backwardness, submissiveness, degradation.

So seeing educated, modern women like Naheed Mustafa embrace *hijab* as something liberating, as giving women control over their bodies, as a way of coping with the frustrating and often intolerable sexism of our culture, dismays and mystifies me, as I'm sure it does other women.

There are many worthwhile and admirable practices in Islam that we should know about in the West. Wearing *hijab* is not one of them.

What Kind of Men Are These?

BY MICHAEL IGNATIEFF

This essay was sparked by recent events in Bosnia, but it could have been based on a thousand other atrocities around the word. The point is not that people from one particular group killed people from another, but rather what is inside us that makes some of us do such things.

It was a small house, the British soldiers said, which they reached through a green iron gate on rusty hinges. They found a bicycle lying by the garage, a baby-sized rubber boot on the grass, some cows grazing in the backyard and inside the front door two burned corpses: a father and his son lying together with a carbonized rifle beside them. In the basement, the soldiers discovered five more burned bodies: three women, two children. From the way the children's hands were pressed to their faces, it seems likely that they had been burned alive. It also seemed likely that those who had set fire to them had watched them burn.

This happened in the village of Ahinici in central Bosnia. Croatian irregulars, drunk on plum brandy, armed with rockets, mortars and small arms, as well as fire and dynamite, went through the village destroying every house that was not Croatian. They finished off the livestock in the barns, shot each chicken pecking in the yard and each dog growling on its chain. When the British soldiers tried to remove the more than 40 bodies for burial, snipers opened fire upon them.

Such terror does have its reasons. The more bestial the atrocity, the more efficient it is. If the Croatian goal was to cleanse the areas granted it under the Vance-Owen plan of anyone who might one day resist them, Ahinici was undoubtedly an efficient action. Word of what was done in that cellar will travel with the speed of a cold desolate wind through the hills of central Bosnia.

Most atrocity is born in atrocity, as crime is born in crime. Ahinici probably has a place on some dark descending spiral of reprisal and counter-reprisal. The torching of that cellar might be one man's revenge for another murder in another cellar. Who knows?

When you have understood all this, you are still left with a deficit of explanation, a void that words and reasons cannot fill. A man watches children burn. What kind of a man is that? Is he any kind of man at all?

There seems to be two possibilities. Watching a child die might be a natural thing for a man to do. We cannot be sure that it isn't. As Shakespeare said, killing is man's work. It may only be a desperate liberal illusion that there is a barrier of natural restraint within us all that we must cross before we can kill. Perhaps it is easy, and only gets easier with each corpse we leave behind.

I do not want to believe this. I would prefer to suppose that a man cannot watch a child burn unless something inside him has long since been burnt out. I want to believe that there must be some natural barrier to atrocity that must first be overcome. A complex inner disintegration coupled with a willed cauterization of the moral instincts that distinguish man from beast must first occur. I want to believe, in other words, that there is a goodness inside us all which must first be forsaken. For if there is goodness, there might be hope. But you cannot return with anything like hope from a trip down those cellar stairs.

We are poorly served by our available language when it comes to understanding the process that burns men out and turns them into killers. The idea that some men are innately evil seems to evade the real difficulty, which is to explain how ordinary fathers and husbands can be slowly degraded, by the dull impulsion of carnage, into the sort of person who torches a basement with women and children inside. We seem to be in need of an idea of the soul but are embarrassed to speak of it. We want to assume that human beings have a kinship with one another that runs deeper than merely the shared faculty of calculating moral consequences. When we speak of the soul, we have in mind some instinct that would make us shudder at the thought of incinerating a child. Yet there were, roaming through the darkened streets of Ahinici, drunken men who had long since thrown away their souls.

It is often said that it was the madness of nationalism that did this. Had they not been taken over by the delusion that ethnicity is all there is to a human being they might have seen that there were fellow members of their species cowering at the bottom of that cellar. Instead, all they saw were dirty Muslims, a nest of vermin to set afire.

In the moral madhouse of nationalism there is no atrocity you cannot commit, that you cannot blame on the antecedent atrocity of the other side. Such is the moral infantilism to which nationalist feeling reduces us all. Even the simple decencies of shame or sorrow can be fended off with, "He started it."

What passes for moral dialogue in the Balkans is actually a pornographic exchange of atrocity stories in which all sides end up absolving themselves at the expense of the other. All of this is very human and none of it is a Balkan specialty. Nationalism everywhere exists to lift the burden of responsibility from a believer's shoulders.

Perhaps even the killers of Ahinici are sitting in a bar in the next village telling anyone who will listen that their actions were the tragic result of necessity or of history. In no time, they will have delivered the causes of their crime safely back to the dim and bloody mists of time.

But again, it may be a liberal illusion to suppose that men need to give themselves moral permission of any sort before they set fire to a cellar full of human beings. Perhaps they need no excuses at all. Perhaps the process of self-degradation is more like desire, more like the hot rush of sexual feeling, with moral excuses and nationalist self-extenuation following solemnly after. For the thing that can make you truly despair about what happened at Ahinici is the possibility that someone really enjoyed doing it. We really must entertain the possibility that with such beings there is no moral frontier whatever to cross, no internal censor to silence with drink or self-delusion. It is quite possible that they wanted this abomination. They took their pleasure there. For destruction is power and the destruction of human life is the greatest power of all.

There is no profit in such thoughts, no lesson to be drawn, no easy moral to point to. Thinking about it is merely the respect that despair pays to horror. For what we know—but can never fully understand—is that there were two children at the bottom of the cellar stairs, and that as the flames drew nigh, they had time to see the light in their killers' eyes.

The Evolution of the Teddy Bear

BY JAY INGRAM

There are black bears and grizzly bears, polar bears and—teddy bears?

It's hard to imagine children growing up without a teddy bear to cuddle, but the teddy bear is actually a relative newcomer, a creature of the twentieth century. Yet a careful study of teddies shows that even in this short time, the animal has been changing shape steadily and dramatically. In a world where evolution is measured in millions of years, this is a remarkable development. The evidence for it was published in the scientific journal *Animal Behavior* by two Cambridge University biologists, Robert Hinde and L.A. Barden, who made their discovery after examining all the teddy bears in an exhibit at the Cambridge Folk Museum.

The teddy bear was named for American president Teddy Roosevelt. Roosevelt had gone to Mississippi in November 1902 to settle a boundary dispute between Louisiana and Mississippi. During his stay he did some hunting, but had no success. On the last day, someone produced a pitiful little bear, tied up, and apparently encouraged the president to fire away. Roosevelt is reported to have said, "I draw the line. If I shot that little fellow, I couldn't look my own boys in the face again." A cartoon called "Drawing the Line in Mississippi" appeared in the *Washington Post* the next day, showing the president refusing to aim his rifle at the tethered cub. The cartoon had political implications—that the president was reluctant to impose the presidential power on what was essentially a local issue—but it was Teddy's bear that became famous. Although humanlike bears were already popular subjects in children's stories, this incident prompted toy manufacturers to begin making cuddly toy versions. Within five years of Roosevelt's trip to Louisiana, toy teddies were flooding the market.

According to Drs. Hinde and Barden, in those early days teddy bears looked like real bears, with low foreheads and long snouts. But that head shape has changed gradually, and the teddy bear's eyes have crept down lower and lower on the face, creating a higher and higher forehead. At the same time, the long snout has been shortening, although the authors note that this change was more or less complete by the 1930s. Today's teddy bear is an animal with a high forehead and a short muzzle, quite unlike his forebears.

One 1916 bear in this study was a particularly intriguing specimen, because it had, at that early date, the head shape and proportions of a fully modern teddy. Evolutionists can only speculate on why that particular line died out, even though it foreshadowed what was to come.

The teddy isn't the only animal to have evolved with dramatic speed over the decades. Stephen Jay Gould, the Harvard scientist and writer, noted several years ago how Mickey Mouse has changed since his introduction in the late 1920s. His eyes have become much larger, his snout thicker (giving the impression of shortness), and his ears have moved back, making his forehead look higher. These changes are similar to those seen in teddy bears, yet these are two completely unrelated species (the ancestral lines leading to bears and mice had already split when the dinosaurs were still around), with very different habits. However, they do have one outstanding trait in common: their very existence depends on their ability to charm humans.

What charms humans? The Nobel Prize-winning expert in animal behaviour, Konrad Lorenz, was the first to point out that adult humans respond to certain kinds of facial and cranial features in other humans and even animals, features that encourage nurturing and affection in the humans who see them. These include a large head, high forehead, big eyes set low in the face, chubby cheeks, short and stocky arms and clumsy movements. In other words, everything that human babies have. And everything that puppies and kittens and other baby animals have. These are the physical features that trigger the reaction "Ooooooooooooohhh, isn't he sooooooo cute." A baby's survival is, of course, enhanced if its physical features elicit feelings of parental protection and love.

In a laboratory test of Lorenz's hypothesis, students at the State University of New York at Stony Brook were shown slides of a variety of line drawings of human faces and asked to rate them on a scale of one (unattractive) to seven (cute). The faces themselves differed in the location and/or size of the facial features. The eyes, nose and mouth could be near the bottom of the face, leaving a very high forehead, or at the top, producing a giant chin. Eyes varied in width and height, and even in the diameter of the iris. Only one feature was changed in every slide, so there was a bewildering array of faces, but even so, one face stood out in the ratings. It was a baby-like face with all the features that Lorenz had predicted: large eyes set low in the face, exposing a high forehead.

Both the teddy bear and Mickey Mouse have been evolving to secure their place in the human heart by tending more and more to infantile features. This process, well known in zoological circles, is called neoteny. Any species that is evolving in this manner prolongs its juvenile stage and so delays adulthood. The result is that the adults of today look like the young of past generations.* Neoteny is seen in organisms as diverse as salamanders—some of which reach sexual maturity without ever losing their gills—and flowers. One species of larkspur has slowed its development so much that the mature flower looks more like the buds of other species. This juvenile tubelike flower is suited to pollination by hummingbirds, a lucky break for both plant and bird.

As Hinde and Barden point out, there are other interesting physical changes seen over the years in toy bears. One particular specimen, which first appeared in the 1920s, was striking because of its tiny brain case—measurements revealed a very short distance between its eyes and the top of its head. These anatomical data support the unusually well-documented behaviour of this bear, as copious field notes attest to the animal's apparent lack of intelligence. He is known as Winnie-the-Pooh.

This study is an important step in paleoanthropology. Hinde and Barden have been able to trace the evolution of the teddy in detail from its initial appearance in the fossil record to the modern form—rarely is such a

---

*In fact, humans have evolved by that very process. We have become humanlike rather than apelike by slowing down our development and retaining fetal or childlike physical characteristics into adulthood. An adult human looks much more like a fetal chimpanzee than an adult. We also presumably look much more like a fetal *Homo erectus* than an adult. You could easily speculate that if this trend continues, future human adults will have even flatter faces and bigger heads relative to their bodies, like modern human fetuses.

complete record available. Their data confirm the Lorenzian speculation that evolution will favour high foreheads and short muzzles to foster parental nurturing behaviour. And most important, any hitherto unclassified teddies discovered in cottage or attic excavations can be placed in their appropriate position in the teddy bear family tree by a simple measurement of their cranial dimensions.

A Walk on the Wild Side

BY ALICE MUNRO

A plea to keep a little bit of nature accessible to everyone.

Where I grew up, on the rural west side of the town of Wingham in southern Ontario, the Maitland River was at the foot of our property. The river flats and the bottomlands were generally too stony for crops, but made good pasture. There were scattered trees where the cattle could shelter from the sun, and the river provided drinking water. From the rough natural vegetation of the bottomlands and river flats, the grazing cattle produced a grassy parkland that reached to the foot of our property in a grove of elm trees within sight of the house.

Downstream to the west, and visible from our place, a wide curve of the river had broadened the flats, and to the north it had undercut a high steep bank covered with trees—the whole being, in effect, a great amphitheatre half a mile or more in width, floored with elm and maple parkland. On the high, distant skyline back from the amphitheatre was Roly Grain's farmstead—house, barn, and silo. To the south, where Roly Grain's sideroad joined Highway 86 just at the bridge where the river completes its curve, the village of Zetland once thrived—remembered by my father, but in my time utterly vanished. When I was young, the skyline with Roly Grain's farmstead seemed to me the end of the world, and the vanished village whose time had ended somehow filled out that idea.

This scene—an amphitheatre floored with parkland and reaching to the end of the world and joined to us by the river—was my first access to the countryside of southern Ontario, which was and has remained magical. When I was very young, I dreamt I saw a pure white horse with a jewelled bridle come down to drink at the river—but I didn't think that was a dream. When I lived in British Columbia, I longed for the sight of Ontario landscape—the big solitary oaks and beeches and maples looming in a summer haze in the open fields, the carpet of leeks and trilliums and bloodroot in the sunny woods before the leaves come out, the unexpected little rough hills with their hawthorns and tough daisies, the creeks and bogs and the long smooth grassy slopes. On a motor trip home via the state of Washington, we came out of the splendid mountains and forest onto the great rolling country of the Palouse-Big Bend wheatlands, and I felt as if I had retrieved a lost part of myself, because it was something "like home."

Some 15 or so years ago, I returned to Ontario to live, not to the place where I grew up but to a small town nearby and to essentially the same landscape. But things have changed. The elm trees are gone—the last one on our flats, a seeming survivor of the Dutch elm disease, fell in a storm in 1977. The bottomlands are no longer pastured, for reasons I have not investigated, and have grown up in coarse vegetation—tall grasses, stinging nettle, joe-pye weed, wild parsnip, thistles, goldenrod, hawthorn, and scrub willow, to name only a part of it—and the walkable land is gone. The local rivers and streams are not poisonously polluted but are often choked with various kinds of algae and water plants overstimulated by fertilizer runoff from cultivated fields. Even if I were to hack my way through the jungle of vegetation, the river doesn't have the swimmable water I once knew.

The amphitheatre in the curve of the river belonged to our neighbours, but I regarded it as mine, or ours, or not anyone's—accessible to everyone not afraid of cows. This was generally the rule—you could walk the countryside on private property without fear of being hauled up for trespass. Now, more and more rural land is posted against trespass, and when I walk in the country, I would seldom think of cutting across a piece of private land, posted or unposted, unless I had the owner's permission. The countryside of southern Ontario was once an unofficial recreation area for local people. For a variety of reasons—too many people, larger cultivated fields, the unpastured bottomlands—that day is gone. There has been no adequate replacement.

Two years ago my husband and I discovered the walking and bicycling trails in Wisconsin that have been converted from abandoned railways. Near Blue Mounds, a little west of Madison, on a fine summer morning, we came upon the Military Road Trail. When we are travelling, we find that our staying power is improved if we get about an hour's walk a day, and the trail was exactly what we were looking for. We walked from Blue Mounds to Barneveld, had lunch there in a pub right beside the trail, and walked back to Blue Mounds. We were so elated by this walk that we decided to change the itinerary of our trip to visit the other Wisconsin trails, and we were not disappointed. We talked about the reasons for our exhilaration and came up with something like this: "One of life's great pleasures is to feel possessive of your homeland, and one way to get that feeling is to see the country as a landscape that belongs to you and to which you belong, and to see it close up and at not too great a speed."

But Wisconsin is not our homeland. It was good to know that there was a government there that had taken this trouble to provide for its people—to recognize that the need to walk is as important as the need to drive on a highway. But it wasn't our government. So we came home with the hope that this sort of program could be started in southern Ontario, where at this very time so many railways are being abandoned. Recently one Sunday, we toured along the abandoned sections of the CPR from Credit Forks to Wingham, which has a branch to Fergus. Near Credit Forks, where the line crosses a secondary highway, we found 12 cars parked. They belonged to people who were walking the line, having clambered over the ridge of earth the company has bulldozed up to block passage to vehicles. At another crossing, we saw cyclists throwing their bikes over the barrier. All along the line from Wingham to Credit Forks we encountered people walking and cycling, including a farmer who owned adjoining land. He said he would like to see the abandoned line become a trail. When you see valiant cyclists pumping along the thin edge of paved highways with the traffic roaring by, you can appreciate the appeal a controlled trail has for them, and you can also appreciate that the Ontario government, despite its advocacy of out-door exercise, is doing nothing to facilitate cycling as an activity that large numbers of people could enjoy.

If the line west out of Credit Forks follows the same history as other abandoned railway lines in Ontario, there will be a brief period during which people will walk and bike along it, and then the adjoining landowners will close it down, whether by legal purchase or not. One fence across the line effectively closes the whole section between road crossings. All across the province, bits and pieces of abandoned lines can be found, fragmented by closure by adjoining landowners. These potential trails are being lost. And they are not just trails but existing corridors of vegetation. Along the Guelph to Goderich line, we saw banks of wild strawberries, thimbleberry and wild raspberry bushes, tame cherry trees and lilac bushes gone wild, and many, many young elm trees—enough, perhaps, to form a reservoir within which an immunity could be developed to the Dutch elm disease. Wouldn't it be worth preserving our vegetation, our nurseries of elm trees? (And trees growing up along the tracks would provide privacy for the landowners.)

I've turned my celebration of southern Ontario countryside into a plea, because I really believe that access to the land is a right and a necessity, just as paved roads and schools and hospitals are. I believe that it's important to our well-being. I think that people who see the landscape in this way will give thought to protecting and preserving it. The railways have been heavily subsidized, so surely we all have some claim on the lines when they are abandoned. If the provincial government would just accept custody of these lines, it would make possible a period in which interested parties could lobby for various plans, and the corridors wouldn't be immediately fragmented and lost. I hope they won't be.

No New Worlds

BY ADRIAN FORSYTH

"As average North Americans, our per capita consumption of energy and its attendant environmental damage are equivalent to that of 531 Ethiopians. In terms of impact, then, the Canadian population is the equivalent of 14 billion Ethiopians."

The small hotel is hot, but Hadi, lying in his bunk, shivers violently. He cannot get warm. His liver is swollen and tender. Sweat beads on his brow as a quarter of a billion parasites burst out of his red blood cells, and he shudders as wave after wave of the protozoans pours through every artery and capillary in his body. It is Hadi's third bout with malaria since he arrived as an immigrant in Irian Jaya, the Indonesian half of New Guinea.

Irian Jaya is a thinly populated, resource-rich New World frontier for landless Indonesians, but Hadi's prospects are grim. Malaria is rampant, and Hadi's wages from the hotel where he works are too low for him to afford antimalarial medicine. Hadi might soon die. If he does, the physiological agent of his death will be malaria, but the ultimate cause of his premature end will be human overpopulation.

Hadi was raised on the island of Java, one of the most densely populated regions on the planet. On Java, more than 90 million people crowd into an area the size of New Brunswick and Nova Scotia combined, and even the countryside swarms with up to 2,400 people per square kilometre. At these densities, it can be said fairly that Java is ground zero in the population explosion and is sending people such as Hadi forth like human shrapnel, cutting into even the most remote corners of our planet.

Hadi knew about the malaria, but he saw no alternative to emigration. On Java, he says, "there is no work, there is no land." And indeed, the land-less poor who stay to fight it out face a horrendous existence. Jakarta, the capital, is crisscrossed by canals—open, sluggish sewers stinking of deter-gent and human excrement—where thin people with basket nets try to sieve out the hardy minnows that survive in the fetid slurry. When the flat-bed garbage trucks arrive at the dumps, ragged, desperate souls swarm over them even before they stop, gleaning food, cardboard to sell or to live under—anything that is not absolutely putrid. The smell and smoke of burning rubbish complete the hellish vision.

It was not always so. A century ago, fewer than four million people lived on Java, and travel writers extolled it as "the Garden of the East," an island blessed with some of the most fertile land in the Tropics. But in spite of its natural abundance, nature is now nearly dead in Java. Virtually every metre of level land has been deforested and converted to paddies. Day and night, people are busy digging away at a landscape now wholly subservient to meeting human needs. Most of the wildlife, having lost its once lush hab-itat, teeters on the edge of extinction.

In the two decades that I have spent working in tropical countries, I have come to see Java not as an exception to but as a microcosm of the glo-bal population predicament. The island is the crest of a corrosive wave of human life, a rising flood of 5.5 billion human beings, 250 billion kilograms of protoplasm, that is eroding the diversity of life. The effect is everywhere. Seas remote from human habitation are losing their fish. Forests that until last year felt only the tread of an indigene's bare feet are today being carried away by monstrous machines from afar.

My work in the Tropics has seen a pronounced shift in recent years. I used to study rain forests; today, I try to save them. Ecologist Norman Myers has pointed out that the planet's biological "hot spots"—areas such as the tropical forests of the Brazilian coast, western Ecuador, West Africa, Madagascar, Sarawak, Irian Jaya—harbour as much as 50 percent of all life forms. But now, seemingly overnight, the burgeoning human population is usurping their habitat, eliminating species after species at an unprecedented rate. Sociobiologist E.O. Wilson estimates that as many as 140 species are becoming extinct daily, a rate some thousand times higher than that which would occur without a human presence. In the next 30 years, we stand to eliminate up to 25 percent of the planet's species.

Certainly, in just 20 years, I have witnessed a sudden, frightening invasion of humans into regions rarely visited before. And critically, the intrusion is not only of poor and benign souls like Hadi, who come seeking land, but also of the economies of cities and nations thousands of kilometres distant that bring people to log, mine, fish, farm and otherwise consume the world's most biologically vital areas. It is this—the insidious combination of swelling human numbers and a technologically powerful globalized economy of consumption—which poses the greatest threat to *all* the Earth's species.

The number of human beings alone, however, is staggering. Two billion people cut trees for firewood today, and still, two-thirds of them cannot get enough. Another billion cannot get enough food to eat. Yet each year, with only 50 million deaths to subtract from 143 million births, there are 93 million new mouths to feed, clothe, shelter and employ. And there will be even more of us added to the tally next year and in the years to come. Although birth rates have, in terms of absolute numbers, declined somewhat in recent years, we are in a period of massive expansion. Fully a third of the world's population is under 15 years old and ready to breed. Demographers point out that "the brunt of the population explosion has yet to come"; indeed, our numbers will double in the next 40 years.

Imagine a world where a country with the population of Mexico bubbles into being each year, a world where a city of 250,000 people erupts each and every day, bursting like a rampant grey cancer across the green, living surface of the planet. That world is ours—and it is one radically different from that which even our grandparents knew. If one plots a graph of human numbers against time, the curve is almost flat at first. For millions of years, we numbered in mere millions, and it was not until our great-grandparents and grandparents were being born that we suddenly awoke to discover we were a billion individuals. Then, in just four brief generations, the growth curve rockets almost vertically. We are soaring toward 6 billion, and United Nations demographers estimate that, given current trends, it will be the year 2150 before the curve tops out—with a population of just under 12 billion.

Mathematicians and ecologists label such slow-start, fast finish growth as exponential. Two centuries ago, English economist Thomas Malthus suggested that human populations expand exponentially, while the resources we depend on, such as space and water, remain fixed. Few have heeded his message, but one who has, Stanford University ecologist Paul R. Ehrlich, uses the example of pondweed to illustrate exponential growth. Consider a small pond that takes 30 days to become completely overgrown with duckweed, a floating aquatic plant that doubles itself each day. If a small population of duckweed colonizes the pond and begins to grow exponentially, it takes the duckweed a relatively long time to cover half the pond—29 days, in fact. Then suddenly, on the very next day, day 30, duckweed chokes the entire pond.

We find it difficult to comprehend exponential growth, but it may prove to be our fatal blind spot. Malthus and his successors have consistently been dismissed as doom-saying Cassandras for their premature predictions of disaster, and the reason is apparent. For a long while, we have been at the equivalent of day 29 in the duckweed pond, which has been lightly occupied until this century. Now, though, the curve shows that day 30 is upon us, and we are beginning to experience the choking of our planetary pond. In even my short time as a conservationist, I have watched colonists flood into some of the biologically richest regions of the world and convert them into what amount to biological deserts. The once verdant forests of western Ecuador, for example, have been replaced by monocultures of oil palm trees: thousands of species destroyed to produce cheap margarine and potato chips.

Can we blame simply our numbers for this devastation? Ever since Malthus posed the question of how many people the world's resources could sustain without irrevocable damage, the answers have been hotly disputed. Certainly, there remains disagreement over how much fault should be assigned to human population growth as such. In the current debate, overpopulation appears as a knot of related problems not only about human numbers but also about how much those humans consume, what technologies they use and their effects on the environment, even how their economic and social systems distribute them and their resources.

Throughout, however, one factor dominates. It is not the number of humans alone but the impact of human activity and consumption that matters. And the impact, considering that we are but one species among an estimated 10 million, is impressive: humans consume far more than their fair share of the Earth's natural productivity. We eat only 3 percent of the world's annual yield, but in order to extract that amount, to produce food, fibre, machines and profits, we have had to degrade biologically 40 percent of all nature.

From an ecological perspective, overpopulation is a level of human activity that leads to the extinction of other species and to the loss of eco-system health and productivity. The reason for this definition is that the human hallmark is our use of, and dependence on, a wide variety of other species. The things that enhance the quality of human life—a diverse diet, medicines such as penicillin, spices, our finest fibres—derive primarily from other species. Yet human activities are eliminating species we have still to discover, let alone understand, appreciate and use. By this measure, places we might otherwise judge underpopulated are already overpopulated.

Consider, for example, Canada's prairies. The sweep of sky and former grassland contains few people, but the entire topography, from horizon to horizon, is devoted to agricultural production. It is only because the people who eat the grain live elsewhere that there exists the impression of freedom and space. The diverse flora and fauna and the original peoples that the prairies once supported have been reduced to tiny remnants by European colonists fleeing the crowded conditions of their homelands.

One of the advantages of looking at overpopulation as impact rather than head count is that it helps clarify the environmental responsibilities of nations. Nearly 80 percent of the world's population, for instance, lives in developing countries, yet it is developed countries, with their habits of vora-cious consumption, that are responsible for most of the environmental deg-radation. As average North Americans, our per capita consumption of energy and its attendant environmental damage are equivalent to that of 531 Ethiopians. In terms of impact, then, the Canadian population is the equivalent of 14 billion Ethiopians.

Obviously, the relative global ecological impact of 27 million Canadi-ans is huge. We have yet to deplete our vast New World resources and have caused only a few extinctions at home, but developed, consumptive econo-mies such as ours drive many of the large-scale habitat alterations witnessed elsewhere. Our appetite for cheap hamburger and a little fruit on our morn-ing cereal nurtures the wholesale transformation of rain forest into cattle ranches and banana plantations. Little by little, however, such depletions are coming closer to home. Recently, with the feeding grounds of Canadian seals and whales being vacuumed of fish to be jetted off to European house-holds, we may well have witnessed the collapse of Canada's cherished mar-itime livelihood and thus gained a sense of what could be in store. For those who understand the importance of, and delight in, life's diversity, the future harbours a grim prospect. Our consumptive growth is converting a world of antelopes, eagles and grizzlies into a world of cockroaches, garbage gulls and sewer rats.

A number of people argue that our global environmental problems are less a matter of population growth than of glaring social inequities in land and resource distribution. In Latin America, 1 percent of the population controls 40 percent of the arable land, a lamentable state of affairs that does indeed have disastrous social and ecological consequences. In Brazil, the nation with the most inequitable land ownership in the world, the productive southern farmlands could support vast numbers of small holders. The landless, however, are trucked and bused to the agriculturally unproductive Amazonian frontiers, where they wreak havoc on the world's greatest reservoir of biological diversity and, despite their efforts, continue to live in misery.

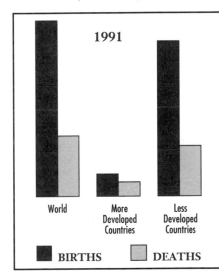

1991

World | More Developed Countries | Less Developed Countries

■ BIRTHS   ☐ DEATHS

A comparison of human births and human deaths reveals not only the scope of the population crisis but also the vastly different rates of growth between the developing and the developed nations. In 1991 in the developed countries, there were 17.6 million births and 11.4 million deaths, leaving a net gain of 6.2 million. In the developing nations, there were 125.3 million births and 39 million deaths, for a net gain of 86.3 million. Combined, the world's net gain was just short of 92.5 million new human beings.

For all its merits, though, the notion that a more equitable distribution of land would solve our global environmental ills has its limits. It would only slightly alleviate population pressure in places like El Salvador, Java and China. In those places, the press of people alone is overwhelming the land's capacity to support them. In China, for instance, there is only one-tenth of a hectare of arable land for each person.

Some who believe in resource redistribution swear that the planet can support many Chinas. The Catholic Church claims we can feed as many as 40 billion people. It may be right, but the assertion raises some questions: For how long? At what ecological cost? And entailing what kind of human life? Feeding our current population is already causing extinctions. The area of the Earth's surface converted to agriculture has grown steadily for the past 150 years, from roughly 900 million hectares in 1850 to nearly 1.5 billion hectares today. The good land is already in production, but in many regions, yields are boosted by irrigation that depletes ground water and carries off soil nutrients accumulated over thousands of years. The loss has to be made up by putting more natural habitat to the plough.

Equally devastating is the fossil-fuel consumption associated with modern agriculture. Fertilizer production, combined with mechanized farming, has increased our annual need for crude oil from 100 million tonnes in 1850 to nearly a trillion tonnes today. The result is a massive contribution to global warming and ozone depletion—phenomena that, ironically, lower agricultural productivity.

As more land and fuel are devoted to agriculture, food security—the ability to produce enough food of enough types to guard against variable harvests—is falling steadily. Only 10 of the estimated 150 developing countries with agriculture are able to export food, and just 3 countries in the world account for 80 percent of grain exports. Over the past three years, while populations have increased by 5 percent, food production has decreased by 5 percent. In a good year, food supply exceeds demand by only 20 percent, a thin buffer against destabilizing events such as global warming and climatic change.

By pursuing the logic that we can produce more food and thus support a far larger population simply by extending our current practices, we are drawn into an ecologist's vision of hell. For instance, let us make every rain forest a tree plantation, producing a mixture of tropical fruits. Let us pulp and replant every boreal forest into a mix of aspen, alder and spruce for fast-growing wood fibre. We can turn every coral reef into farms for giant clams, seaweed and fish. Our tractors can plough up every grassland for wheat, millet and soybeans. The deserts can be bulldozed and groomed to produce edible prickly pear and buffalo gourds. Each marsh and pond might be bermed and fed with treated sewage to yield an abundance of carp and duckweed.

We could go further. If need be, we can live beneath sunlit plastic domes, eating a solution of blue-green algae and perhaps yeasts and fungi, the most efficient of all organisms. Bacterial cultures feeding on human wastes, minerals, carbon dioxide and sunlight could produce immense quantities of food. Add to the equation tranquillizers and chemical regulators of behaviour to prevent social unrest, and it might be possible to maintain, year after year, 100 billion people. The scenario of such a dismal life on such a mutilated planet may seem absurd, yet it is precisely the trajectory we are now following. Perhaps most discouraging, no one seems to be asking why we should want to pursue it further.

Those who can change our path, the world's decision-makers—politicians, planners, economists and industrialists—are largely urban dwellers, unschooled in biology and ecologically ignorant. They have yet to accept the importance of population, in large part because they are insulated from its impact and do not see the ecological and evolutionary outcome of their decisions. Such myopia is politically imaginable because globalized trade makes it possible to achieve economic growth, high population levels and high consumption without much environmental or political cost to a developed country.

Expanding industrial economies typically extract resources and transform habitats thousands of kilometres distant. I recently visited Bintuni Bay in Irian Jaya, the last great mangrove forest in the Asian Pacific, a superbly productive ecosystem that is home to a fishing-gathering people and much wildlife. Using capital from Japan's Marubeni Corp., Indonesian companies are turning the forest into raw, low-value wood chips, which are exported to Japan to make high-value calligraphy and facsimile paper. The operation, if left unregulated, will destroy the breeding grounds of a valuable banana prawn population and the traditional foraging grounds of the peoples indigenous to the mangrove forests. The densely aggregated Japanese consumers and corporations benefit, while distant ecosystems and the local Irianese, who still live in balance with the ecosystem, pay the price.

The Japanese economy, which most nations seek to emulate, is a classic example of an economy that is thriving but eroding biological diversity. Laudably, Japan, with 125 million people and a high standard of living, has increasingly good energy-conservation, pollution-abatement and recycling systems at home. What goes unmentioned, however, is that its economic success depends on its drawing in boatload after boatload of resources from states that lack sound environmental controls. The true cost of Japan's economic success is stripped rain forests and plundered oceans. Japan prospers because there are still countries that are willing to absorb its environmental impact in exchange for rapid economic growth. This is not new: the wealth of Europe was created by harvesting the resources of the colonies.

Not everyone believes that the combination of economic and population growth is a liability. Specifically, there is a school of economists who believe that the population explosion is the forerunner of human improvement and rising fortunes, who see the population explosion not as a cause of poverty but as a means of eliminating poverty, and who argue that human population growth inspires rather than retards development. They are known as "cornucopians," and their most vocal proponent is Julian L. Simon of the University of Maryland.

The cornucopian theory goes like this: More births means more future consumers; more consumers means more industry and business. The larger market allows for economies of scale; production runs increase, and cost per item goes down. The growing economy means more profit, and more profit means more prosperity for everyone. Capital flows in a circle through the economy, releasing human ingenuity and increasing productivity.

This is, in fact, exactly what appears to be happening in Java, which has acted as a steadily accelerating engine of the Indonesian economy for the past 15 years. Foreign investment and development money pours into the region. Textile factories materialize amid the paddies. Great shining glass and steel towers spring up regularly in Jakarta, and the streets are crowded with new cars—all signs of recent wealth. Even the human surplus, landless people like Hadi, have a role in this vision. Hadi is part of the low-cost labour that fuels the textile mills of Java and the lumber camps, mines and newly sprouting plantations of the Indonesian frontier.

Perhaps some of the growth economists will admit that a Java or a Bangladesh or a Haiti may already have more than enough people like Hadi. But perhaps not. Simon claims that historically, one of the characteristics of prosperous societies has been a rapidly expanding population. He sees real benefits to high-density living and has suggested that it might be worth having all the people living west of the Mississippi in the United States move east because "such a change would bring about major benefits in shortening transportation and communication distances, a factor that has been important in Japan's ability to closely coordinate its industrial operations so as to reduce the costs of inventory and transportation." Simon recognizes that this would destroy much valuable farmland. Such a loss, however, is acceptable. As he points out, "Less than 3 percent of U.S. income comes from agriculture," and besides, "greater population concentration forces social changes... that may be costly in the short run but, in the long run, increase a society's ability to reach its economic and social objectives."

It seems that Simon's ideal world would be a continuous Tokyo or Hong Kong. "Drive around on Hong Kong's smooth-flowing highways for an hour or two," he has written. "You will then realize that a large concentration of human beings in a small area does not make impossible comfortable existence and exciting economic expansion."

The great failing of Simon's vision, as with so much current economic thought, is that it ignores, utterly, ecological facticity. He has not noticed that all of Hong Kong's birds hang in bamboo cages. He seems not to have realized that a Hong Kong cannot be replicated without inflicting tremendous damage elsewhere. He has failed to appreciate that there are few employment opportunities on a dead planet.

It is tempting to consider growth economists like Simon as part of an antiquated fringe whose ideas belong to an earlier era. In fact, their basic premise enjoys wide currency. In 1991, the Economic Council of Canada produced a $1 million study that argued for greatly increasing Canada's population by raising immigration levels. Newspaper headlines blared, "Wanted: 100 million people to make Canada efficient." The argument made by the economists was that by increasing Canada's population by 400 percent, we could raise the Canadian standard of living by 7 percent. That this is considered a serious argument and a valid trade-off, that there are still well-educated people who believe it is worth sustaining 400 percent more traffic, pollution, resource consumption and loss of space for a 7 percent increase in material wealth, is a cause for concern.

Yet the belief in the necessity of growth is obviously still strong. In spite of the manifest horror of places like Haiti, Bangladesh and Java, there is no shortage of people clamouring for increased population growth for reasons of national political or economic interest. Canadian politicians and economists are joined by people with political motivations, all calling for the multiplication of their particular constituency. Colonel Muammar el-Qaddafi of Libya, arguing that Arabs will survive only if they are able to increase their numbers from the present 150 million to 1 billion, has stated that "all family-planning measures in the Arab countries should be abolished." The president of Malaysia urges that his already deforested country increase its population by 500 percent, from 14 million to 70 million.

Faced with these attitudes and statistics, one might conclude that trying to change current population trends is a hopeless task. That is wrong. Relatively minor reallocations of human resources can make significant differences. The scope for improvements is tremendous. In Africa, Latin America and Asia, respectively, only 16, 59 and 56 percent of married women, and far fewer men, practised contraception in 1990. Furthermore, women's access to education is for the most part appalling, as is their chance of improving their general lot in life.

Investing in women's rights and allowing women control over fertility will pay huge dividends, both by lowering birth rates and by raising the prospects for proper care of the children who are born. Revamped education programs and tax systems could create major changes in the consumption patterns of the developed nations while generating a net savings through the elimination of waste.

Do we have the money to buy a healthy future? For much less than the $12 billion North Americans spend annually on chocolate bars, we could stabilize the world population at between 8 billion and 12 billion people. The World Federation of Family Planning Associations estimates that just $8 billion a year could do the job by encouraging adequate family planning. The amount equals a little more than $1 a person each year, a trivial price, given the cost of unchecked population growth.

We have not one but two clear priorities. First, we must increase our financial commitment to family planning. Currently, less than 1 percent of international-development aid goes to family planning. Second, and equally vital, we must act to protect the most fundamental reservoirs of biological diversity. Hot-spot areas now receive only a few million dollars for the creation and management of conservation systems. A few billion is needed; again, it is a small price when weighed against the consequences of our current neglect.

The task can also be made much easier by instituting reforms in the way we manage our natural resources. By encouraging conservation and reducing waste, we will create a world better able to support 12 billion souls.

But even if things go optimally, we will still have to rethink what it means to be developed. Reducing our consumption is near the top of the agenda for change, but it will also be the most difficult task to accomplish because it will require altering human values. How difficult? Consider the words of Danish economist Bernard Gilland: "It is very likely that affluent industrial society is a brief historical interlude made possible by a mineralogical bonanza... but this does not constitute a grounds for dismantling it. Why should we not continue the burst of production and consumption as long as we can?"

Why not? Why not just use it up in one short blaze of consumer glory? The answer depends on what we choose to value.

My response is to ask why we persist in measuring the Canadian standard of living by the price of the latest electronic trinkets. Why not some other measure with a built-in sense of posterity and diversity? The ease of finding water fit to drink, fish fit to eat and loons fit to call across a northern lake would make a more ecologically appropriate measure of the quality of Canadian life.

We have not yet lost the battle. Much of the world's biological diversity remains intact. We still have loons and clean northern lakes. Fish without names still swim the seas. The Tropics still harbour deep forests where streams run clear and birds of paradise display their fiery plumage. But these organisms are virtually without defence against human competitors and predators. If these species, the most beautiful and necessary elements of the planet, are to remain with us, we need to accept and limit the completeness of our ecological conquest. We need to stop growing. There are no New Worlds.

Hardball

BY MARGARET ATWOOD

A grim look at how things might turn out if we let the environment collapse.

ere comes the future, rolling toward us like a meteorite, a satellite, a giant iron snowball, a two-ton truck in the wrong lane, careering downhill with broken brakes, and whose fault is it? No time to think about that. Blink and it's here.

How round, how firm, how fully packed is this future! How man-made! What wonders it contains, especially for those who can afford it! They are the elect, and by their fruits ye shall know them. Their fruits are strawberries and dwarf plums and grapes, things that can be grown beside the hydroponic vegetables and the toxin-absorbent ornamentals, in relatively little space. Space is at a premium, living space that is. All space that is not living space is considered dead.

Living space is under the stately pleasure dome, the work-and-leisure dome, the transparent bubble-dome that keeps out the deadly cosmic rays and the rain of sulphuric acid and the air which is no longer. No longer air, I mean. You can look out, of course: watch the sun, red at all times of day, rise across the raw rock and shifting sands, travel across the raw rock and shifting sands, set across the raw rock and shifting sands. The light effects are something.

But breathing is out of the question. That's a thing you have to do in here, and the richer you are the better you do it. Penthouse costs a bundle; steerage is cramped, and believe me it stinks. Well, as they say, there's only so much to go around, and it wouldn't do if everyone got the same. No incentive then, to perform the necessary work, make the necessary sacrifices, inch your way up, to where the pale-pink strawberries and the pale-yellow carrots are believed, still, to grow.

What else is eaten? Well, there are no more hamburgers. Cows take up too much room. Chickens and rabbits are still cultivated, here and there; they breed quickly and they're small. Rats, of course, on the lower levels, if you can catch them. Think of the earth as an eighteenth-century ship, with stowaways but no destination.

And no fish, needless to say. None left in all that dirty water sloshing around in the oceans and through the remains of what used to be New York. If you're really loaded you can go diving there, for your vacation. Travel by airlock. Plunge into the romance of a bygone age. But it's an ill wind that blows nobody any good. No more street crime. Think of it as a plus.

Back to the topic of food, which will always be of interest. What will we have for dinner? Is it wall-to-wall bean sprouts? Apart from the pallid garnishes and the chicken-hearted hors-d'oeuvres, what's the main protein?

Think of the earth as a nineteenth-century lifeboat, adrift in the open sea, with castaways but no rescuers. After a while you run out of food, you run out of water. You run out of everything but your fellow passengers.

Why be squeamish? Let's just say we've learned the hard way about waste. Or let's say we all make our little contribution to the general welfare, in the end.

It's done by computer. For every birth there must be a death. Everything's ground up, naturally. Nothing you might recognize, such as fingers. Think of the earth as a hard stone ball, scraped clean of life. There are benefits: no more mosquitoes, no bird poop on your car. The bright side is a survival tool. So look on it.

I'm being unnecessarily brutal, you say. Too blunt, too graphic. You want things to go on the way they are, five square meals a day, new plastic toys, the wheels of the economy oiled and spinning, payday as usual, the smoke going up the chimney just the same. You don't like this future.

You don't like this future? Switch it off. Order another. Return to sender.

from The Real World of Technology

BY URSULA FRANKLIN

We live in a time when new technologies seem to be altering the way we work and live every few years. Terms like "global restructuring" and "future shock" make it seem that the technologies we have created are out of our control.

This essay is abstracted from the 1989 Massey Lectures, a series of talks on radio by scientist Ursula Franklin. She explains some of the processes that happen when new technologies arrive.

What follows is taken from the fifth talk, but includes explanatory remarks from an earlier talk. Ellipses (. . .) indicate where paragraphs have been moved from their original position, with the author's permission.

... I start from the premise that we are living in a very difficult, very interesting time, a time in which a major historical period is coming to a convoluted end. I think we live in a time in which the social and political upheaval is as great or greater than it was at the time of the Reformation.

As I see it, technology has built the house in which we all live. The house is continually being extended and remodelled. More and more of human life takes place within its walls, so that today there is hardly any human activity that does not occur within this house. All are affected by the design of the house, by the division of its space, by the location of its doors and walls. Compared to people in earlier times, we rarely have a chance to live outside this house. And the house is still changing; it is still being built as well as being demolished. . . .

I want to distinguish between two very different forms of technological development. The distinction we need to make is between *holistic technologies* and *prescriptive technologies*....

Holistic technologies are normally associated with the notion of craft. Artisans, be they potters, weavers, metal smiths, or cooks, control the process of their own work from beginning to end.... This first kind of specialization, by product, I call holistic technology, and it is important because it leaves the doer in total control of the process. The opposite is specialization by process; this I call prescriptive technology. It is based on quite a different division of labour. Here, the making or doing of something is broken down into clearly identifiable steps. Each step is carried out by a separate worker, or group of workers, who need to be familiar only with the skills of performing that one step. This is what is normally meant by "division of labour."

This type of division of labour is most familiar to us as it arose in the Industrial Revolution in Britain. The factory system of the time resulted from large-scale applications of such divisions of labour. However, this kind of division of labour is actually much older. We find it among the late Romans, whose Terra Sigillata pottery or Samian ware was produced by a prescriptively controlled technology. But even a thousand years earlier there was the production of Chinese bronze vessels, organized as a prescriptive technology *par excellence*, with clearly defined process-determined divisions of labour....

The division of labour characteristic of prescriptive technologies has resulted in the acculturation of people into a culture of conformity and compliance. And that has very many significant consequences....

All social interactions proceed according to a certain characteristic internal logic. Actions are carried out in a particular manner in the expectation of a commensurate reaction, whether it is the tit-for-tat logic of strife or a turning of the other cheek. Where prescriptive technologies are structured to perform social transactions, these transactions will be organized or reorganized according to the logic of technology, the logic of production. Thus, as more and more of daily life in the real world of technology is conducted via prescriptive technologies, the logic of technology begins to overpower and displace other types of social logic, such as the logic of compassion or the logic of obligation, the logic of ecological survival or the logic of linkages into nature.

In order to clarify the mechanisms by which the logic of technology suffocates other forms of social logic, I want to look at the patterns that emerge during the introduction of different technologies into a society. Historians of technology point out that there are general stages in this process of introduction.

In the early stage of a particular invention, a good deal of enthusiasm and imagination is generated. There are efforts to explore and explain just how wonderful and helpful the new invention will be. Science fiction often gives a framework for such imaginary explorations. The dreams of flight, of fast private transportation, of instant communication across continents, and of helpful machines all stress liberation from hard physical labour at work or drudgery at home. Wellsprings of creativity and freedom from toil seem to be just around the corner. In this phase technologies create human bonds and a sense of excitement in people who feel grateful to be part of such wonderful, progressive times. The voices of reservation sound like disgruntled skeptics, fearful of change—like the old lady who said that if God had wanted us to fly, she would never have given us the railways.

During the Industrial Revolution there were "Odes to the Steam Engine"; the great exhibitions at the turn of the century were filled with public displays of light and sound and they depicted a much better and more exciting life almost within the reach of ordinary people. In the course of this phase of youthful exuberance, technologies achieve broadly based entry into the public mind and the public imagination. Yes indeed, people feel, it might be nice to try out a car or a telephone, or work with some of these fancy machines.

After this phase, with its flights of imagination, human contacts, and excessive hopes, a new phase appears. This is the phase of the stern father saying, "What do you really want to do when you grow up?" This is the phase of growth and standardization of the technology. From here on the involvement of people, whether workers or users, is drastically reduced.

Take, for instance, the motor car. In its young phase, it could be quite appropriately called a "mechanical bride," the term used by Marshall McLuhan to describe the relationship between car and owner. Care was regularly lavished by young men upon their vehicles, polishing and tuning them, repairing them and improving their performances. There was a sense of camaraderie among the owners and they would admire one another's mechanical brides. Little is left of this era in todays' real world of technology. In the automobile's technological middle age, it is hard, if not impossible, to tune or repair one's own vehicle—other than by taking out inter-changeable parts and popping in identical replacements. Cars are costly to buy and to maintain, but for many owning a car is neither a joy nor a luxury but a necessity. The mechanical bride has turned into a demanding but essential business partner.

Technical standardization of cars has occurred, and with it the elimination of the user's access to the machine itself. At the same time, the infrastructures that once served those who did not use automobiles atrophied and vanished. Some may say they were deliberately starved out. Railways gave way to more and more roadways. And thus a technology that had been perceived to liberate its users began to enslave them. The real joy of owning wheels, the sense of independence that allowed drivers to go wherever and whenever they wanted to go, became muted, because in reality there were usually thousands and thousands of others who wanted or had to go at the same time to the same place.

The early phase of technology often occurs in a take-it-or-leave-it atmosphere. Users are involved and have a feeling of control that gives them the impression that they are entirely free to accept or reject a particular technology and its products. But when a technology, together with the supporting infrastructures, becomes institutionalized, users often become captive supporters of both the technology and the infrastructures. (At this point, the technology itself may stagnate, improvements may become cosmetic or marginal, and competition becomes ritualized.) In the case of the automobile, the railways are gone—the choice of taking the car or leaving it at home no longer exists.

When assessing the individual and social impacts of different technologies, the internal chronologies outlined above must be considered. For instance, within my memory not only cars but audio equipment had a youthful and involved phase, when people talked about matching impedances, building turntables and preamplifiers from kits, and comparing their respective successes in achieving high-fidelity sound reproduction. That phase is gone, too. The market now offers standard plug-in components and owners may listen—but not intervene beyond pushing buttons. We're in the midst of a similar evolution in the use of computers. Today's popular and emotional involvement with the personal computer is very much akin to the mechanical bride phase of the automobile. Once again there is a promise of liberation—there's no need any more for good typing skills or correct spelling, for arithmetic or knowing how to do percentages, no need to keep the files straight. The computer can do it all. It can even recycle that painful letter to Aunt Amelia to other members of the family with only slight modifications.

Manufacturers and promoters always stress the liberating attributes of a new technology, regardless of the specific technology in question. There are attempts to allay fear, to be user-friendly, and to let the users derive pride from their new skills. There is an effort to build up user communities brimming over with warm feelings of sharing newly won expertise. In the computing field the best barometer for these endeavours is the large number of popular computing magazines. They range from the free-of-charge ones, such as *Toronto Computes*, that can be picked up in the neighbourhood convenience store, to the glossy numbers like *PC World*. All of them have similar styles based on a gushy, breathless, gee-whiz kind of journalism. They remind me of nothing so much as the women's magazines that one used to pick up in great numbers at supermarkets, when fancy kitchen appliances and prepared foods were being introduced. Here too were coupons and free gifts, recipe exchanges and user-proven tips for shortcuts or special effects. I urge you to look at some of the computer magazines from the point of view of set-up and style. You'll find columns on "How I found ten more uses for Lotus 1-2-3" and "How I extended the capacity of my Mac beyond imagination." These columns strongly remind me of columns like "How I used a packaged cake mix and even my mother-in-law didn't notice it."

You may well question the validity of this analogy and ask, "Is there really a correspondence between the ways in which prepared and packaged food was introduced and the marketing of home computers?" I think there is, and the argument goes as follows: The postwar period saw considerable advances in the chemistry of food additives, allowing for much longer shelf-lives of products to which these chemicals had been added. At the same time, new machinery made the individual packaging of goods economically viable. New distribution systems—particularly by air—opened up around the same time. Thus foods could be chemically stabilized, industrially packaged, and commercially shipped over long distances. The challenge to advertising and marketing was to stimulate and entice changes in cooking and eating habits that would utilize the new products (and the appliances to go with them).

The chain of evidence then goes from "Betty Crocker" and her recipes, to magazines and gadgets, to frozen food and TV dinners, to today's attempts to market irradiated food (or infant formula in the Third World). The promotion of industrially processed food was geared to make women accept the new products as a liberating and exciting addition to their lives without worrying about chemical additives or increasing costs. I see a very similar scenario in the promotion of computers for individual use, and I think the pitch is quite deliberate. It is aimed at creating an atmosphere of harmless domesticity around the new technology to ease its acceptance. Who could fear these cute and clever things that make life so interesting at home when the kids play games on them? There's also the language of computers to support this image of harmless domesticity. One speaks of booting up and boilerplates; one talks about mouse and menu. The user has the feeling of choice and control, of mastery and a comfortable relationship with the machine and with other users.

But this phase will not last. Behind that pink fluff one already sees the features of global restructuring. The changes in the workplace are there and it is not the workers who exercise control. After you've looked at the gushy computer magazines, you may want to read Heather Menzies' new book, called *Fast Forward and Out of Control*, in which she speaks about global restructuring in terms of the Canadian economy and Canadian workers.

If one doesn't watch the introduction of new technologies and particularly watch the infrastructures that emerge, promises of liberation through technology can become a ticket to enslavement. I'd like to remind you of one example of the doubtful promises of liberation by a new technology. The case is focused, direct, and drastic. Let's look at the introduction of the sewing machine.

In 1851 the mechanical sewing machine became a commercially available device. It was widely advertised as a household appliance that would free women from the chores and drudgery of hand sewing. Whether women sewed at home for their families' use or as seamstresses working for others, the promise was liberation from toil. Not only were individual women to benefit from the new device, but there were high hopes for humanity as a whole. The following paragraph, written in 1860, is quoted by Cheris Kramarae in an article on the history of the sewing machine:

The sewing machine will, after some time, effectively banish ragged and unclad humanity from every class. In all benevolent institutions, these machines are now in operation and do or may do 100 times more towards clothing the indigent and feeble than the united fingers of all the charitable and willing ladies collected through the civilized world could possibly perform.

The authors of this prognostication evidently assumed that the introduction of the sewing machine would result in more sewing—and easier sewing—by those who had always sewn. They would do the work they had always done in an unchanged setting.

Reality turned out to be quite different. With the help of the new machines, sewing came to be done in a factory setting, in sweatshops that exploited the labour of women and particularly the labour of women immigrants. Sewing machines became, in fact, synonymous not with liberation but with exploitation. The sewing machines at home were used less, as machine-sewn household goods and garments began to be readily available on the mass market. These garments were produced by the prescriptive technologies that created a situation in which one seamstress sewed up only sleeves, another worker put them in, another made buttonholes, another pressed the shirts. A strictly prescriptive technology with the classic division of labour arose from the introduction of new, supposedly liberating "domestic" machines. In the subsequent evolution of the garment industry, much of the designing, cutting, and assembling began to be automated, often to the complete exclusion of workers.

The social history of the industrialization of clothing is similar to the current phase in the industrialization of eating. Food outlets put frozen or chemically prepared "unit meals" together like sleeves and collars for shirts—there are "McJobs" and no security of employment. Indeed, women sew less, cook less, and have to work hard outside the home to be able to buy clothing and food.

What turns the promised liberation into enslavement are not the products of technology per se—the car, the computer, or the sewing machine—but the structures and infrastructures that are put in place to facilitate the use of these products and to develop dependency on them. The funny thing is that in the course of this process of spreading technology, the ordinary things—a home-cooked meal, an individually made garment—become prized and special, while what had been prized and extraordinary—for instance, cloth or fruit from the Orient—appears now to be quite ordinary and routine.

To recap: many new technologies and their products have entered the public sphere in a cloud of hope, imagination, and anticipation. In many cases these hopes were to begin with fictional, rather than real; even in the best circumstances they were vastly exaggerated. Discussion focused largely on individuals, whether users or workers, and promised an easier life with liberation from toil and drudgery. Discourse never seemed to focus on the effects of the use of the same device by a large number of people, nor was there any focus on the organizational and industrial implications of the new technologies, other than in the vaguest of terms.

In spite of the exaggerated individual promises, techniques were treated as if they would fit easily into "normal life." Carefully selected phrases used to describe new technical advances could generate an image of chummy communities and adventurous users. But once a given technology is widely accepted and standardized, the relationship between the products of the technology and the users changes. Users have less scope, they matter less, and their needs are no longer the main concern of the designers. There is, then, a discernable pattern in the social and political growth of a technology that does not depend on the particular technical features of the system in question....

The Moosehide Gloves

BY ALAN S. KESSELHEIM

"I often hold the gloves to my face and breathe in, as you do the first full fragrance of spring."

My moosehide gloves do not come from the shelves of a store. They are not packaged in plastic and removed from any connection with their source. They come from the tough skin of a moose that I helped to butcher. They were fashioned at the hands of a Chipewyan grandmother whom I know. When I slip my hands into them, I feel in contact with the North. The power of that rock-bound land lying beneath the stunning stretch of tundra, of the people who live there, graces my hands.

The gloves are permeated with a cured smell that is as evocative as a drug. I often hold the gloves to my face and breathe in, as you do the first full fragrance of spring. That smoked, pungent, wild smell sends me on image-rich journeys. With its aid, I recapture the soft lime-green of reindeer lichen on rocky knolls. I remember wall tents in winter camps, piquant with spruce boughs. I taste the stringy dryness of smoked caribou meat. I curse clouds of black flies. I feel the rapacious sword of winter winds, and I hear the sweet dip of wood paddles and the splash of a bow wave on a dawn-quiet lake.

The moosehide came from a large bull surprised by native hunters while crossing a lake narrows. They killed him with one neck shot at close range. The hide was cut away from the body with great care, keeping the valuable skin intact. Yet the hunters worked with a slashing quickness.

Angela, the wife of one of the hunters, prepared the heavy hide during the fall months. The process is a lengthy and arduous one, an ancient, crucial skill passed on through generations. That knowledge is a threatened legacy now, less essential than in the past, but still treasured by many Chipewyan.

First, Angela soaked the hide to loosen the hold of hair and soften bits of membrane that still adhered to the inner skin. After sufficient time, she scraped the hair from the hide and cleaned away any fat or tissue.

She used a serrated scraping tool her husband had fashioned from the leg bone of a black bear. Angela prized that tool, worn to the shape of her grip. She kept the bone tool wrapped in canvas and tied up securely in a soft square of caribou skin.

When the hide was cleaned, it was thoroughly rubbed with a concoction whose most essential ingredient was the brain of the moose. Angela produced a caribou skin bag full of leather thongs, which she laced through the edges of the hide and pulled tightly to stretch the hide on a simple wooden framework. Then the skin was set out to dry.

A second soaking, with water, further softened the stretched hide. Its pliability was then ensured by a thorough pounding. Finally, the supple skin lay draped over a rock under which there was a smoky fire built with rotten wood. The hide was cured to the desired colour and given its heady fragrance, the very essence of the North.

Angela's hands seemed ready for retirement, like they'd put in their time and then some. Firm of grip, calloused and tough, gnarled with arthritic knobs, they were hands that had spent a lifetime pounding and cutting meat, stitching canvas and leather, hauling water and kindling, and gripping various kinds of tools.

These were working hands. They were incongruously delicate and agile hands. Watching them work, I was mesmerized by their economy and grace. Angela's hands were intelligent at their tasks, exerting just the correct pressure or twist.

She worked surely and quietly. The steps, the patterns, the designs seemed so deeply ingrained that they might as well have been in her blood and marrow. Her motions maintained a rhythm, a flow, an expression of heritage. They no longer required thought.

When Angela began the pair of gloves, she referred to no pattern for size. She imagined the hands of a man and cut the pieces to fit that hand. She laid out the leather and stitched it together in the manner that has been

found most satisfactory over time. The gloves were made to let in the least cold and moisture, with the least possible number of seams.

Before the gloves were put together, however, she attended to the matter of decoration. When completed, the beadwork design is what sets handmade gloves apart from something you'd buy in a store, wear out, and discard. The gloves become pieces of art.

Distinct patterns and colours are used in the beadwork of different Chipewyan and N.W.T. Dene groups. Within each, there is room for individual creativity. My gloves are beaded in a floral pattern, distinctive of the Chipewyan band of Fond-du-Lac, Saskatchewan. If asked where she learned the designs, Angela would answer that she picked them up from her mother. Where else? She would not, it seems, even consider beading in a style outside the inherited set.

As with the stitchwork of the gloves and the process of preparing the hide, the beadwork designs are taught by old, knobby hands to young, smooth ones. The information is never written down, but simply passed on from hand to hand, mother to daughter.

Angela made no declarations regarding these simple old ways. She made me a pair of gloves, adorned them in the way she saw fit, and constructed them with the best materials at hand.

When I put on my moosehide gloves, run my fingers over the tightly beaded flowers on their backs, and smell the odor of wood smoke and animal, my enjoyment is tinged with regret. The gloves whisper of the North, while they remind me that the way of life on the land may be passing into history.

It's Yer Genuwine High-Tech

BY DAN STRICKLAND

Beneath the bantering tone, this essay presents a serious comparison between the power of our technology and the infinite depths of nature.

We dare say that most people are fascinated by new gadgets. This being so, what an age to be living in! With today's digital sound, versatile computers, and powerful microchips, the sky seems to be the limit. New and better devices are coming out all the time, and the old saying about building a better mousetrap and having the world beat a path to your doorstep has never seemed to be truer.

We confess to being as impressed and amazed by all the new gadgetry as anyone else, but sometimes we get the feeling that the supposedly unsophisticated natural world is getting short shrift. This was brought home to us with special vividness one day last week when we were riding down to the new visitor centre with a visiting journalist. The man was proudly showing off his new cellular phone when a Short-tailed Shrew about five centimetres long ran across the highway right in front of us. And do you know something? Without a word of a lie, the man never even stopped talking about his phone and, as far as we could tell, didn't even look at the shrew.

Incredible! After all, a cellular phone is a nice example of some pretty fancy high-tech, but it can't hold a candle to a Short-tailed Shrew! There's just no comparison.

Now, we want to say right away that no one should feel bad if they have to own up to knowing as little about Short-tailed Shrews as our newspaper friend. In fact, we bet there are lots of folks in exactly the same boat. It's not a crime not to know about Short-tailed Shrews, but it certainly is a shame because they are about as interesting and as "high-tech" as can be. So, if you are in the dark about these little creatures, allow us to take a few minutes and fill you in.

First of all, these particular shrews are just one among hundreds of kinds found throughout the world and one among the five found here in Algonquin Park. Most people are at least vaguely aware that shrews superficially resemble mice but are much smaller and lack the big, constantly growing front teeth of a rodent. Several of our Algonquin shrews weigh around five grams whereas most mice would be four or five times as big (20 to 25 grams). Being so tiny, shrews lose heat very quickly to the surrounding air and are famous for killing prey and burning up energy at truly prodigious rates. Small shrews must eat their own weight in food every 24 hours and will starve to death in a day if they are unable to keep up this rate of intake. Imagine what it would be like to eat about 70 kilograms of insects, snails, slugs, and earthworms every single day on pain of starvation and you will have some idea of what it would be like to be a shrew.[*]

The above generalities apply more or less to the Short-tailed Shrew as well, but there are also important differences. For one thing, Short-tails are much bigger than most shrews. They weigh in at 10 to 20 grams, making them almost as big as some mice. Short-tails also seem to be much more common than our smaller shrews. On average there may be 25 Short-tailed Shrews per hectare although, as with many small mammals, populations can fluctuate dramatically. A few Algonquin old-timers can still remember the fantastic summer of 1947 when Short-tailed Shrews may have reached densities of 250 per hectare or even higher. All in all, this particular shrew is sufficiently different from—and more plentiful and more important than—the other smaller kinds that many naturalists prefer to use the Latin name *Blarina* (instead of "shrew") to reflect its distinctiveness. Now, when any animal is obviously more successful than its relatives, we may legitimately suspect it has one or more special adaptations that give it an edge over the competition.

---

[*]With a diet like that you might prefer starvation, especially when the best you could hope for would be one or two years of life. By then your teeth would be worn out and your body an ancient wreck, and you would starve to death anyway. Such is the short life of a shrew.

In fact, Blarinas have three special adaptations that account for their success. The simplest of all is that Blarinas smell bad—and presumably taste about the same. This has the effect of protecting them from all but the hungriest of predators and apparently allows them to proliferate much more rapidly than would otherwise be the case.

The second key to the Short-tailed Shrew's success was inadvertently discovered back in 1889 when a man named Maynard was bitten by a Short-tail he was trying to capture. The skin of his hand was barely punctured—but within 30 seconds he felt a burning sensation followed by intense shooting pains in his arm. The pain and swelling reached a maximum after an hour, but he still felt considerable discomfort more than a week later. Mr. Maynard had learned first-hand that the saliva of the Short-tailed Shrew is deadly poisonous! Subsequent studies have shown that the poison is produced by the salivary glands in the Blarina's lower jaw (saliva produced by two other sets of glands in the animal's mouth is completely harmless). Very little of the saliva is sufficient to kill a mouse, and this enables Blarinas to tap into a major food supply that is completely unavailable to smaller, non-poisonous shrews. Even though a Blarina is still appreciably smaller than a mouse, all it has to do is get in a few nips and wait for the deadly saliva to do its work. Within a few minutes the hapless mouse is dead or so lethargic that it can't resist when the Short-tail starts to devour it. The idea of being paralyzed and then eaten alive is not particularly interesting for the victim, but the advantage to the shrew is considerable. You will remember that shrews risk starving to death if they don't eat their own weight in food every day. The problem is that they aren't guaranteed to find the necessary steady supply every single day. Under these circumstances, the ability to store excess food for later use could make the difference between life and death. Short-tailed Shrews do indeed paralyze mice and smaller prey with their saliva, bury them for safekeeping, and then return a day or two later. Being still alive, the victims have not rotted, and the shrew can derive maximum nutritional benefit from its surplus food supply.

As macabre as this little twist may be, however, it is nothing compared to the final, ultra-sophisticated feature of our supreme little mouse-killing machines. Shrews operate mostly at night and in tunnels under the soil and leaf litter. Their keen sense of smell helps them zero in on prey under these conditions, but neither this sense nor their small eyes help much with the more basic problem of getting around through complicated underground tunnel networks in almost complete darkness. Most shrews do indeed blunder into things and uselessly poke their way up blocked tunnels—at least until they have memorized the local travel routes. The Short-tailed and a few other shrews, however, have made a major breakthrough, enabling them to navigate in total darkness in completely unfamiliar surroundings. As with bats, these shrews can "see" their environment through "echolocation." By sending out high-pitched clicks and then listening to the echoes, the Short-tailed Shrew generates in its brain a three-dimensional picture of its underground world, which it can then use to make navigation decisions. Like all shrews, Short-tails lack the big, sound-collecting external ears of bats (not very practical in a world of narrow underground tunnels), but they can nevertheless distinguish some very small features of their environment. Even from 30 centimetres away, for example, a Blarina can detect an opening barely half a centimetre wide. Even more amazing, by sending a burst of ultrasonic clicks down a tunnel from its entrance, a Short-tailed Shrew can "see" if the tunnel is blocked farther down, and can do this even if the tunnel is bent or curved. In other words, shrews can use their echolocation capabilities to almost literally see around corners.

Imagine being a mouse "safely" curled up in your subterranean nest when a Blarina comes into your tunnel network. We don't know if mice can hear the ultrasonic clicks of an approaching Short-tail, but if they can it must be something like one of those Second World War submarine scenes where the crew members all hold their breath listening to the sonar "pings" from the dreaded destroyer passing overhead. The trouble is, in the case of a cowering mouse, the echolocation signals and data processors (brains) of a Short-tailed Shrew can distinguish between different surfaces such as soil, leaves, and fur....

We think it nothing less than astounding that a minuscule 10-gram package of flesh can so completely eclipse the capabilities of the high-tech gadgets about which everybody gets so excited these days. Imagine paying more attention to a crude trinket like a cellular phone than to a sophisticated marvel like a Short-tailed Shrew. And if anybody from Sony, IBM, or Mitsubishi comes along with some hype about a better mousetrap, you might just ask them a few questions. Do their high-tech gadgets contain enough toxin to kill 200 mice? Can their mousetraps actually track down their victims and then clean up the mess? Is their technology capable of seeing around corners in complete darkness and resolving the data into a useful, three-dimensional picture on a computer screen tiny enough to fit inside a shrew's skull?

When these companies begin to manufacture products with even some of the abilities of a Short-tailed Shrew, then we'll start to take them seriously. In the meantime we will always pay keen and respectful attention whenever we're lucky enough to see a Short-tailed Shrew run across the highway. They may look simple and unsophisticated, but they truly are the world's best and most awesomely high-tech mousetrap.

Or, as people always say in these parts, "If it's a better mousetrap you want, then gettin' some of them there Blarinas would be a shrewd move."

THE WRITER'S IMAGINATION 4

Twenty-five Dollars and a T-4 Slip

BY SUSAN MUSGRAVE

"'The cheque is in the mail' is the story of most writers' lives."

e **L**ast week I received payment for three poems published in one of Canada's more prestigious literary journals. I got twenty-five dollars and a T-4 slip. That's roughly $8.33 per poem—enough to drive a poet to drink, or journalism.

As I stood wondering how not to spend my twenty-five dollars all in one place, I got a phone call from a local realtor. He was planning a book on the art of the real estate deal, but before he quit his day job he wanted my professional advice on what tax breaks were available to writers.

Tax breaks! I'd had too many of these phone calls lately. After giving the realtor my unprofessional opinion, I called Ma Bell to request an unlisted number.

"Occupation?" asked the clerk, after all the easy questions.

"Writer," I must have mumbled.

She didn't even hesitate. "How long have you been unemployed?" she asked.

In our country, where more people are said to have caught AIDS last year than bought a Canadian book, the average annual income from writing is five thousand dollars. Sixty-eight percent of writers make less than ten thousand dollars a year, and nine percent earn nothing. Some writers actually *lose* money writing.

Authors have always been poorly paid. John Milton got ten pounds for *Paradise Lost*, and Swift wrote, "I never got a farthing by anything I writ except one [*Gulliver's Travels*] about eight years ago." Even Shakespeare earned less than eight pounds apiece for his plays.

"The two most beautiful words in the English language are 'cheque enclosed,'" said Dorothy Parker. But "the cheque is in the mail" is the story of most writers' lives. Edgar Allan Poe had to wait a year and a half for the ten dollars he eventually received from the *New York Mirror* for his poem "The Raven." Balzac was so poor he had to find secret lodgings and hide from his creditors while writing *La Comédie Humaine*.

Then there are the Lord Byron types who refuse payment for their work, preferring to write for glory. But there isn't much glory in having to budget twenty-seven-and-a-half cents a week for food, as Thoreau did at Walden, or in cleaning toilets to pay for the groceries, like Carl Sandburg.

Hemingway may have believed that hunger is a good discipline, but these days it's more or less accepted that writers—like everyone else—need to eat. With his next meal in mind, the Vancouver poet Tom Wayman wrote to a Bulgarian editor who wished to include some of his poems in an anthology, *Eleven Canadian Poets*, and had offered a "token" payment. Tom requested his standard permission fee of fifty dollars per poem.

"Dear Tom," replied the editor, "Poetry is a matter of honour and conscience: it has no price that can be estimated in dollars, pounds or marks. The present collection has been compiled and translated in the name of a higher and nobler purpose. Let us forget about remuneration in the name of poetry."

Tom responded, "I appreciate that you have undertaken the task of translating Canadian writers out of interest and good will.... However, the manufacturers of the paper on which the book will be printed will be paid more than a 'token' for their work. The makers of the ink and the printing press will be properly paid for their work. The printers and binders of the volume will be paid. The publishing house, distribution, warehouse and bookstore employees will all be paid. What has been proposed is that the only people whose work goes into the production of this book who are expected to receive a 'token' payment are the original writers. I believe what I write has value, no *more* so but no *less* than the work of those who are employed in paper mills, printshops, binderies, publishing houses, and bookstores."

The anthology has since been shortened to *Ten Canadian Poets*, but Tom and the Bulgarian editor both have their points. Writers need money so they can write, but this doesn't mean they always write for money. As Garrison Keillor, author of *Lake Wobegon Days*, said, "You don't think of it [writing] in terms of an hourly wage. In the end you don't even do it for love. You do it because not to do it would be suicidal."

I cashed my token cheque for twenty-five dollars and attached the T-4 slip to my income tax return. Another year, another loss. In one of my worst moments ever, after twenty years of working as a writer, I realized I had to start looking for a *real* job.

I had almost reached the bottom of the Help Wanted ads, and the conclusion that I was utterly unemployable, when the phone rang again. It was my editor asking when she could look forward to receiving another of my columns.

"Writing is turning one's worst moments into money," J.P. Donleavy said. So I did.

Cosmo Girls

BY MOIRA FARR

"Cosmo, the bible of the enviable modern breed of confident, self-reliant women? Who are we kidding?"

I was standing at the magazine rack, in the lurid late-night light of my nearby Mac's Milk, when for a brief and terrifying moment I thought I'd stumbled into a Twilight Zone time tunnel that had transported me back to, oh, say 1965. "Exactly *How* I Got the Man to Marry Me" is what the throbbing black *Cosmopolitan* cover come-on promised to reveal. The bottom-line, let's-cut-the-shit tone made me laugh out loud. Farther down, in wimpy white don't-let-us-scare-you type, it said "Gloria Steinem on Taking Risks." (Phew, guess I was in the right decade after all!) Dear reader, I bought the magazine.

I should confess that half my life ago, I was a willing supplicant to the Cosmo Zeitgeist. At 16, I had forsaken teeny-bopper rags like *Fave* and *Tiger Beat* for what I considered the more racy, mature pleasures of *Cosmopolitan*. Articles on Tao-inspired love-making techniques and how to serve boffo breakfasts in bed were a little beyond me, but I recall dutifully doing the illustrated exercise routines (Yoga for Urban Hothouse Flowers), following the recommended cleansing regimens (using products advertised in the magazine *of course*) and taking to heart the results of the regularly featured quizzes—I was quite smug when I scored highest of all my friends on "How Sensuous Are You?", which gauged sensuality through such revealing factors as how you eat ice cream cones. In the narcissistic pits of my adolescent ego, I believe I was convinced that with the right make-up, lighting, and fab designer gown, I too could be one of those Scavullo-shot models pouting from the covers, or (as the come-ons of those rip-off modelling agencies put it) "just look like one." Yes! I was, to quote one of Helen Gurley Brown's early gushatorials, "a grown-up girl, interested in whatever can give you a richer, more exciting, fun-filled, friend-filled, man-loved kind of life!"

I couldn't have known then how demographically perfect, how very ripe I was to absorb Cosmo's pseudo-liberated mythology, so succinctly articulated by HGB herself in the issue that recently marked her 25th anniversary as Cosmo's editor: "I like to think the occasion was about an American dream—somebody starting with ordinary looks, no money, no college education or family influence... and getting from there to here." For Gurley (it really should be Girly) Brown, "here" was a glamorous New York party in honour of her darling self, at which she was presented with the keys to her very own silver SEL Mercedes-Benz—driver included. Underlying HGB's breathless babble is the touching assumption that us slavering mouseburgers, the term coined by Brown to describe non-Cosmo girls, reading all about it would like nothing better than to be "here" too; though some of us might find ourselves tempted to paraphrase Gertrude Stein, who said of Los Angeles that once you get there, "there's no there there."

But back to the early seventies. Fate, in the form of an older sister who went away to university and came back a militant feminist, eventually thwarted my course on the Cosmo girl trajectory. With the dour insistence of the newly converted, my revered sibling urged me to read books like *Patriarchal Attitudes, Sisterhood Is Powerful, The Feminine Mystique* and a dandy little tract about sexist advertising with the subtle title *Mind Warp*. I soon saw Cosmo in a different light, though the swift grafting of hard-core feminist rhetoric onto the Cosmospeak I had begun to assimilate is no doubt responsible for making me the twisted mess of warring aspirations that I am today.

In all the years since, I've managed to pretty much ignore *Cosmopolitan*, perhaps buying it once or twice to kill time at an airport or train station. Why it catapulted itself so forcefully back into my consciousness by way of that antediluvian headline, I don't know. (The article, incidentally, was a letdown. The author bought satin sheets, served candlelit dinners, wore sexy underwear and tried to be an interesting companion. In her recap of handy pointers that ended the piece, she cautions readers to be careful that you pick the right guy).

But I have begun reading Cosmo again—studying it, actually—in the manner of an anthropologist examining the strange practices of a lost tribe. I am by turns fascinated and appalled. Each issue beams out wildly contradictory messages. Apparently oblivious to its own bizarre irony, one recent cover pitched the following articles: "Does He Bore You? How to Stay Interested," "10 Ways to Find a Man," "How to Look like a Fashion Model" and "Gloria Steinem: We've *Still* Got a Long Way to Go Baby."

I began to form a theory: that in the wake of feminism, the average Cosmo reader is an even more mixed-up, shook-up girl than she was 25 years ago: that the schizophrenic ideal—Be Gorgeous or Be Lonely/Be Liberated like Gloria—is impossible for any rational mind to incorporate without employing a disturbing array of contortions, denials and delusions.

Like most untested notions, this one proved to be wrong, or at best, only half right. In the interests of scholarly rigour, I spent a day at the library going blind and becoming slightly nauseous as I whirred through two and a half decades of microfiched *Cosmopolitan*. But what a joy ride through the pop culture of the late twentieth century it was! I found that, in fact, the Cosmo girl has always been confused. Being a Cosmo girl has nothing to do with historical time—1970, 1990, it's all the same to her. Rather, it's a state of mind, best suited to someone suffering from a multiple personality disorder. And if you don't think this has serious social ramifications, consider that Cosmo is read by millions of women throughout the world (182,000 per month in Canada alone), and that, as Gurley Brown proudly announced in October, 1990, it's "number one on college campuses again."

I was unaware when I first embarked on my research mission that *Cosmopolitan* had led a long and full life before Helen Gurley Brown became its editor in 1965. Pre-HGB, the magazine appears to have been aimed at a more general, though probably still predominantly female, audience—a sort of *People*, *Redbook* and *Life* rolled into one. It wasn't just pulchritudinous women who appeared on the covers. The first one I looked at, dated January, 1964, featured bedroom-eyed Richard Chamberlain, "That Scrubbed Young Doctor Who Attends Fifty Million Women." Later issues also relied on celebrities as cover art—Dick van Dyke and Mary Tyler Moore (a.k.a. Rob and Laura Petrie), Barbra Streisand ("The People-Who-Need-People Girl"), and Virna Lisi, an Italian actress billed as "the most delicious piece of pizza to reach our shores since Sophia Loren," and the nubile star of a movie called "How to Murder Your Wife." That cover line appeared beneath one that said "Why Women 'Need' Wrong Husbands."

Of course, the Cosmo of that era is filled with what seem now hilariously dated sentiments and assumptions. There's the ad plugging Norforms suppositories, "for those most intimate marriage problems," providing "germicidal protection... Norforms eliminate, rather than cover up those embarrassing odours." (It took me quite a while to understand what embarrassing odours had to do with marriage. You're probably not as slow as I am, so I'll let you figure it out.) Another ad touted the charms of a loony garment called Roundez-Vouz: "the all-girl girdle," for those with a "flat derriere." (Can you imagine *any* woman padding her ass today?) Classifieds at the back of the mag flogged everything from Fashion Play Wigs to the Princess Pellatron (a "permanent" hair remover that sounds like it was tailor-made for Barbarella) to training programs for "Big-Pay Glamour Jobs" like executive secretary and medical assistant.

And then there are the articles: James Bond Girls in Furs and Bikinis, PR Girl in an Igloo, Lunch Date with Albert Finney (then 27), Models Attend a Crazy Fashion Party, Far-Out Daughters of British Aristocrats—I could practically hear the Fab Four and the Supremes crooning away in the background as I read. But apart from all the puffy stuff, these pre-Cosmo girl Cosmos also included articles that, to a reader in 1990, seem endowed with an ominous prescience. Betty Friedan on working women's problems; a piece entitled "Anatomy of a Family" that states bluntly, "marriage is in trouble in this country"; and how's "The TV Set: Who Needs a Husband?" for laying it on the line? The illustration shows a paunchy man snoozing in an easy chair, tie loosened, newspaper fallen to the floor, and a woman in a black dress and pearls seated on a sofa, holding a cigarette being lit by a lighter in a man's hand extending from the TV. The opener reads, "American wives, confused about husbands who are lost in the world of business and unwilling to stay at home except to eat and sleep, have taken a new lover to their bosom: that electronically perfect companion, the TV set. Warm, affectionate and understanding, its biggest virtues: it can't talk back, it keeps its problems to itself."

And what *could* the editors have been thinking of when, in late 1964, they published an excerpt from a book entitled *The Useless Sex*, by Italian journalist Orianna Fallacci. Based on observations made during a trip around the world to witness and document the lives of women, it is brilliant, and stunningly ironic in its Cosmo context. More to the point, if read and considered seriously, it completely obviates the raison d'être of the magazine Cosmo was about to become. Fallaci concluded that "from one end of the world to the other, women are living in a wrong way, whether they are segregated like animals in a zoo… or are unleashed like ambitious warriors winning medals in shooting contests with men." From tearful child brides in Pakistan to exhausted factory workers in China, the news was not good. The happiest women Fallacci found were those of Malaya, whose husbands continued living with their mothers after marriage. As for the "sleek career girls" of the United States, Fallacci movingly wrote, "a desperate sadness clouds their hearts… New York seems to tremble with their furious sighing." Everywhere, Fallacci reported, women were "more or less consciously hurtling to… an increasingly complex sorrow."

Well, don't bore Helen Gurley Brown with talk of complex sorrow! There she is, phone to ear in classic editrix pose, staring coyly from the July 1965 issue, as if to say "don't worry, I'll help you ward off that silly ol' desperate sadness." And lest single girls think that being unmarried at least means they won't have embarrassing odour problems, the vertical ad alongside HGB's inaugural editorial announced the arrival of Quest deodorant powder. Promising to deal with those dreadful, disgusting smells that lurk on bras, girdles, and panties, Quest declared itself "safe for intimate use and feminine daintiness." (God only knows what this meant you were supposed to do with it.) Armed with her Quest, the Cosmo girl, as conceived by a woman on her way to realizing her version of the American Dream, was born.

Despite the Cassandra-like warnings about the disastrous state of marriage in those earlier Cosmos, and despite the fact that she was capitalizing on the success of her bestselling *Sex and the Single Girl*, Gurley Brown presided (and continues to preside) over a magazine whose chief obsession is marriage. Getting married, staying married, how to be happily married, what to do if you're not happily married, having affairs with married men, having affairs while married, what to do in and out of bed until you get married, what to do in and out of bed after you get married—name the variation, Cosmo's done articles on it, enough to make you gag. The message hasn't changed a whit in twenty-five years, though these days there's a certain Trumpian feel to pieces such as "Closing the Deal (Marriage!)… No question—it's survival of the fittest time… the man shortage is real!" Cosmo, the bible of the enviable modern breed of confident, self-reliant women? Who are we kidding?

April 1966   May 1994

Being a Cosmo girl has nothing to do with historical time.

Gurley Brown herself, inviting the girls to "step into my parlor" (what is she, a madam?) lo these many years, is an enduring stereotype: best friend as bitch with a heart of gold. She's devoted to you darlin', calls you "pussy-cat" and, in her salty, conspiratorial way, lets you in on the latest gen. She's that ever-reliable, late-night soft shoulder, ready to cry "Harlot!" at any rival girl who steals your man, and there to issue soothing rationalizations when it's you doing the cheating. At your service, sweetie, so "take this issue out to the hammock with your Sara Lee fudge brownies and *begin!*"

I couldn't possibly have read all the Cosmos of the past twenty-five years, so (for the sake of sanity as well as time) I picked several from 1968, the year marked by student radicalism in Europe and North America, and the August 1974 issue, which I must have read as a glum adolescent holed up with a stack of magazines at my parents' cottage.

Back in 1968, Cosmo was, in its own inimitable way, plugged into the tempestuous spirit of the times. "Have you ever wondered how you and Mia Farrow's maharishi would get along?" Gurley Brown asked, by way of introducing "What Is This Thing Called Guru?" by Gail Sheehy. There may have been talk of revolution in the streets, but Cosmo's brand of busting loose was tepid and predictable. There were "The Outrageous Opinions of Jane Fonda," including such shockers as "sex is more than the size of your breasts," and "men should flirt with just one woman."

Cosmo also ruminated on "What Happened to Marion the Librarian?" Debunking the stereotype of the repressed tweed-suit-and-sensible-Oxford wearer, Cosmo claimed to have found librarians who "do the frug, play the vibes, collect Shearing and Brubeck records, read Ian Fleming, come to work in fun furs and mount stepladders in spring pumps." Lest the reader think that these frug-doing, vibe-playing, spring-pump-wearing bibliophiles were going a little *too* far, Cosmo was quick to add that "a reasonable number are married." Well, sock it to me.

Hurtling forward to 1974... different headlines, same obsession. "Love for *One* Person Is Back! Goodbye to the Numbers Game," "Hooked on a Married Man?" "You and Me, Babe: Chuck Barris' Gutsy Love Story of Ambition and Passion." The ads, just as they were in the sixties, are laughably dated, though in a different, even disturbing, way: It's painful to look at spreads for Love's Baby Soft cologne that say, "Because innocence is sexier than you think," and feature an adult woman dressed in little girl's pinafore and sucking a lollipop.

By the seventies, "women's lib" was a buzz concept, as exploitable as anxieties about growing up and having to deal with embarrassing odours. Were you the right kind of woman to wear the Mistress Collection by Funky (pants that bottomed out in bells the size of St. Mary's, shoes with platform soles that could double as barge pontoons)? Well, do you "turn him on during the Monday Night Football game? Worry about women's rights, alimony checks, and the shortage of motels with heart-shaped tubs for two—in that order? Sew satin sheets in your sleeping bag?" If so, you'd probably also go for some Mary Quant gloss pots, advertised just pages later.

Gurley Brown's editorial in that issue is poignant reading now. "Usually I don't do battle for many 'causes,'" she confided, "just the one of getting *you*, my beloved Cosmo girl, and *me*, through the night." Still, she felt moved to discuss *the abortion issue*. She'd even attended a high-profile meeting of the National Abortion Rights Action League, and met Gloria Steinem in person! "What's Gloria Steinem really like? Beautiful... Admirable... *Dedicated* to her causes." Gosh, a bit overwhelming for a Cosmo girl, but HGB soldiered on. "Before the press conference we went to the ladies' room where *I* glued on my false eyelashes and anchored my fall while Gloria ran a comb through her hair and put on some Chap Stick! A contrast in grooming styles but we *both* think we have nice hearts."

Well, at least in 1974, Helen had a heart nice enough to proclaim itself adamantly pro-choice, which is more than I can imagine these days, when her editorials run to lazy "in this issue we feature" roundups and, more spuriously, to unabashed plugs for airlines that fly her and her husband to exotic destinations. Would Moral Majority-addled advertisers ever tolerate an openly pro-abortion stance these days? Oh, why push it, pussycat! A girl over sixty deserves some comforts, after all.

So Cosmo is number one on college campuses once again. Families may disintegrate, divorce rates may rise to even more disastrous levels than those predicted in 1964, yet Cosmo still pushes its relentless old message: there's nothing wrong with a single girl looking good and feeling good, so long as it's in the service of one goal: Matrimony. Same weirdly mixed "now you're liberated, now you're not" message. "The Courage to Heal: Surviving the Nightmare of Incest," "Plastic Surgery: I Decided to Have It All" (written by a 34-year-old woman who compares living with her pre-surgery "superficial imperfections" to "going through life with my slip showing"), "Ways to Make a Man Feel Comfortable," and so on and on and on. Advertisers no longer feel the need to push their products with disingenuous hype about liberation, and it's just as well. And despite news that fuller breasts and rounder bums are in, one recent Dieter's Notebook featured a near-starvation diet, designed to be followed for three days in order to lose three pounds. You can forget Virginia Slims. Now we've come so far baby, we've got *Super* Slims, advertised with a compressed photo of a very elongated woman's body. We've still got odours to worry about, but now they can be conquered with Femicine, a "homeopathic" suppository developed by the friendly sounding Womens' Health Institute. At least the woman in the ad doesn't look embarrassed—and she's in the company of a man!

Deaf to the furious sighs, oblivious to desperate sadness (it's no fun!), Cosmo continues exhorting women to fashion themselves, and their relationships, into stereotypes that are, and always have been, untenable. My advice to latter-day Cosmo readers is to rent the video of Sandra Bernhard's savage film, "Without You I'm Nothing." Bernhard does a wicked send-up of the Cosmo girl as the consummate consumer of commercially generated, socially sanctioned fantasy. With bouncy Burt Bacharach tunes playing in the background, Bernhard cavorts across the stage, the sleeve of her sequined minidress slipping fetchingly from her bony shoulder. She's the "Woman I Could Have Been"—an executive secretary in romantic San Francisco, acing her shorthand and snaring her dreamboat boss. She comes home to her cute bachelor apartment, furnishings courtesy of Pier One Imports; she takes a long hot bubble bath, washes her hair with Herbal Essence Shampoo, rubs herself down with a big cozy Fieldcrest towel and applies lots of Love's Lemon After Bath Splash. "I look," she tells us with a smug purr, "reeeeealllly pretty." The crowning achievement of her young life, she finally reveals with a jubilant shout: "I'M UNDER THIRTY-FIVE AND I'M GOING TO BE MARRIED!!!"

The inspiration for Bernhard's wonderful comic riff was a notorious (and since debunked) study, which concluded that a single woman over the age of 35 had less chance of getting married than being killed by a terrorist. "I asked myself, who is it out there making women feel shitty about themselves?" If we don't know by now, I guess we never will.

Absent-Minded People

BY DEBORAH LEE

The author was inspired to write this after going through a garbage can at the airport, looking for a cheque she had inadvertently thrown out.

There are no support groups for us, and yet our numbers are legion. You can recognize us easily... we lose our keys, our wallets, our train of thought. We rarely lose our sense of humour, as this is crucial to survival. With this in mind (if only briefly), I am starting a support group for us Very Absent-minded Generally Unassuming Eccentrics, or VAGUE.

Recent research indicates that those of us whose minds are here-and-now challenged are actually reacting to stress. Gentle souls that we are, we do not resort to violence to vent our frustration, or develop physical ailments. No, we merely board a plane while wearing our slippers (as a friend's father once did), or jump in a car and race to the maternity ward, leaving our pregnant wife on the front step (another friend's father), or make eggs Benedict and forget the eggs (another friend... O.K., so it was me).

We vaguerants take comfort in the words of the brilliant yet absent-minded Albert Einstein, who once said: "I want to know the thoughts of God—all the rest is merely detail." (Naturally, I forget the exact quote.) We find solace in the acts of kindred spirits.

When I worked in a major downtown hotel, a guest reported his stolen car to police, only to be admonished by his wife: "You danged fool! We flew from Portland!"

A co-worker's sister, in an attempt to foil prospective burglars when she went on vacation, put her camera and Walkman in the oven and— there is no point in continuing; you all know what happened.

We are unintentional sources of comic relief.

"I did a Deb" has become entrenched in my friends' vocabulary. Once we have done something really stupid, we vow never to repeat our mistake; instead, we keep finding new, creative ways of defying belief.

Vaguerancy appears to run in families. My uncle once borrowed his father's car, stopped for gas, went to the washroom, then came out and ran for his usual bus, which was passing by. It wasn't until that evening, when his father asked him about the car, that he even remembered. My grandfather himself, who was taking my grandmother shopping in Halifax after the birth of her 15th child, inadvertently drove her to the Grace Maternity Hospital.

We are, by our very nature, rarely materialistic. Gloves and jewellery make but fleeting appearances in our lives. Cupboards are not for storing our possessions but for staring into, blankly. When we travel, we leave souvenirs. Tony Bennett left his heart in San Francisco; I have left a bra there.

There appears to be no cure for us (although one boyfriend did offer to pay for my operation—to have my keys surgically implanted). Perhaps we should all move to England, where eccentrics rule. I know a successful businessman who, in the 1960s, was walking down a street in London that seemed familiar. He remembered he had once left a ring in the jeweller's there to be repaired. The clerk asked when he had left the ring, and was told: "1942." Unfazed—he was English, after all—the clerk produced the ring.

Until medical technology is able to enlarge our memory glands, I would just ask, on behalf of countless absent-minded professionals and other light-minded individuals, for a little tolerance, compassion, and perhaps another cheap umbrella.

A last personal request—that after I am gone, someone will take my ashes and then, as is only fitting, forget them on a bus.

At a Loss for Words

BY ROSE BORRIS WITH PAULETTE JILES

When she was forty-six, Rose Borris decided it was time to learn to read and write. This is her experience.

One of my sisters, she used to pretend that she knew how to read. I didn't pretend. I said, "There's nothing I can do. I don't know how and that's it!" This was common in my parents' time, that people couldn't read or write. My father never went to school and my mother only went for a bit. My father could sign his name, but it took him 10 minutes. My mother knew a little bit more. But to them, it wasn't important. My mother said she wanted the house clean, she didn't like paper lying around. That's how it was. Your life was in the bush and when my father went there to work my mother took all the kids along. There were 14 of us altogether. Only five ever learned to read.

I was born in 1932 in a little place called Maltais, New Brunswick. My grandmother always told me I looked like a bear when I was born, I had hair all over me. And she said to my mother, "Caroline, you didn't have a kid, you just had a bear." My grandmother had a baby herself, a month after. She came to help my mother, and then my mother went to help her. This is the way it is with big families.

In Maltais the school was our neighbour. Just a one-room school. But sometimes the people couldn't pay their taxes so there was no teacher. And then somebody burned the school down so they would have some work building it again. I was five maybe, my brother and I saw a man go to the school at night with a can of gas. I remember our dog, Siffleur, barked and barked. Nobody reported the man, people were tired of the tax. Everybody was cousins anyway.

Before I was eight years old, we didn't have any money. But we had enough to eat, because of relief. It was the same with everybody in Maltais. You had a paper to go to the store and now and then people would come to your home and check your supplies to see if you had anything left over. If you did, then they would cut you off. My mother would hide the stuff we had under a rock out in the field—beans, brown sugar—and she would trade it to other people for the things she needed.

We had a little bit to eat from our farm—my father had a horse, a cow, and a few pigs and chickens. Every summer, we used to pick blueberries by the Northwest river. I once saw seven bears in the blueberry patch. We stayed in a black tar-paper thing, like a tent, and everybody slept on spruce boughs. I took care of the younger kids.

When I was eight I went to school, but in February I had an abscess on my knee and I couldn't go back. Anyway I didn't like it, I didn't have nice clothes and the kids would laugh. And if I hit somebody, my mother would beat me for it. The trouble was, I didn't speak very well. We had to read out loud, and I couldn't pronounce words and I was afraid and I forgot everything. Boy, I hated school. I was happy when we left for the bush.

I don't even remember the first time my family went into the bush. We would stay there five or six months, the whole winter. The camp buildings were made with logs so we had to chink them again every winter. There were always porcupine quills stuck in the bark. The buildings had only tar-paper roofs with dirt on top. My mother always had a little baby two or three months old, and sometimes the snow fell in our faces. All the children helped. We carried water and helped to cook for the men and washed dishes and put them out again, the plates upside down. We finished our work about 10 o'clock at night.

When I was 10, an Englishman took a big contract for 100 men to cut wood and work in the forest at Upsalquitch. He talked to my mother and we never came home to the farm again. This camp was big, a place where my father could make more money. But we had to work much harder.

We had three stoves, big ones. We made soup and meat and beans every day, and sometimes a roast with gravy in a big iron pot. We cooked the bread at night. Breakfast was beans and hot biscuits and bread. We made lunch for the men too—cold meat, bread, butter molasses cookies, molasses cake, and white cake. We also had to make all the beds in the morning when the men weren't there. But it was the first time we kids had a room of our own to sleep in, even if I never had my own bed.

We never had time to play. But we talked a lot and we fought a lot, we made jokes and laughed—I miss this. I love people around me all the time. You smell food cooking, you wash the floor, and the wood smells so good, your stove is always red—this is life.

This was wartime, too. My father's cousin Emile Maltais went to war. His mother cried so much. He later said he fought and killed people. Awful thing, to kill people with a gun! And telegrams came saying people were dead, so if somebody went to be a soldier people thought he would never come back.

My uncle listened to the radio, but he didn't understand it too well. He would say: "And now the Germans are going to take that place there! Now they're going to take this place!" The way people talked, I thought the war was just behind home, maybe five miles from Maltais.

Our neighbour didn't want to be a soldier, so he hid in the bush and every day a girl went to feed him. They never caught him. In a little place like Maltais, everyone was his friend. It rained sometimes so the girl couldn't go, and once he went two days without food. He fell in love with that girl, they got married and had a big family after the war. You know, he *had* to marry her. But that's what happens when you take food to a guy in the bush, eh?

At the camps you didn't have to work so hard in the spring, and always some old people would sit down and tell stories. There's never one that's the same. Old Ouellet was a very good storyteller and he never read in his life. Sometimes a story would last two, three nights. And it was so nice when they'd say, "We ain't going to finish tonight." All the kids would listen, we loved this so much, and sometimes the small ones fell asleep. But I don't think I ever fell asleep. This was how I learned to tell stories. They'd say, "Tell us a story, Rose!" and everyone would come to listen.

There were lots of stories about Ti-Jean. He was a little man, maybe he comes from the moon. These stories have kings in them and dragons and princesses. A story like this would come over from France a long time ago, and people would repeat it and change it all the time. So beautiful!

And then there were also stories about local people. *Le vieux Joseph*, my father said, had eyes so shining that he knew when the moon was changing to full. Then this man would turn himself into the werewolf, the *loup garou.* He would take a walk into the bush and push his knife into a log. It was a magic knife, no one could touch it or he would die. Then *le vieux Joseph* would walk out on the roads and kill people in the dark.

We lived at Upsalquitch for two years. On the Upsalquitch River there were big timber rafts, and we would stand and watch them pass. The family moved when there was no more wood to cut. We moved many times, that's the way it was.

It was when we were living at Upsalquitch that my sister Stella and I took First Communion. I was 11 and we had to get on the bus, and go to the church at Kedgwick. We stayed with my grandmother Maltais. You can never get married if you are unable to pass your First Communion.

We had to learn the catechism. I had trouble because I couldn't read and my mother was not the kind of person to teach us at home. After a week of going to church I thought it was all finished. But I didn't go to confession and I didn't know I needed to. On Sunday, the first thing I know, all the people got up and went to Communion. When I saw the little kids, five, six years, going up, I said to Stella, "It's time we go. If we don't go, we're not going to pass." Some of the women knew that you had to go to confession before you can take Communion, but they didn't stop me. And the priest didn't know and he gave us Communion.

These women told the priest after Mass. And the priest was so mad, he made us get on our knees in front of everybody and stay there for an hour. He said that God was going to come and get us, and we were never going to be saved. We were so afraid we were shaking.

He asked us, "What kind of a father do you have?" The priest didn't know we were in the bush all wintertime. He said, "We never saw people like this in our lives!" I never believed a priest again.

After my brother Leo was born, my mother met some people who had visited Montreal. They said there was a convent where the nuns had a school for girls six to 14 years old. The people said Stella and I could go there, and work for room and board and learn to read and write. We would get $12 a month. That was good money in 1945. I was 13, Stella was 12. I thought about this and finally I said yes.

My mother and father put us on the train. You know, I was afraid. On the train we met a sailor, he was drinking liquor and he tried to catch us. I got mad and I told the conductor, but after he found us a room with a bed that opened up the conductor came in and tried to lift our blankets. After that we were so afraid we didn't sleep all night.

I had heard so many people say, "It's a very big place, Montreal!" You see, my father's cousin used to buy horses in Montreal to take them back to New Brunswick. When the train stopped, I never saw any horses so I never thought we were in Montreal. We waited a long time. The train started to move and the conductor came to find us. He said, "This is Montreal!"

I said, "What? Montreal!" I thought it was some other city, I was waiting for the horses.

The conductor told us to go up the escalator. It was the first time I was on one and I was scared. Two sisters were waiting at the top for us, they were always in pairs. They took us to the convent on a streetcar.

The convent was a big place, very beautiful. There was a curtain to close off your room, and a washroom, and water—you could take a bath. But I said to Stella, "You know, I don't like this too much." When you come from a big family, you feel so lonesome in such a place.

We had to work hard. I had to take care of seven tables in the dining room. When the kids wanted something, I had to go and get it. When they finished eating, I had to wash all the dishes and dust the tables and set them again. I also had to clean the hall and wash and wax the floor all the time. Every day I had to clean each washroom.

I learned many things there that I never knew before. Cut the sandwiches fancy, place the plates and forks very fancy. I learned how to run those huge laundry machines, and we ironed and pressed the clothes with the big ironing machines. I started to like the laundry because there was a nun there who was very nice. She wasn't yelling at me all the time, you know?

But the nuns wanted us to read and write. And I was ashamed. The way I spoke, it wasn't good French like they spoke. The little girls there, eight or nine years old, they knew how to read and write. I used to pass by the classrooms and think, "There's no way we can learn this. They're smart." Later when you're grown up, you think: "They're smart, but they've got their problems too."

We were not allowed to talk to the kids. The only time we played outside was when the kids weren't out there. We could play outside for an hour, and after that we had to go to the chapel. We had to pray every morning and every night.

Seven months I stayed there, and the first thing I found out was who could write. You see, I had to make some of the kids write for us. I had learned to spell my name when I was smaller but I never used it, so I forgot. When you never have a book at home, you even forget how to sign your name. If a letter came, the nuns didn't read it to us right away, they had to know what was in the letter first. I was not allowed to touch it. Oh, how I hated this! My own mail.

Then the kids started leaving school for the summer and I had to do more and more. I worried about getting the rooms clean and waxing the floors. The first thing I knew, I was sick for two days and I didn't even eat. Then the eczema started. I had it for two years, I think. I was poisoned from the floor wax, so I borrowed six dollars from Stella to go home on the train.

After I arrived home from the convent, we moved to a place called Squaw Cap. We had a store there. In the store, I found every box was a different colour or there was something different about it so I could tell what it was. I couldn't read the labels. I don't know why, but "tomato" I could read. I guess it was because I loved tomato soup. What I hated was when they started to put the salt in bags like the sugar.

My mother was expecting another baby that fall, and my father said if she left to go in the bush with him everything was going to freeze up at the store. He said, "Rose, if you come instead, you'll be head cook at the bush camp. Five dollars a day, good money."

I wanted to bring my brother Normand with me to carry water. He was eight years old. We had to wait till the river froze, then we took all our stuff and moved in. I had to get up at four in the morning and peel 75 pounds of potatoes, cook beans, make bread and pies and cakes and cookies all morning, and then make all the lunches. I cooked for 49 men. Nobody helped me, only Normand.

Now I was 14 when I started to fall in love with a man. His name was Edmond, he was 18. He used to come to our house every night. When he went out with me, I just talked to him. When he tried to kiss me one time, I hit him in the face.

I had my fifteenth birthday when I was in the bush. I never wanted to turn 15. I wanted to stay 14 forever. I guess I was afraid that at 15 you had to get married.

Then I went to work in Campbellton. I lived in a boarding house with five other girls and I washed dishes in a restaurant. I enjoyed the job—it was hard work, but I was used to that. Campbellton was English, but I couldn't be a waitress because I couldn't read the menu anyway. You also had to buy your dinner at the restaurant. I had learned how to say "pork chops" from my brother, so I ordered pork chops all the time. Sometimes I wanted something else, but what can you do?

One night a circus came to town and Edmond's cousin Albert Borris came to take me. He was a mechanic, but he used to chop wood when he was a boy for 25 cents a day. I won a doll there—I wanted one so bad. It was just a porcelain head, without any hair, but it was the first doll I'd ever had.

And then Albert asked me to meet his family. They were nice, a big family like mine. He was a good mechanic, I trusted him to have money in his pocket. Maybe that's why I kept going out with him: I cared for him, he respected me. I was afraid of the men who worked in the bush.

But Stella started to bug me about going to the convent again. She made my mother write to the nuns. They wrote back and said, "We don't need any girls to work but we know another convent where they can go." I made up my mind and said yes. Albert was coming around all the time but I wanted to be free. I was young, eh?

This time the convent was a little bit outside Montreal, on the St. Lawrence River. It was a beautiful place. But the first thing the nuns told us was, "You have to take all your clothes out of your trunk. We want to see everything you have there."

I said, "What do you mean, you? This is *our* stuff."

She said, "This is the rule."

I had a cigarette pack in there. "You're not going to make me take my stuff out!"

I got mad and cut the cord around my trunk and opened it. Then I took my cigarettes and kept them in my hand and threw everything else out. She didn't see that. I had time to put the cigarettes under the mattress.

That night I went to bed and I cried. I slept for maybe two hours. I felt like I was in prison. The walls were so high and I knew the place was strict from the way they talked.

In the morning I got up and they showed me everything. I had the same job as in the other place. All those tables to take care of, the windows to wash and the stairs and the floors—and the same wax again.

I didn't mind the work. But every night we had to go to church. And they wanted me to put my hat on, and I didn't want to put it on. And this nun I hated, Sister Vachon from the kitchen, she didn't want us to wear lipstick. The nun took a Kleenex and grabbed Stella and wiped the lipstick off. She was a big nun, almost 200 pounds.

The nuns didn't trust anyone, they only trusted themselves. I couldn't live where there's no trust. My mother trusted us, but here there was none at all. I wanted to write my mother. I tried to make a little orphan girl of 11 years write for me, and the nuns found out and punished the little girl.

Then Stella said, "We're going to say yes for the nun to write. But we're going to make all kinds of lies and we're going to laugh at them and enjoy ourselves."

That night the old nun began a letter for us. She said, "You want me to say how much you love it here?"

I said, "No, say 'I hate this place so much, if I don't get out of here I think I'm going to kill somebody. Hurry and send me money because I want to go home.'"

She wrote, "Your little girl, she likes it here very much and she's a good girl and works very hard… "

Then Stella started. Stella had a boyfriend too.

"Tell him I miss him so much I don't know what I'm going to do."

The nun said, "Who is this?"

Stella said, "It's my brother."

She knew we came from a big family so she said, "Oh, your brother."

I told her, "Say hi to Albert. Tell him I miss him a little bit."

"Who is this Albert?"

"It's my brother, he's a baby, he's only seven months old."

She liked this. But later, we got a letter from my mother.

"Albert is fine, he still drives his truck and he stops by here and asks how you feel and misses you so much." And with Stella it was the same. Our letter stayed in the office two days, I saw it there, but there was no way I could take it. And the nun, she was so mad.

I was in that place three months. I wanted to go home right away. No way I can phone, no way I can write. To be in a jail and I couldn't even do anything!

Anyway, the nuns had to let me go. And before I left, they made me a cake. A fruitcake, they are very expensive. "We know you want to get married soon, and this is your present." The nuns felt sorry for me because they thought I was going to get married soon.

They brought me to the train and they gave me a rosary and told me, "Sit by yourself. Make sure you don't talk to anybody. Promise us this: think about God." And they waited until the train started.

I threw the rosary away as soon as I could.

Everyone was at home and I was so happy to see all the family again. But after a while my mother went to the bush camp and I had to make the food and look after the store. The baby, Aline, was 15 months old and there were four other children to take care of too.

At Christmas Albert bought me a watch. My father said, "He loves you very much, that man."

I was only 15. But around there, everybody got married at that time.

Albert came to see me. He said, "You're going to have to listen. I have something to say." It took him four hours, and he finished by asking me to marry him. I had to say yes. You know, when you get married, you always marry a stranger. You never know how it's going to work.

I got married in a big church close to Campbellton. I remember I didn't sign the marriage certificate—the priest said, "Make a cross." And my father made a cross too. Albert could sign his name, he had been to school a little bit, he knew enough to fill out a paper. But he's not fast and he hates to read.

We had a big dinner and a party, and we went back to sleep at Mrs. Borris's at Val-d'Amour, we had a room there. Albert wanted to leave at 11 o'clock. I didn't want to go, I loved to dance. If it were today I'd tell him, "Go by yourself!" He wanted to go before his parents came, to be first in the house. We went into the bedroom and I started to look at the presents, I was so embarrassed I didn't know what to do. I went to another room and put on my nightgown over my brassiere.

Then Albert's brother came home. Albert said, "Hurry up!" And he caught me and we fell to the bed.

What I found hard was to get up in the morning. Mr. Borris was there and he said, "And how did you pass the night, Rose?" If I got married again I would never stay in the same house as my in-laws.

Ten years later I had five kids: Clayton, Garry, Betty-Ann who is deaf, Shirley Ann who died as a baby, and Jerry. But one of my brothers had moved to Toronto and he said it was beautiful. Then my father got a job in construction and my parents moved to Toronto. I missed my family.

Then Albert asked me to move. When he found a job at Master Buildup we moved to Cabbagetown. I loved Toronto. It was the best of all the places that I have lived. I said, "This is where I want my life, not in a camp. In a house where you have water, hot water."

At first we stayed at my brother's place. I was 27 and Jerry was only 15 months. Albert said, "At first, Rose, it's going to be hard in the city because we're not going to make enough money." But I saw some of my relatives had rooming houses and I wanted one too. One of my cousins, he was a bootlegger on Carlton Street. He got caught and had to sell his home. I said to my mother, "I'm going to go get this." Albert was afraid. But I borrowed the money from my mother to rent the house and buy the furniture and pay my cousin's fine.

Now I had everything. A big house, 10 rooms, with my own bedroom and my own kitchen. Pretty soon my brother had two houses, then more of the family did the same, and first thing I know there were 11 rooming houses around me.

I was never afraid when my boarders drank—it made me mad. When they fought too much I'd just go and yell at them to shut up. If they didn't do that, I would hit them. Sometimes people would come in with no money. But I found I would get my way. I always have.

I didn't speak good English but I was learning it all the time. Every time I got mad, I learned some new words. I had to learn English because Betty-Ann was already in English school, the school for the deaf in Belleville, and I only knew French. Betty-Ann didn't understand French at all. I said to myself, "The time will come when she's going to be able to talk to me, I've got to be able to understand her." It was hard. We had to go up to Belleville every week. She was so lonesome, she was like me at that convent I hated so much.

It is hard to make people believe that you can't read and write. In Toronto, it's awful. You go into an office and they give you a paper to fill out and they say, "This is easy."

"All right, it's easy for you!"

"You're *sure* you don't know how to read? It's not hard."

And I say, "Well, do you speak French then?"

And they say, "Oh, but we don't know how to speak French."

"But I don't know how to read and write! Don't you understand this?"

And they say, "Oh, we're very sorry. We didn't believe you couldn't read."

When I was first in Toronto, my son Clayton wasn't old enough to fill out a cheque. I would buy a money order, and use it to pay the gas and telephone bills. The woman at the post office put on the address. And my mother, she knew all the rules for a rooming house. She said, the first thing you do is put up a sign, NO LIQUOR ALLOWED IN THE HOUSE. There's always somebody in the house who can read and write.

It's not hard to get around in the city and not be able to read. With the streetcar, I knew where I was going and you can see if it's stopping at the place where you live. But the subway, I hate this. I was afraid to go underground. The trains go so fast and I find it's not fair—they should have somebody to call out the names of the stations. If I wanted to go to a place where I've never been before, I would take a taxi. Then the second time I'd know where to go.

When Albert and I would go to a restaurant, we always asked for the special. You ask for the special and they tell you what it is. If you like it, you get it. People used to ask me, "How do you know a washroom when you stop in a restaurant?" This isn't hard—you look around and see a woman get up and leave, then you go where she goes.

I know numbers, so I always knew where to find an address. We had to learn numbers as children, my father and mother were very good on this. But when I would go in a building where they have names, I hated it. I had to ask people where to go.

I enjoyed my job. But if I had known how to read and write, you think I would have had a rooming house? No, I would have had a big restaurant on Yonge Street. The kids used to show me their report cards and they had to make sure they passed—this was very important to me. I made them so scared of not passing, they would shake.

I think when you get older, you don't like yourself as much as before. Some people hate themselves because they're getting old, or they hate the job they do, but there's no way you can stop. They're too chicken to change their lives. Then other people, they want to stay the same and there's no way you can do this. Everybody has to change.

I was thinking about my family. My sister Aline hanged herself, and my brother Ted drowned. I was at my doctor's many times. I was dizzy when I got up or when I moved. He told me it was my nerves. I didn't believe him at first. But later I said, "I'm going to do something for myself. I'm not going to wait to have a breakdown. I'm going to make myself a road."

Now I had lots of reasons to learn how to read and write. My kids had started to leave home and I was thinking: "If I'm left on my own, what am I going to do?" I'm independent, but I knew it would be hard. Even if I wanted to phone someone, I had to wait for somebody to look up the name in the book.

When I was younger, I didn't have a phone. And in New Brunswick, when I wanted to order something from the catalogue, I would walk to my girlfriend's and she would do it for me. But now every weekend, at our cottage north of Belleville, people would come to visit and sit around on the beach, or underneath a tree, and read. And others would walk in with a newspaper. This killed me.

People would ask, "Did you read this? You know what happened here?" Oh boy, that made me mad. I would listen to the news on the radio but it was never like the paper. I said to my son Clayton: "It sure must be nice to know how to read and write."

Betty-Ann sent me a card and her little girl, Roxanne, made an X. She was only two years old. It was all that I had learned since I was small, because when somebody wrote a letter to Betty-Ann for me I always used to make many Xs, many kisses. The first thing I know, Roxanne would know how to read and write. If she can learn, what's wrong with me? But I didn't know how to start.

Just before Christmas 1977, I went up to the cottage for three months with Albert. He had a bad leg and I was stuck there, so stuck. I had to wait for somebody else just to come and read my Christmas cards. Albert wanted me to stay, he didn't want me to learn how to read. We moved back to Toronto in February and I started to watch "Sesame Street." But all the letters went by so fast. I'd try this and I'd try that but later I'd forget.

Then it was Clayton's birthday, the thirty-first of March. Clayton's the one who has made the movies about our family. He did *Paper Boy* and *Alligator Shoes* and *One Hand Clapping*, and he made *Rose's House* about my boarding house in Cabbagetown. Now he's making movies in Hollywood. I said to my son Jerry, "I want you to write, 'Happy Birthday Clayton, it's going to be a beautiful party.'" He wrote it and it took me over half an hour to copy the message down on the card. I would look at the letters and then forget what they looked like. It's hard, you know. They were not very nice letters.

Clayton found this beautiful that I wanted to read and write. He went and put my name down at Jones Avenue School in Toronto. I started there in October 1978.

It's hard to get out of home when the man doesn't want you to do this. You're lucky if you can get out the door. That's why I didn't start in September—I had to fight with Albert all the time because he wanted me at home. He said I was never going to learn. Maybe he was afraid. But one day he said, "It's no use, Rose, I can see what you want. I can't stop you." I said, "No, you can't stop me."

But when I was first at school, I was so depressed. After two months I phoned my mother. I was crying and I said, "I made a mistake, I should never have said, 'Rose is going to school.' I was crazy to think I could learn."

And she said, "Rose, you got nothing to lose. You did the best thing." I was 46 years old. I had always helped other people, but now I had to ask for help. This was hard to do.

At first I hated all the teachers. I didn't understand how they could go so fast, and I was just a little thing in the corner. But then I understood why I hated them. It's because I was thinking about the nuns in Montreal. You couldn't trust those people.

I went to school five days a week for three years. Once I started to trust people, I was O.K. It was strange, I had always bought school supplies for the children, and now I had to buy them for myself. The other people in the class were from all over the place—China, Vietnam, Quebec. It was so hard! I remember sitting in the library, trying to read a book for an hour and I understood six words. Maybe it would have been easier if I'd been learning in French. But I don't speak French the way they do in books.

I didn't understand so many things. *That apple is red—that apple is not red*—it's funny when you're not used to it. "Why do you say it's red when I know it's red? If it's red, then why do you say it's not red? Why do you change your mind?" I thought that probably my eyes were different. It's hard on the eyes. The first thing you know, I had to change my glasses.

But I kept on going to school. And after I was there seven months, I wrote a letter to my principal. This is what I wrote:

Jones School, Tuesday, June 12, 1979.

The first day I came at school, I was lost and nervous. I saw all around. The principal gave me a paper. I forgot the room and my names for one week. I was always thinking about my house and I felt stupid and crazy. I hated the teacher, the principal, and myself so much. Not now. I was thirty years at home. It was strange, when my teacher Susan talked to me I jumped. Here it is nice, because we have a private teacher every day in the library. Today I'm happy because I didn't stop my school. I read and I write today, I like my two teachers very much.

Rose Maltais Borris

And at the bottom of my letter, the principal wrote: "This is an excellent piece of work."

Albert used to say to me: "You're crazy!" But now, I read in front of him. And the first thing I know, he was trying to read too, a Bible. I laughed at this: he's trying to find out what happened to his wife and he hasn't found out yet and he's probably never going to find out. Not in there!

Margaret Laurence: In Memory

BY TIMOTHY FINDLEY

This is the eulogy one of her friends delivered on radio the morning after Margaret Laurence died.

Mind must be the firmer,
Heart the more fierce,
Courage the greater
As our strength diminishes.

These are lines from an old English poem that was cherished by Margaret Laurence—cherished, rehearsed over time, and implemented. Wherever she found these words—whenever it was they first refused to go away and leave her alone—that moment must be counted as one of the most important in all the sixty years of her life. As words, as articulation, they became a cornerstone of her resources. They inform not only her writing: they also inform whatever we know of how she lived and how she died.

Margaret Laurence was a great believer in simplicity. She was also one of its greatest practitioners. This is where the *firmness* came in. Firmness, for Margaret Laurence, was one of simplicity's most important synonyms. "I will" and "I won't" were two of her absolutes. She would not and could not tolerate anything less than her full capacity to make words work on paper. Nor would she tolerate anything less than her full capacity to stand for what she believed in.

As time progressed and her capacities expanded, she also progressed from *firm* to *firmer*. If you knew Margaret Laurence, you had to contend with this sometimes difficult part of her will. And if you knew her well, you wished, in a way, you could protect her from it. Part of her firmness and, of course, an extremely potent part of her will was her rejection—which was total—of any kind of safety: personal, intellectual, or physical. She struggled thirty years or more at her table to produce on the page an account of what was in her mind—and that, as any serious writer knows, is a struggle utterly without the benefit of self-preservation. The onslaught of fictional men and women, ideas, and events—all of whom and all of which can achieve their existence only if the writer succeeds at giving them articulation—has a strange, seductive power to suggest that articulation "cannot be achieved." Unless you are firm.

So Margaret Laurence stayed there at her table, no matter how long it took to get things right. And when she rose and when she handed over what she had written, she said: "This is it, the way it should be, the way it must be, the way it is and the way it will stay."

This is it: the way it will stay: *The Stone Angel, A Jest of God, The Fire-Dwellers, A Bird in the House, The Diviners*: firm, firmer, firmest.

The fierceness in her was mighty.

Margaret Laurence had to contend with a body whose nervous system tended to betray her just when she needed it most to be strong. She shook. Her knees gave way. Her hands could be seen from almost any distance, reaching for the backs of chairs and the tops of tables—anything to hold her up and stop her from shaking. Rising to speak—choosing, against all odds, to rise at all—in order to tell what she believed—these were the harshest enemies she had whenever it came to speaking her mind. But speak her mind she must—and fiercely. She said something once that gave the essence of all her beliefs: her certainty that we, her beloved humankind, were capable of wilful, self-determined sanity if only we would *try*.... Margaret Laurence believed, with a passion so profound it almost puts me to shame to think of it, that war and hatred must *and can* be put aside. And she devoted, even to the point of exhaustion, all the latter years of her life to activities supporting this belief. But her open espousal of peace through nuclear disarmament brought her, as it must, a host of enemies, name-callers, finger-pointers: people who called her a "fool," a "red," and the word that disturbed her most, "subversive." What Margaret Laurence said to these accusers was said with the kind of ferocity that only absolute certainty can justify. "If the quest for peace," she said, "is subversive, then what, in the name of God, is war?"

Fierce, fiercer, fiercest.

One day the word came that Margaret Laurence was going to die. No backing off, no second chance at survival, nothing to mitigate the certainty. Up to about a year before this day arrived, those of us who knew and loved her had been aware of her struggles to take up the pen again and write. Her last major piece of work had been published in 1974. This was her masterpiece, *The Diviners*. But since that year, her writer's output had been meagre: three books for children and one of essays written in the past. Her time was given over to antinuclear and peace activities. She was also—with great success and personal popularity—the chancellor of Trent University. But what she wanted—besides these things—was one more book. And it wouldn't come.

What very few people knew was that, during this time, Margaret Laurence was slowly going blind with cataracts. She couldn't properly wield the pen. She couldn't properly type, though both activities were still producing a vast outpouring of letters to students and fans and friends. And then there was a "miracle." A plastic lens was implanted in one of her eyes—and she began to write again. She could barely believe her good fortune. What she wrote, and what she completed, and what, in a not-too-distant future, will be published was a book devoted to the theme of motherhood: a memoir. She worked on this until the week before she died.

Brave, braver, bravest.

Euripides told us: "Never that which is shall die."

He didn't mean people, I guess. I guess what he meant was ideas and truths and things like that. I think he meant, too, that whatever goes into life—the whole of what is alive—is alive forever. Margaret Laurence is dead. But so—we are told—is Euripides. I'm sure you know exactly what I mean. Goodbye, Margaret Laurence. And thank you.

The Importance of Teaching

BY ROBERT STEWART

"To a large extent, teachers are in charge of the future. The fate of people in the future depends on how well they are taught today."

Teaching is one of those things, like editing a newspaper or managing a baseball team, that everybody thinks he or she can do better than the experts. Everybody has taught something to somebody at one time or another, after all. We begin our amateur teaching careers as children by imposing our superior knowledge on our younger siblings and playmates. As students, we pass judgment among our peers on this or that teacher's capabilities. As adults, those of us who do not teach professionally stand ever ready to criticize those who do.

An educator himself, Bergan Evans once struck back at people who presume that any fool could be a teacher. Commenting on George Bernard Shaw's aphorism, "He who can does. He who cannot teaches," Evans wrote: "The common inference from this much-quoted statement, that the teacher is a sort of failure in the world of action, greatly comforts anti-intellectuals. But almost to a man successful men of action (all of whom think they could be teachers if they turned aside to it) have proved failures as teachers." He did not document his information, but it rings true.

In any case, Shaw's quip does not stand up to logic. Teachers *can* do something, and *do* do something; they teach. Like any other professional activity, teaching requires a cultivated ability. To be done exceptionally well, it also requires a special talent and a sense of vocation. There are "born teachers" just as there are "born statesmen" or "born musicians."

Practised diligently by men and women of talent, teaching is as much of an art as Shaw's métier of play-writing. The trouble from the teacher's point of view is that there are a lot more teachers than playwrights or men of action like generals or financiers. Education is one of our nation's biggest industries. Because of the sheer number of those who teach in schools, colleges and universities, they have become part of the landscape. Like the familiar features of a landscape, they tend to be overlooked.

Still, there are probably many more great teachers labouring among the crowd than there are great authors or actors basking in the spotlight. They could be found anywhere in the educational system from a graduate to a country school. Teaching, as measured by its results, does not lend itself to a division between the big and the bush leagues. Those results come in the form of the quality of the people it shapes.

Unlike sports, politics, entertainment, the arts or the law, teaching does not give rise to "stars." Nobody ever got a Nobel Prize for teaching achievements. True, many academics have come in for high honours, but always for something other than their work in the classroom—a book, an economic treatise, a ground-breaking scientific experiment.

Schoolteachers, as opposed to university professors, are particularly underrecognized. Who is to say that a woman conducting a kindergarten class may not be contributing as much to society as the most degree-laden university president? Given the evidence that our very first brush with education leaves a permanent stamp on our characters, that teacher could be moulding a future Abraham Lincoln or a Madame Curie. More likely, though, she is moulding a whole class of the type of responsible citizens upon whom the well-being of our society depends.

Teaching is a creative act, never more so than in primary and secondary schools. Good teachers, like good artists, have their own individual styles of performing. They also respect the individuality of their students in the realization that everybody learns through his or her own perceptions. The story is told of a legendary teacher who was asked at the start of the term what his course matter would be. "I don't know," he said. "I haven't seen my students yet."

It would be a wonderful world if every teacher deeply understood each and every child and put that understanding into effect, but that would be asking too much of human nature. Teachers can become tired and impatient, and give up on troublesome or backward children. They have their personal prejudices, and it is sometimes a struggle with their own personalities to give every pupil the attention he or she requires.

The world would be equally wonderful if every youngster came to school to learn. There is an element of truth, however, to the old teachers'-room joke that for every one who wants to teach, there are 20 not wanting to be taught. The teacher has the peculiar dual task of inculcating knowledge while at the same time breaking down resistance to its inculcation. It is part of the challenge of teaching to bring promising students around to the point where they are willing and even eager to learn.

forceful knowledge

Because instruction is an interpersonal affair, different teaching styles work on different students. An abrasive performer might drive his more timid students into their shells. But then there was Rudyard Kipling, who, in his autobiography *Something of Myself*, recalled his English and classics master. "He had a violent temper, no disadvantage in handling boys used to direct speech, and a gift of schoolmaster's sarcasm which must have been a relief to him and was certainly a treasure trove to me... Under him I came to feel that words could be used as weapons, for he did me the honour to talk to me plentifully... One learns more from a good scholar in a rage than from a score of lucid and laborious drudges."

Kipling's phrase, "a good scholar in a rage," should remind us of the point, often forgotten by those who belittle teachers, that the best of them have a broad and deep range of knowledge. First-class teachers seek to ignite in their students an enthusiasm for their subjects by example and leadership. They are more than instructors; they are role models for students. "The mediocre teacher tells. The good teacher explains. The superior teacher demonstrates. The great teacher inspires," William Arthur Ward wrote.

Just what makes a first-class teacher has always been a matter of debate between educational liberals and conservatives. Even the traditional method of teaching by terror—spare not the rod and spoil not the child—has its supporters among parents who feel that permissiveness in the schools has gone too far. On the other hand, there seems to be general agreement that the traditional technique of making students learn by rote produces not rounded human beings but programmed automatons. An anonymous principal once warned his staff: "Don't think that the mind is a warehouse, and that you are here to stuff it full of goods."

On the other hand, a certain amount of didactic learning is necessary to show the student the way. "Some flabby persons try to make education painless," one-time teacher W.E. McNeill wrote. "'Do not,' they say, 'ask students to learn facts, but teach them to think.' O thinking—what intellectual crimes are committed in thy name! How can a man think if he doesn't know?"

At the same time no one would dispute that the aim of education should be to produce individuals able to think for themselves and not merely follow what someone else has told them. And the way for teachers to accomplish this is to concentrate on what M.F. Ashley Montagu called "the drawing out, not the pumping in." Teaching should excite a youngster's natural curiosity. Instead of giving pat answers, it should raise questions. It was a wise mother who asked her young son after school not "What did you learn today?" but "What questions did you ask today?"

It has been said a thousand times in different ways that education should not stop at school; that the proper role of the school is to prepare the mind for lifelong learning. The theory is that you do not get an education in a classroom; you learn *how* to get an education, which in the long run you can acquire only by yourself. In fact, the word "educate" comes from the Latin *educere*, which means "leading out" the student into a wider world of knowledge. It is by stimulating a zest for learning in general that teachers can perform their greatest service to those in their care, for a zest for learning is a zest for life. And a zest for life is what allows people to live contentedly for all of their days.

As in writing, teaching is at its most efficacious when it shows instead of tells. The best teachers make their points by way of illustration. Better still, they demonstrate wherever possible. Any teacher would do well to keep in mind the Chinese saying: "I hear and I forget. I see and I remember. I do and I understand."

"The method of teaching which approaches most nearly to the method of investigation is incomparably the best; since, not content with serving up a few barren and lifeless truths, it leads to the stock from which they grew," wrote Edmund Burke, who possessed one of the best-conditioned minds in history. By investigating ideas, the teacher becomes a participant in the act of learning. "To be a teacher in the right sense is to be a learner," Kierkegaard wrote.

Given what is now known about the psychology of learning, everyone ideally would be taught in a small group with the teacher acting as a participant, leading the students in the pursuit of ideas and motivating them to think about life in all its aspects. Instruction would be tailored to the learner's personality, and tightly focussed on individual weaknesses and strengths.

In a world that is far from ideal, that is not the reality. "In education, we have long given lip-service to the fact that all human beings are different," said Earl C. Kelley, professor of education at Wayne University. "But we have proceeded as if this were not so."

The exigencies of economics lead to uniformity. Even in prosperous jurisdictions, education is strapped for funds. At its worst, inadequate funding makes for overcrowded classrooms, and education becomes a kind of mass production process, complete with a fair percentage of rejects. Teachers being human, there is always a temptation to treat students as so much raw material to be fed through a diploma-producing factory. The temptation is compounded by the fact that the educational system can be satisfied by filling "production norms."

This helps to explain why, for instance, it is possible for some young people to graduate from high school unable to read and write adequately. When such things happen, the cry goes up: "Where were their teachers, for heaven's sake?" But to blame teachers for the failings of modern public education is a classic case of shooting the messenger. Teachers did not invent the system, nor do they run it. It is the product of politics, and it is administered by educational bureaucrats whom teachers often regard as their sworn enemies.

If the public, through its elected and appointed delegates, opts for a levelling process in which no student is allowed to fail, or curricula so soft that youths can loaf through their school days, it is not the fault of the teaching profession. If parents are careless enough or dumb enough not to notice that big Johnny can't read, they are hardly entitled to protest.

"If a doctor, lawyer or dentist had 40 people in his office at one time, all of whom had different needs, and some of whom didn't want to be there and were causing trouble, and the doctor, lawyer or dentist, without assistance, had to treat them all with professional excellence for nine months, then he might have some conception of a classroom teacher's job," wrote Donald D. Quinn, himself an experienced teacher. Faced with this daunting situation, some teachers tire of catering to individual needs and striving for professional excellence.

"A teacher is like a candle which lights others in consuming itself," wrote Giovani Ruffini in an early description of teacher burnout. In inner-city schools such as the one referred to in Tom Wolfe's *The Bonfire of the Vanities*, where student behaviour ranges from "cooperative to life-threatening," burnout must be a terrible professional hazard.

You do not have to look as far as the slums of New York to see where social trends have added to the already heavy burden borne by teachers. Broken homes, teenage promiscuity and drug and alcohol abuse are common in nice middle-class neighbourhoods too. Parents are often too apathetic or busy to meet their parental responsibilities. Problems of youth that were once dealt with at home have been dumped into the schools.

In a materialistic society, young people have their attitudes shaped by a commercial prepackaged youth culture that encourages precocity and contrariety toward authority. Materialism also permeates parental attitudes. In his recent admirable book *The Closing of the American Mind*, Allan Bloom wrote: "Fathers and mothers have lost the idea that the highest aspiration they might have for their children is for them to be wise—as priests, prophets and philosophers are wise. Specialized competence and success are all they can imagine." In this spiritual vacuum, it is often left to teachers to instil whatever higher values a youth might have.

Society has always expected an awful lot from its teachers, and now we are expecting even more from them. We expect them to serve to a large degree as surrogate parents, dealing with the emotional tangles and torments of the adolescent years. Teaching is one of those rare jobs in which one's work is wrapped up in one's personality. It is very demanding psychologically. The abdication of responsibility within so many homes has added to the psychological drain.

Yet at the same time as the complications and vexations of teaching life multiply, the public persists in undervaluing the teacher. Every thinking person would agree that the hope of the human race lies chiefly in education, but most of us pay little attention to the people who provide this precious service, nor do we give them much support in the vital job they do.

Fidel Castro had his priorities straight when he declared: "We need teachers—a heroine in every classroom." Teaching is not usually associated with heroics, even though it takes actual physical courage to face up to the lurking threat of violence in some North American high schools today. The only teacher-hero in recent popular literature who readily comes to mind appears in Thomas Flanagan's novel *The Year of the French*, in which the protagonist risks imprisonment to instruct poor Irish children in illicit schools proscribed by the English in the interests of keeping the Irish in subjugation. He and his enemies appreciated just how important education can be when freedom is at stake.

More commonly, however, the heroism is not so dramatic. "If I had a child who wanted to be a teacher, I would bid him Godspeed as if he were going to war," wrote James Hilton, author of the great novel of teaching, *Goodbye Mr. Chips.* For indeed the war against prejudice, greed and ignorance is eternal, and those who dedicate themselves to it give their lives no less because they may live to see some fraction of the battle won."

Not every teacher is a hero or heroine, of course. There are good, bad and indifferent ones, ranging from those who totally devote their lives to their students to those who totally devote their lives to themselves. Our social priorities do not make it easy to encourage the best and the brightest to teach. Surveys of students who consistently get top marks in university show that they intend to go into more prestigious and more lucrative professions. To a large extent, teachers themselves tend to be diffident about their occupation. "I beg of you," said William G. Carr to a representative teacher, "to stop apologizing for being a member of the most important... profession in the world."

"Teaching is not a lost art, but the regard for it is a lost tradition," Jacques Barzun wrote. If this society knows what is good for it, that regard will be restored. Parents and other concerned citizens will do all they can to make a teacher's life less troublesome and give due credit to the profession. To a large extent, teachers are in charge of the future. The fate of people in the future depends on how well they are taught today.

A House without Books: The Writer in Canadian Society

BY TOM WAYMAN

A writer explores the place of literature in a country that apparently does not want to read it.

An incident that best sums up for me what it means to be a writer in Canada occurred in the summer of 1986 when I was on holiday at the north end of Vancouver Island. I was taking the ferry from Port McNeill to Alert Bay, to visit the Indian museum there. On the deck of the ferry, standing by my car, I fell into a conversation with another driver. He was a fisherman, maybe in his mid-fifties, headed over to Alert Bay to pick up a net. He mentioned that his home port is Pender Harbor, on the Sunshine Coast north of Sechelt. Now Pender Harbor is not a large place, and happens to be the home of my friend, publisher and fellow poet Howard White. So I asked the fisherman if he knew Howie.

Howard White is somewhat of a legend in the B.C. literary world. By trade he is a heavy equipment operator, and still has the contract to manage the Pender Harbor dump. This means besides spending most of his time at his computer pushing large amounts of words around, he spends several hours a week at the controls of his bulldozer pushing large amounts of garbage around. And in addition to running his vital and thriving publishing house, Harbour Publishing, Howie edits the highly successful magazine about the B.C. coast, *Raincoast Chronicle*. On the side, he is a well-received poet and his oral history books routinely appear on the B.C. bestseller list.

But standing then on the deck of that ferry, I watched the eyes of the fisherman darken as I mentioned Howie's name. "Howie White?" the fisherman said, recoiling away from me. A certain tone entered his voice, the tone people reserve for talking about in-laws they despise, or child molesters. "Sure, I know him. Doesn't he *write?*"

This attitude of utter disdain expressed by the fisherman toward writing encapsulates for me the relationship of Canadian authors to their society. At best a Canadian writer is a marginal figure. But that marginality leads a majority of Canadians to view writers as people engaged in a socially unacceptable, if not perverse activity.

Before I continue, though, let me quickly define my central terms. When I speak of a Canadian writer here, I mean writers of prose fiction, drama, or poetry. Also, when I speak of Canadian society, I refer here to mainstream English-language society. In my experience, literary authors associated with ethnic minorities have a different relationship to readers within that minority than they do to English-speaking Canadians as a whole. For instance, Andrew Suknaski is a nationally recognized writer who has detailed in his poems the lives of Ukrainian settlers in rural Saskatchewan. Because of this, Suknaski's work has been received with enthusiasm by many member of the Ukrainian-Canadian community. But when Suknaski turns to address the general Canadian population, not as a representative of a minority but simply as a *poet*, he faces the same unease and scorn that greets the rest of Canada's literary practitioners.

Now since cultural values are transmitted by education, I believe a root cause of the marginal status accorded Canadian authors is our school system. One of the triumphs of mass public education in Canada is that we have been able to teach the overwhelming majority of people to read while simultaneously so turning them off reading that, once they are out of school, most never read a book again.

In my experience, a majority of people who endure our high school or university English classes do not afterward regard reading books—and especially literary titles—as a means of enhancing their lives. Those few who do continue to read see literature mainly as entertainment, fantasy, escape. I sometimes hear poetry mocked at as irrelevant because "hardly anyone reads poetry." As far as I can see, hardly anyone reads any kind of literature. In the course of my life, I go into house after house where there are *no books*. In the homes of many of my friends, although most of them at least finished high school, there are *no books*—of any kind.

* * *

When I taught in the early 1980s at David Thompson University Centre in Nelson, B.C., we set a little quiz for students entering the writing program in which, among other things, we asked if they could name three Canadian writers. Almost none could. And these were students who not only were interested enough in learning to seek post-secondary education, but were presumably interested enough in literature to enter a creative writing program. Most recently, I have been teaching at a community college in a Vancouver suburb. One of my assignments asks each of my students to give a presentation to their classmates on something they learned about how to write from their reading of a contemporary novel, book of short fiction, play script or collection of poems. I find the response depressing. "But I don't *read*," is one protest I hear *every* term when I announce this assignment. Most students eventually choose to discuss the work of authors like the popular U.S. horror writer Stephen King. One student last term came up to my desk clutching a newspaper clipping of a personal advice column by Ann Landers. The student inquired: "Is it O.K. if I do my presentation on this?"

I am convinced that by what we teach, we teach a system of values. If the majority of our population decides the reading of good literature is irrelevant to their lives, and looks with indifference or suspicion on those who produce literature, these are value judgments that Canadians have acquired through their schooling—since school is the *only* place most of us ever meet people whose job it is to try to show us the worth of literature.

When we examine most high-school English curriculums, it is not difficult to see why students might conclude literature is pointless, boring or escapist. I worked some years ago in a suburban Vancouver high school as an English Department marker. The students whose papers I marked were bothered by the usual issues facing adolescents—and the rest of us—today: sex, drugs, family break-up, the uncertainty of long-range occupational goals, immediate employment opportunities in a province where the official unemployment rate is 10 percent, and—if any work can be found—job conditions. The assigned novels for Grade 11 in those days were *Lord of the Flies*, a science-fiction tale about a group of English schoolboys marooned on a tropical island during World War III, and *A Separate Peace*, about some boys at a private boarding school in rural New England during World War II. If you set out to *design* a reading curriculum more removed from contemporary suburban Canadian high-school students' lives, you'd be hard pressed to come up with better titles. Plus, these students would write in their essays over and over again—presumably echoing or mis-echoing what they were taught in class—how *Lord of the Flies* portrays a microcosm of human existence. I'd patiently scrawl across their papers: "But there are no *women* in that book."

For it was the women's movement that showed us that if in our teaching of literature we omit an accurate account of the experiences of women, we teach that those experiences have no value. My own mission as a writer has been to add that if in our teaching of literature we omit an accurate account of the experiences of daily work, we teach that such experiences have no value. Generations of Canadians have grasped that when the literature we are taught omits the experiences of Canadians—as a people who share a history and geography, as well as individuals who must function in a society and workforce organized in a particular way, then this literature teaches us that our own experiences—past, present and future—have no value.

English classes where this literature is taught thus obliterate who we are and what we have so painfully managed to accomplish and to discover about our world. It's no wonder a majority of us don't want to pursue reading any further, except for whatever escape from daily cares some reading offers. And no wonder we look with disbelief and contempt at anyone who wants to actually write *more* stuff that says we and our lives are worthless.

Let me hasten to acknowledge, however, that here and there in the educational system are English teachers who work very hard to right this great wrong. These marvelous women and men approach even the authorized curriculum with tremendous imagination and energy and often succeed in inspiring readers from among their students. Unfortunately, as house after house without books in Canada incontestably reveals, such teachers are definitely the exception. This very Monday, in educational institutions all across Canada, most students will be back learning that literature has nothing to do with them. Their only *possible* revenge is to have nothing to do with literature.

But the marginalization of Canadian writers is not solely caused by the schools. Canada in its twelve decades of existence has managed to transform itself from a colony of Britain into a colony of the U.S.A. Since one of the hallmarks of every colony is a lack of self-confidence, even if we *were* a nation of readers, we would be mainly readers of British and American books.

I can still get a rueful laugh in high-school classrooms I visit when I talk about how when I was a young student I thought poetry was something written by dead Englishmen. My sense is that the curriculum in poetry hasn't changed all that much. Many of my literature professors at the University of B.C. were live Englishmen, or Canadians who thought like Englishmen. I can still remember the comment of one when a fellow student raised a question to do with U.S. authors. "*American* literature?" the professor sneered. "Ah, yes. I really must sit down and read it some *afternoon*." You can well imagine this professor's attitude toward *Canadian* literature.

And to demonstrate the present economic and cultural power of the behemoth we live beside, one anecdote should do. On the same holiday trip I referred to earlier, I was camped for a time on a beach on northern Vancouver Island's west coast, at San Josef Bay. After about a week, we had to hike out for more food, and so headed for the nearest store, at Holberg. Holberg, though nominally a village, really is a large logging camp, but the camp commissary serves as the grocery for the region.

Looking for something to read, I discovered in the Holberg commissary a wire rack of novels, such as is found in urban drugstores or supermarkets. Inserted into a holder on the top of the rack was a computer-generated printout listing the current week's bestsellers as compiled by the *New York Times*.

Such is the awesome might of the U.S. industry, that they can supply the Holberg commissary, many kilometres in the bush at the northern tip of Vancouver Island, with the list of what someone in New York City has determined *that same week* to be the latest bestsellers. What's more, most of these U.S. bestsellers were available in the commissary. I don't have to tell you that the list did not include any Canadian books, nor that a list of current B.C. or Canadian bestsellers was not posted at Holberg. I don't have to tell you that there were no Canadian books of any kind for sale in the Holberg commissary.

People are sometimes shocked by the economic consequences of this marginalization of the Canadian writer. Sales of Canadian literary titles are for the most part staggeringly low. A novel typically will sell about 2000 copies in hardback over a couple of years. If the novel sells for, say, $22.95 and the author gets the standard royalty of 10 per cent, the writer earns about $4,600 from his or her creation—over two years. "But what about Margaret

Atwood?" people sometimes object. "She gets six-figure advances." O.K. But according to a 1985 *Financial Post* survey, out of the dozens of novels by Canadians published in Canada each year, only *five* will reach sales of 5000 copies—the mark of a Canadian bestseller. Priced at $22.95 those 5000 copies will net each of those five, extremely rare, bestselling Canadian fiction authors the glorious sum of $11,500 before taxes. That $11,500 is not much for the amount of time, thought and energy a novel takes to produce. And it certainly isn't adequate to live on.

The numbers for poetry sales are of course worse. An ordinary Canadian book of poems will sell about 400 copies a year. At a retail price of $8.95, that brings the author the grand total of $358 for her or his creativity, sweat and tears.

In fairness, I should mention that the determination and know-how that enables the U.S. book industry to service the Canadian hinterlands where the Canadian book industry apparently is unable to go does not mean the average American author is better off than a Canadian one. *Publishers' Weekly* reported in 1981 a survey of U.S. literary and nonliterary writers that concluded "figures for authors from households of varying size suggest that writing income places most authors below the poverty line." In fact, despite the articles on rich and famous writers in *People* magazine, *Publishers' Weekly* reported only five percent of U.S. authors can support themselves from their writing. This is partly because, although the U.S. population is 10 times larger than the Canadian one, most books in the U.S. do not sell 10 times better than their counterparts in Canada. For example, a book of poems in the U.S. usually sells about 1000 copies and can sell as few as the equivalent book in Canada. Most novels, also, don't do much better in the U.S. than here. A 1980 survey of the U.S. children's book authors who had been writing for 20 years or more found half of them earned less than $1,000 a year from their writing, and two-thirds earned less than $5,000 a year from their writing.

As in Canada, writers in the U.S. have no safety net of income indemnity plans, extended health-care programs, or other job benefits. Concerning pensions, James Lincoln Collier, who wrote the 1981 *Publishers' Weekly* article I mentioned, makes a ghoulish observation. He points out that a successful writer's best hope for retirement is to fall face down over his or her keyboard from a heart attack while his or her markets are still holding up.

In the U.S., as here, most authors must support themselves by working at another job as well as writing. Like anyone in the workforce who moonlights, authors who have two jobs often seriously damage their ability to relate meaningfully to other human beings—threatening both family and social life, and negatively influencing the message of what these authors write. In Canada, as in the U.S., a network of public and private granting agencies provides some additional writing-related revenue for authors. But none of it, save an occasional grant providing subsistence income for up to 12 months, fundamentally alters the writers' economic status. In this country, the Canada Council provides support for public readings by authors, and organizes payment to writers for the use of their books by libraries. Yet both of these programs have financial caps: readings are limited by the Council to seven a year, or $1,400 maximum annually, and the library use payment is capped at $3,000 a year. Very few authors receive the maximum in these programs. Once again, the economic marginalization of the Canadian writer is in no way changed by such government aid.

If things are so bleak for writers in Canada—sociologically, culturally, economically—why do any of us continue to write? I think each of us finds a satisfactory answer, or stops writing. For myself, I observe that although only a few people make a living and/or are considered culturally significant because they can dance, nevertheless millions of Canadians enjoy getting out on the dance floor. A similar observation can be made of people who, for example, fly kites or play guitar.

I believe writing, for at least this Canadian author, is no different than kite-flying or guitar-playing is for someone to whom kite-flying or guitar-playing has become a central part of their existence. In such circumstances, building and flying kites represents more than a hobby, although not a livelihood either. Rather, the challenges and sense of accomplishment kite-flying provides approach being an obsession. I have written elsewhere of why I am convinced what I have to say as a writer is important—even if no one is listening. I am fascinated, too, by the difficulty of trying to express myself in a manner that delights a reader while it acquaints that reader with information I believe is crucial. This is a task that seems unquestionably worth a lifetime of struggle, of small achievements and large defeats, even if this is a battle about which a majority of my fellow citizens couldn't care less.

From Batman, through G.A. Henty, to *All Quiet on the Western Front*

BY MORDECAI RICHLER

Novels can betray you when you least expect it.

Reading was not one of my boyhood passions. Girls, or rather the absence of girls, drove me to it. When I was thirteen years old, short for my age, more than somewhat pimply, I was terrified of girls. As far as I could make out, they were only attracted to boys who were tall or played for the school basketball team or at least shaved. Unable to qualify on all three counts, I resorted to subterfuge. I set out to call attention to myself by becoming a character. I acquired a pipe, which I chewed on ostentatiously, and made it my business to be seen everywhere, even at school basketball games, pretending to be absorbed by books of daunting significance: say, H.G. Wells's *Outline of History*, or Paul de Kruif's *Microbe Hunters*, or John Gunther inside one continent or another. I rented these thought-provoking books for three cents a day from a neighbourhood lending library that was across the street from a bowling alley where I used to spot pins four nights a week.

O my God, I would not be thirteen again for anything. The sweetly scented girls of my dreams, wearing lipstick and tight sweaters and nylon stockings, would sail into the bowling alley holding hands with the boys from the basketball team. "Hi," they would call out, giggly, nudging each other, even as I bent over the pins, "How goes the reading?"

The two ladies who ran the lending library, possibly amused by my pretensions, tried to interest me in fiction.

"I want fact. I can't be bothered with *stories*," I protested, waving my pipe at them, affronted.

I knew what novels were, of course. I had read *Scaramouche*, by Rafael Sabatini, at school, as well as *Treasure Island* and some Ellery Queen and a couple of thumpers by G.A. Henty. Before that there had been *Action Comics*, *Captain Marvel*, *Batman* and—for educational reasons—either *Bible Comics* or *Classic Comics*. All these treasures I bought under the counter, as it were. They were passed hand to hand on dark street corners. Contraband. Our *samizdat*. The reason for this being that in 1943 the dolts who prevailed in Ottawa had adjudged American comic books unessential to the war effort, a drain on the Canadian dollar. So on the home front we were expected to make do with feeble black-and-white indigenous comic books for the duration, a blow to my crowd's morale.

Novels, I knew, were mere romantic make-believe, not as bad as poetry, to be fair, but bad enough. Our high-school class master, a dedicated Scot, had been foolish enough to try to interest us in poetry. A veteran of World War I, he told us that during the nightly bombardments on the Somme he had fixed a candle to his steel helmet so that he could read poetry in the trenches. A scruffy lot, we were not moved. Instead, we exchanged knowing winks behind that admirable man's back. Small wonder, we agreed, that he drove an ancient Austin and had ended up no better than a high-school teacher.

My aunts consumed historical novels like pastries. My father read *Black Mask* and *True Detective*. My mother would read anything on a Jewish subject, preferably by I.J. Singer or Sholem Asch, though she would never forgive Asch for having written *The Nazarene*, never mind *Mary* and *The Apostle*. My older brother kept a novel, *Topper Takes a Trip*, secure under his mattress in the bedroom we shared, assuring me that it was placed at just such an angle on the springs that if it were moved so much as a millimetre in his absence he would know and bloody well make me pay for it.

I fell ill with a childhood disease, I no longer remember which, but one obviously meant as a rebuke for those girls in tight sweaters who continued to ignore me. Never mind, they would mourn at my funeral, burying me with my pipe. Too late they would say, "Boy, was he ever an intellectual!"

Aunts, who still took me for a child, brought me really dumb books *in which animals talked*. I was appalled. But the ladies from the lending library also dropped off books for me at our house. The real stuff. Fact-filled. Providing me with the inside dope on Theodore Hertzl's childhood and *Brazil Yesterday, Today, and Tomorrow*. One day they brought me a novel: *All Quiet on the Western Front*, by Erich Maria Remarque. The painting on the jacket that was taped to the book showed a soldier wearing what was unmistakably a German army helmet. What was this, I wondered, some sort of bad joke?

Nineteen forty-four that was, and I devoutly wished every German on the face of the earth an excruciating death. The invasion of France had not yet begun, but I cheered every Russian counterattack, each German city bombed and, with the help of a map tacked to my bedroom wall, followed the progress of the Canadian troops fighting their way up the Italian boot. Boys from our street were already among the fallen. Izzy Draper's uncle. Harvey Kugelmass's older brother. The boy who was supposed to marry Gita Holtzman.

All Quiet on the Western Front lay unopened on my bed for two days. A time bomb ticking away, though I hardly suspected it. Rather than read a novel, a novel written by a German, I tuned in to radio soap operas in the afternoons: "Ma Perkins," "Pepper Young's Family." I organized a new baseball league for short players who didn't shave yet, appointing myself commissioner, the first Canadian to be so honoured. Sifting through a stack of my father's back issues of *Popular Mechanics*, I was sufficiently inspired to invent a spaceship and fly to Mars, where I was adored by everybody, especially the girls. Finally I was driven to picking up *All Quiet on the Western Front* out of boredom. I never expected that a mere novel, a stranger's tale, could actually be dangerous, creating such turbulence in my life, obliging me to question so many received ideas. About Germans. About my own monumental ignorance of the world. About what novels were.

At the age of thirteen in 1944, happily as yet untainted by English 101, I couldn't tell you whether Remarque's novel was (a) a slice of life, (b) symbolic, (c) psychological or (d) seminal. I couldn't even say if it was well or badly written. In fact, as I recall, it didn't seem to be "written" at all. It just flowed. Now, of course, I understand that writing which doesn't advertise itself is often art of a very high order. It doesn't come easily. But at the time I wasn't capable of making such distinctions.

I also had no notion of how *All Quiet on the Western Front* rated critically as a war novel. I hadn't read Stendhal or Tolstoy or Crane or Hemingway. I hadn't even heard of them. But what I did know was that, hating Germans with a passion, I had read only twenty, maybe thirty pages before the author had seduced me into identifying with my enemy, nineteen-year-old Paul Bäumer, thrust into the bloody trenches of World War I with his schoolmates: Müller, Kemmerich and the reluctant Joseph Behm, one of the first to fall. As if that weren't sufficiently unsettling, the author, having won my love for Paul, my enormous concern for his survival, betrayed me in the last dreadful paragraphs of his book:

> He fell in October 1918, on a day that was so quiet and still on the whole front, that the army report confined itself to a single sentence: All quiet on the Western Front.
>
> He had fallen forward and lay on the earth as though sleeping. Turning him over one saw that he could not have suffered long; his face had an expression of calm, as though glad the end had come.

The movies, I knew from experience, never risked letting you down like that. No matter how bloody the battle, how long the odds, Errol Flynn, Robert Taylor, even Humphrey Bogart could be counted on to survive and come home to Ann Sheridan, Lana Turner, or—if they were a sensitive type—Loretta Young. Only character actors, usually Brooklyn Dodger fans, say George Tobias or William Bendix or Dane Clark, were expendable.

Having waded into the pool of serious fiction by accident, as it were, I was not sure I liked or trusted the water. It was too deep. Anything could happen.

There was something else, a minor incident in *All Quiet on the Western Front* that would not have troubled an adult reader, but, I'm embarrassed to say, distressed that thirteen-year-old boy colliding with his first serious novel.

Sent out to guard a village that had been abandoned because it was being shelled too heavily, Katczinsky, the incomparable scrounger, surfaces with suckling pigs and potatoes and carrots for his comrades, a group of eight altogether.

> The suckling pigs were slaughtered, Kat sees to them. We want to make potato-cakes to go with the roast. But we cannot find a grater for the potatoes. However, the difficulty is soon got over. With a nail we punch a lot of holes in a pot lid and there we have a grater. Three fellows put on thick gloves to protect their fin-

gers against the grater, two others peel the potatoes, and the business gets going.

The business, I realized, alarmed—no, *affronted*—was the making of potato *latkes*, a favourite of mine as well as of Paul Bäumer's, a dish I had always taken to be Jewish, certainly not a German concoction. What did I know? Nothing. Or, looked at another way, my real education, my lifelong addiction to fiction, began with the trifling discovery that the potato *latke* was not of Jewish origin, but something borrowed from the Germans and now a taste that Jew and German share in spite of everything.

I felt easier about my affection for the German soldier Paul Bäumer once I had been told by the ladies from the lending library that when Hitler came to power in 1932 he had burned all of Erich Maria Remarque's books, and in 1938 took away his German citizenship. Obviously Hitler grasped that novels could be dangerous, something I had learned when I was only thirteen years old. He burned them; I began to devour them. I started to read at the breakfast table and on streetcars, often missing my stop, and in bed with the benefit of a flashlight. It got me into trouble. I understood, for the first time, that I didn't live in the centre of the world but had been born into a working-class family in an unimportant country far from the cities of light: London, Paris, New York. Of course this wasn't my fault; it was my inconsiderate parents who were to blame. But there was, I now realized, a larger world out there beyond St. Urbain Street in Montreal, a world that could be available to me, even though—to my mother's despair—I had been born left-handed, ate with my elbows on the table and had failed once more to come rank one in school.

Preparing myself for the *rive gauche*, I bought a blue beret, which I didn't dare wear even in the house if anybody else was home. I looked at but lacked the courage to buy a cigarette holder. But the next time I took Goldie Zimmerman to a downtown movie and then out to Dinty Moore's for toasted sandwiches, I suggested that, instead of milkshakes, we each order a glass of *vin ordinaire*. "Are you crazy?" she asked.

As my parents bickered at the supper table, trapped in concerns far too mundane for the likes of me—what to do if Dworkin raised the rent again, how to manage my brother's college fees—I sat with, but actually apart from them in the kitchen, enthralled, reading for the first time, "All happy families are alike but an unhappy family is unhappy after its own fashion."

* * *

Erich Maria Remarque, his family of French descent, was born in Westphalia in 1897. He went off to war, directly from school, at the age of eighteen. He was wounded five times. He lost all his friends. After the war he worked briefly as a schoolteacher, a stonecutter, a test driver for a tire company and an editor of *Sportbild*. His first novel, *Im Westen Nicht Neues*, was turned down by several publishers before it was brought out by the Ullstein Press in Berlin in 1928. It sold 1.2 million copies in Germany and was translated into twenty-nine languages, selling 4 million copies throughout the world. A reviewer for the *Manchester Guardian* called it the greatest of all war books, and the critic for the London *Times* wrote, "It has certain of the marks of genius which transcend nationality." The novel has been filmed three times—the first time, memorably, by Lewis Milestone in 1930. The Milestone version, with Lew Ayres playing Paul Bäumer, won Academy Awards for Best Picture and Best Direction.

Erich Maria Remarque, who lived in the United States for the duration of World War II and then moved on to Switzerland, wrote nine other novels before he died, in 1970, but none had the impact of *All Quiet on the Western Front*, a novel that endures as a testimony to a wasted generation.

Because *All Quiet on the Western Front* once meant so much to me, I picked it up again with a certain anxiety in 1986. After all this time I find it difficult to be objective about the novel. Its pages still evoke for me a back bedroom with a cracked ceiling and a sizzling radiator on St. Urbain Street, mice scrabbling in the walls, a window looking out on sheets frozen stiff on the laundry line, and all the pain of being too young to shave, an ignorant and bewildered boy of thirteen.

Over the years the novel has lost something in shock value, even as I am now missing something in purity. Once, I would happily fork out three cents a day for the pleasures any novel might have to offer; now there are editors foolish enough to pay me to pronounce. I don't know what that hungering thirteen-year-old boy would make of this fat middle-aged writer and, what's more, I don't want to know. On the other hand, what did he know anyway? He didn't really understand *Anna Karenina* the first time he rented it, and only insisted on taking it out of the lending library because one of the ladies said, "Don't you think you ought to wait a few more years before tackling Tolstoy?" He was scornful of his father for never missing an issue of *Black Mask*, but now these magazines are collectors' items, the subject of endless literary essays.

The original jacket copy of the 1929 edition of *All Quiet on the Western Front* warns the reader that it is "at times crude" and "will shock the super-sensitive by its outspokenness." Dr. Henry Seidel Canby, in his Book-of-the-Month Club report of May 1929, cautions members that the novel includes a "liberal share of grossness which accompanies war because it must." Obviously we've come a long way. After *The Naked and the Dead*, *From Here to Eternity* and *Catch-22*, not to mention a spate of Vietnam war novels, contemporary readers—far from being shocked—will be amused by the novel's discretion, the absence of explicit sex scenes, the unbelievably polite dialogue of the men in the trenches. The horrors are still there, of course. The endless artillery bombardments. The gas attacks at dawn. The bayonet warfare:

> The bayonet frequently jams on the thrust and then a man has to kick hard on the other fellow's belly to pull it out again; and in the interval he may easily get one himself. And what's more, the blade is often broke off.

And of course the rats. The fat corpse rats.

> They have shocking, evil, naked faces, and it is nauseating to see their long, nude tails.
> They seem to be mighty hungry. Almost every man has had his bread gnawed. Kropp wrapped his in his waterproof sheet and put it under his head, but he cannot sleep because they run over his face to get at it. Detering meant to outwit them: he fastened a thin wire to the roof and suspended his bread from it. During the night when he switched on his pocket-torch he saw the wire swinging to and fro. On the bread was riding a fat rat.

The novel also has its poignant moments, both in the trenches and when Paul Bäumer goes home on leave, an old man of nineteen, only to find insufferably pompous schoolmasters still recruiting the young with mindless prattle about the Fatherland and the glory of battle. Strong characters are deftly sketched. Himmelstoss, the postman who becomes a crazed drillmaster. Tjaden, the peasant soldier. Kantorek, the schoolmaster. On the front line the enemy is never "the Frogs" or "the Limeys," but the insanity of war itself. It is the war, in fact, and not even Paul Bäumer, that is the novel's true protagonist. In a brief introduction to the novel, Remarque wrote: "This book is to be neither an accusation nor a confession, and least of all an adventure, for death is not an adventure to those who stand face to face with it. It will try simply to tell of a generation of men who, even though they may have escaped its shells, were destroyed by the war."

Since World War I we have become altogether too familiar with larger horrors. The Holocaust, Hiroshima, the threat of a nuclear winter. Death by numbers, cities obliterated by decree. None of this, however, diminishes the power of *All Quiet on the Western Front*, a novel that will endure because of its humanity, its honour and its refusal to lapse into sentimentality or strike a false note. It is a work that has earned its place on that small shelf of World War I classics, alongside *Goodbye to All That*, by Robert Graves, and Ernest Hemingway's *A Farewell to Arms*.

Growing Up Native

BY CAROL GEDDES

"It didn't matter who was carrying me—there was security in every pair of arms."

I remember it was cold. We were walking through a swamp near our home in the Yukon bush. Maybe it was fall and moose-hunting season. I don't know. I think I was about four years old at the time. The muskeg was too springy to walk on, so people were taking turns carrying me—passing me from one set of arms to another. The details about where we were are vague, but the memory of those arms and the feeling of acceptance I had is one of the most vivid memories of my childhood. It didn't matter who was carrying me—there was security in every pair of arms. That response to children is typical of the native community. It's the first thing I think of when I cast my mind back to the Yukon bush, where I was born and lived with my family.

I was six years old when we moved out of the bush, first to Teslin, where I had a hint of the problems native people face, then to Whitehorse, where there was unimaginable racism. Eventually I moved to Ottawa and Montreal, where I further discovered that to grow up native in Canada is to feel the sting of humiliation and the boot of discrimination. But it is also to experience the enviable security of an extended family and to learn to appreciate the richness of the heritage and traditions of a culture most North Americans have never been lucky enough to know. As a filmmaker, I have tried to explore these contradictions, and our triumph over them, for the half-million aboriginals who are part of the tide of swelling independence of the First Nations today.

But I'm getting ahead of myself. If I'm to tell the story of what it's like to grow up native in northern Canada, I have to go back to the bush where I was born, because there's more to my story than the hurtful stereotyping that depicts Indian people as drunken welfare cases. Our area was known as 12-mile (it was 12 miles from another tiny village). There were about 40 people living there—including 25 kids, eight of them my brothers and sisters—in a sort of family compound. Each family had its own timber plank house for sleeping, and there was one large common kitchen area with gravel on the ground and a tent frame over it. Everybody would go there and cook meals together. In summer, my grandmother always had a smudge fire going to smoke fish and tan moose hides. I can remember the cosy warmth of the fire, the smell of good food, and always having someone to talk to. We kids had built-in playmates and would spend hours running in the bush, picking berries, building rafts on the lake and playing in abandoned mink cages.

One of the people in my village tells a story about the day the old lifestyle began to change. He had been away hunting in the bush for about a month. On his way back, he heard a strange sound coming from far away. He ran up to the crest of a hill, looked over the top of it and saw a bulldozer. He had never seen or heard of such a thing before and he couldn't imagine what it was. We didn't have magazines or newspapers in our village, and the people didn't know that the Alaska Highway was being built as a defence against a presumed Japanese invasion during the Second World War. That was the beginning of the end of the Teslin Tlingit people's way of life. From that moment on, nothing turned back to the way it was. Although there were employment opportunities for my father and uncles, who were young men at the time, the speed and force with which the Alaska Highway was rammed through the wilderness caused tremendous upheaval for Yukon native people.

It wasn't as though we'd never experienced change before. The Tlingit Nation, which I belong to, arrived in the Yukon from the Alaskan coast around the turn of the century. They were the middlemen and women between the Russian traders and the Yukon inland Indians. The Tlingit gained power and prestige by trading European products such as metal goods and cloth for the rich and varied furs so much in fashion in Europe. The Tlingit controlled Yukon trading because they controlled the trading routes through the high mountain passes. When trading ceased to be an effective means of survival, my grandparents began raising wild mink in cages. Mink prices were really high before and during the war, but afterward the prices went plunging down. So, although the mink pens were still there when I was a little girl, my father mainly worked on highway construction and hunted in the bush. The Yukon was then, and still is in some ways, in a transitional period—from living off the land to getting into a European wage-based economy.

As a young child, I didn't see the full extent of the upheaval. I remember a lot of togetherness, a lot of happiness while we lived in the bush. There's a very strong sense of family in the native community, and a fondness for children, especially young children. Even today, it's like a special form of entertainment if someone brings a baby to visit. That sense of family is the one thing that has survived all the incredible difficulties native people have had. Throughout a time of tremendous problems, the extended family system has somehow lasted, providing a strong circle for people to survive in. When parents were struggling with alcoholism or had to go away to find work, when one of the many epidemics swept through the community, or when a marriage broke up and one parent left, aunts, uncles and grandparents would try to fill those roles. It's been very important to me in terms of emotional support to be able to rely on my extended family. There are still times when such support keeps me going.

Life was much simpler when we lived in the bush. Although we were poor and wore the same clothes all year, we were warm enough and had plenty to eat. But even as a youngster, I began to be aware of some of the problems we would face later on. Travelling missionaries would come and impose themselves on us, for example. They'd sit at our campfire and read the Bible to us and lecture us about how we had to live a Christian life. I remember being very frightened by stories we heard about parents sending their kids away to live with white people who didn't have any children. We thought those people were mean, and that if we were bad we'd be sent away, too. Of course, that was when social workers were scooping up native children and adopting them out to white families in the south. The consequences were usually disastrous for the children who were taken away—alienation, alcoholism and suicide, among other things. I knew some of those kids. The survivors are still struggling to recover.

The residential schools were another source of misery for the kids. Although I didn't have to go, my brothers and sisters were there. They told stories about having their hair cut off in case they were carrying head lice, and of being forced to do hard chores without enough food to eat. They were told that the Indian culture was evil, that Indian people were bad, that their only hope was to be Christian. They had to stand up and say things like "I've found the Lord," when a teacher told them to speak. Sexual abuse was rampant in the residential school system.

By the time we moved to Whitehorse, I was excited about the idea of living in what I thought of as a big town. I'd had a taste of the outside world from books at school in Teslin (a town of 250 people), and I was tremendously curious about what life was like. I was hungry for experiences such as going to the circus. In fact, for a while, I was obsessed with stories and pictures about the circus, but then when I was 12 and saw my first one, I was put off by the condition and treatment of the animals.

Going to school in Whitehorse was a shock. The clash of native and white values was confusing and frightening. Let me tell you a story. The older boys in our community were already accomplished hunters and fishermen, but since they had to trap beaver in the spring and hunt moose in the fall, and go out trapping in the winter as well, they missed a lot of school. We were all in one classroom and some of my very large teenage cousins had to sit squeezed into little desks. These guys couldn't read very well. We girls had been in school all along, so of course we were better readers. One day the teacher was trying to get one of the older boys to read. She was typical of the teachers at that time, insensitive and ignorant of cultural complexities. In an increasingly loud voice, she kept commanding him to "Read it, read it." He couldn't. He sat there completely still, but I could see that he was breaking into a sweat. The teacher then said, "Look, she can read it," and she pointed to me, indicating that I should stand up and read. For a young child to try to show up an older boy is wrong and totally contrary to native cultural values, so I refused. She told me to stand up and I did. My hands were trembling as I held my reader. She yelled at me to read and when I didn't she smashed her pointing stick on the desk to frighten me. In terror, I wet my pants. As I stood there fighting my tears of shame, she said I was disgusting and sent me home. I had to walk a long distance through the bush by myself to get home. I remember feeling this tremendous confusion, on top of my humiliation. We were always told the white teachers knew best, and so we had to do whatever they said at school. And yet I had a really strong sense of receiving mixed messages about what I was supposed to do in the community and what I was supposed to do at school.

Pretty soon I hated school. Moving to a predominantly white high school was even worse. We weren't allowed to join anything the white kids started. We were the butt of jokes because of our second-hand clothes and moose meat sandwiches. We were constantly being rejected. The prevailing attitude was that Indians were stupid. When it was time to make course choices in class—between typing and science, for example—they didn't even ask the native kids, they just put us all in typing. You get a really bad image of yourself in a situation like that. I bought into it. I thought we were awful. The whole experience was terribly undermining. Once, my grandmother gave me a pretty little pencil box. I walked into the classroom one day to find the word "squaw" carved on it. That night I burned it in the wood stove. I joined the tough crowd, and by the time I was 15 years old I was more likely to be leaning against the school smoking a cigarette than trying to join in. I was burned out from trying to join the system. The principal told my father there was no point in sending me back to school, so with a Grade 9 education I started to work at a series of menial jobs.

Seven years later something happened to me that would change my life forever. I had moved to Ottawa with a man and was working as a waitress in a restaurant. One day, a friend invited me to her place for coffee. While I was there, she told me she was going to university in the fall and showed me her reading list. I'll never forget the minutes that followed. I was feeling vaguely envious of her and, once again, inferior. I remember taking the paper in my hand, seeing the books on it and realizing, Oh my God, I've read these books! It hit me like a thunderclap. I was stunned that books I had read were being read in university. University was for white kids, not native kids. We were too stupid, we didn't have the kind of mind it took to do those things. My eyes moved down the list, and my heart started beating faster and faster as I suddenly realized I could go to university, too!

My partner at the time was a loving supportive man who helped me in every way. I applied to the university immediately as a mature student, but when I had to write Grade 9 on the application I was sure they'd turn me down. They didn't. I graduated five years later, earning a bachelor of arts in English and philosophy (with distinction)....

Today there's a glimmer of hope that more of us native people will overcome the obstacles that have tripped us up ever since we began sharing this land. Some say our cultures are going through a renaissance. Maybe that's true. Certainly there's a renewed interest in native dancing, acting and singing, and in other cultural traditions. Even indigenous forms of government are becoming strong again. But we can't forget that the majority of native people live in urban areas and continue to suffer from alcohol and drug abuse and the plagues of a people who have lost their culture and have become lost themselves. And the welfare system is the insidious glue that holds together the machine of oppression of native people.

Too many non-native people have refused to try to understand the issues behind our land claims. They make complacent pronouncements such as "Go back to your bows and arrows and fish with spears if you want aboriginal rights. If not, give it up and assimilate into white Canadian culture." I don't agree with that. We need our culture, but there's no reason why we can't preserve it and have an automatic washing machine and a holiday in Mexico as well.

The time has come for native people to make our own decisions. We need to have self-government. I have no illusions that it will be smooth sailing—there will be trial and error and further struggle. And if that means crawling before we can stand up and walk, so be it. We'll have to learn through experience.

While we're learning, we have a lot to teach and give to the world—a holistic philosophy, a way of living with the earth, not disposing of it. It is critical that we all learn from the elders that an individual is not more important than a forest; we know that we're here to live on and with the earth, not to subdue it.

The wheels are in motion for a revival, for change in the way native people are taking their place in Canada. I can see that we're equipped, we have the tools to do the work. We have an enormous number of smart, talented, moral Indian people. It's thrilling to be a part of this movement.

Someday, when I'm an elder, I'll tell the children the stories: about the bush, about the hard times, about the renaissance, and especially about the importance of knowing your place in your nation.

Another Country

BY JANICE KULYK KEEFER

Janice Kulyk Keefer writes of her need to know about the land her grandparents came from.

e— **O**ne evening, not long ago, I came into the possession of an envelope—plain, brown, 8 x 12—on which two words were marked, in my dead grandmother's handwriting. A foreign language, a different alphabet. Yet however much of my Saturday-school Ukrainian I'd forgotten, I couldn't fail to know these words by heart. They were the reason translation was necessary in the first place—translation from one country, language, future into another. "Moyèh pòleh: my fields."

Paszport: Rzeczpospolita Polska—contents inscribed in Polish and French. In Latin, official recognition of private life: *Testimonium copulationis: Thomas Solowski, aetas 20, Helena Lewkowycz, aetas 18*. A map of fields narrow as piano keys: the land my grandparents still own in a vanished country. From the Polish Transatlantic Shipping Company, a Notice to passenger Helena Solowska (34) and daughters Natalja (14) and Wira (12). Disclaimer of responsibility—in English, Polish, Ukrainian, German, Finnish, Lithuanian, Latvian, Romanian, Czechoslovak, Serbian, Yiddish, and Croatian. And finally, on cream-coloured, durable paper: Certificate of Canadian Citizenship, Helen Solowska. Address, Toronto, Ontario, Canada. Place of birth: Poland. Distinguishing Marks: None.

Confirmation in paper, ink, official stamps of a world I know only as memories and stories: a country as different from my own as "Rzeczpospolita Polska" and the crowned eagle is from Canada and its scarlet maple leaf.

The land with which I've been obsessed ever since I was old enough to know how to remember.

Where to begin with something that's as much a web of gaps and silences as words? Thanks to the envelope I have, at last, something definite, concrete: Pid-Volochiska, the name of the village, though it may now be called by another name. I know that my grandfather, Tomasz Solowski, was Polish: my grandmother, Helena, Ukrainian. And I know from history books that Ukrainians living in Poland weren't allowed to speak or read their mother tongue, that the language had to survive underground, in the fields and in the home. The village in which my mother grew up was then on the border between Poland and Russia: my grandmother told me of how she once went to market in the nearby town and bought a fine pair of pigs only to have them run away and end their days as Russian bacon. More than pigs escaped—young men were always being shot at the border, trying to cross into the worker's paradise. My aunt has stories of how she and my mother would play "mourner," draping themselves in black scarves, following the coffins to the burial ground; eyes streaming for strange young men buried with no more ceremony than if they'd been dead birds or barn cats. And there were *Liebestods*, as well—I have heard of the beauty of the young men, and that of girls in shifts stiff with blood-red embroidery, their long braids glistening, roped around them. Dead because their parents had forbidden them to marry, dead because nothing but landlessness, the kind of poverty which means starvation, could come of love. They'd hang themselves or slit their throats: I have been told about the open coffins the whole village would parade to see: protruding, purple tongues cut off; chins propped, necks scarved: that's how it was then, that's the kind of thing which happened there.

Unless, like my grandparents, you spat in Death's face. The story of their meeting I have heard and reheard, embroidered so that I can't tell, and do not wish to ask, what I've made up and what is memory. My grandmother, a mere fifteen, the youngest in a family of girls where only sons were wanted. My grandfather, a soldier, a cavalry man, going to a dance in the village. Tomasz Solowski: uniformed, handsome, tall—the girls a storm of doves around him. Of them all, he asks my grandmother to dance. She is wearing a kerchief on her head, even though young, unmarried girls may wear their long hair loose and unconfined. And while she is dancing with Tomasz, the girl who was her best friend runs up to them and whips the kerchief from my grandmother's head. Instead of thick, wheat-coloured hair, there is just a downy fuzz, like that of baby chicks: she has had typhus—her hair is only beginning to grow in. Shamed, she runs into the garden—would there have been flower gardens in a Polish village? Never mind, I want a garden here, a river, nightingales and pear blossom…. Tomasz follows her, his uniform kindled by the white-fire moon. He comforts, kisses her. They are married within the next month.

Against both parents' wishes. She was to have been matched with a farmer whose lands were adjacent to her father's: he was to have married his stepsister, so that the land would not go out of the family. All this is true, and yet I have embroidered, misheard: I have their marriage certificate now, from the envelope—the *Testimonium Copulationis*. They were not fifteen and eighteen, as I'd always believed, but eighteen and twenty. I also have the photograph—whether it really is of my grandmother's mother I do not know, but it is her only possible likeness: a woman encased in a black dress, with a black scarf clamped round her head, cutting off her forehead, the way a nun's coif would do. And with no band of white for relief: just black, even the shadows out of which her stone eyes peer. My great-grandmother, come to witness my mother's birth: I have been told that she sat with folded arms outside the room in which her daughter screamed. Sat, and spoke only once, saying, "You wanted Tomasz: you've got Tomasz." I've also been told that my grandmother spent only a few hours resting after her labour. She had to get back into the fields—there was planting to be done, and no money to hire help on the land.

The land, always the land: moyèh pòleh. Thin strips marked out on the tissue-paper map, snipped ribbons of land, scattered through the village, handfuls of earth to be halved and quartered between what was to have been four children: my mother and her sister and then the twins who would die before they were a year old, for whose sake, the day after their birth, my grandfather went off to Canada. I have my grandfather's Certificate of Immigration, earned by a voyage, third class, on *The Empress of France*, to earn Canadian dollars and buy a few more strips of Polish land. And here, another story, one that people tell me cannot possibly be true; one that I've entirely invented. That the man in the sepia photograph stapled to the immigration card was shipped from Quebec to Saskatoon, and found himself forced to work for a farmer who treated his labourers worse than he did his livestock. How my grandfather, who'd not been a farmer back in Poland, but a soldier, set out in October to walk east to the city, any city. And through freezing rain, tempests of snow, walked all the way to Toronto, where he found work in a foundry, a place no less hellish than the farm he'd abandoned. Somewhere in my mother's house is a memento of his days in that foundry: a metal nutcracker he cast, in the shape of a dog: you press the tail down and the jaws smash whatever's caught between them.

I picture my grandmother and her daughters, leaving the port of Gdynia, bound for a country that's no more than a foreign word, the stamp inside a passport. The crossing—my grandmother sick as a dog in her stifling, third-class berth—while her daughters dance to the accordion music sailors play on tilting, windy decks. Young girls coming down to their mother, calling her to wake up, dance, look at the moon's face, or nets of sunlight on the waves, and she'd push them away, groaning in the belly of that reeking, rolling ship. For my aunt and my mother, a time of the first leisure, the first freedom they have ever known, or would know for a long time after. No school work and no farm work, but dancing, careering round and round the decks. Until the day they dock, and officials come aboard to inspect the cargo. The blunt, purple stamp of the Health Officer on my grandmother's immigration card. And my mother remembering this: a room full of naked women, women forced to strip to the skin to assure their new countrymen they carry no hideous disease, bear no contagion. My mother thinking that the older women are all wearing aprons, until she looks again, and sees that the aprons aren't cloth but flesh: sagging breasts and bellies of women worn and wrung out like scrubbed clothes, hung on the racks of their own bones to dry.

Now it is the dockyards at Halifax, the porter who helps them onto the train. My mother cannot say please or thank you—not just because she doesn't know any English, but because she is dumb with fear. For this man is black, she has never seen a black person before, and the village priest has told them only devils are black. This man with his uniform, his jaunty whistle and wide smile, this is the devil helping them onto, shutting them into a train bound for what, where? How did they survive that journey, sitting upright in the coaches whirling past a landscape indecipherable as the language of its people? Of the journey, my mother has told me only one thing: how she stepped out of that hot and smoky train into the night of a strange city, to find not stars but letters scrawled across the sky. Fiery, enormous, unfathomable: Sosa Sola, Sosa Sola. When she learned to read them not in the Cyrillic but the Latin alphabet; when she read them, not in electric letters on the sky, but round a Coca-Cola bottle, were they more or less meaningful? What sort of clue did they furnish to this place where nothing grew—where you had to go to the store for bread and milk and eggs? So that my grandmother would lock herself in the bathroom of their rooming house (having had to patiently queue for her turn). Would let the taps gush in order to cry without being heard—cry for everything she had left behind, the orchard filled with pear trees, the cows and geese and chickens, fields of wheat and rye, root cellars stocked with potatoes, onions, beets.

I remember my grandmother remembering how she'd wept: how, the only time I asked her if she wished she'd never taken that boat to Halifax, she couldn't answer me, as if my question were not only meaningless, but lunatic, like asking if you wished to be unborn. I remember for myself the backyard of her house on Dovercourt Road, the narrow strip of grass at the back, bordered by prodigally fertile earth: roses and zinnias and phlox and asters: beans and tomatoes and garlic which, once harvested, would hang in wreaths on the cellar joists: cucumbers for pickling: raspberry canes and strawberry beds her grandchildren were free to harvest. That narrow strip of garden fed my aunt's family as well as my own—could the land my grandmother had left behind in Poland, those paper fields, have ever produced so much? Could that earth have been any richer, blacker?

Blacker, yes, because the dead were there, my mother's sister and brother, twins who'd died in infancy. For years the ghosts of that unknown aunt and uncle haunted me: I would scour the old albums and find pictures of babies which I'd persuade myself were them, Ivan and Marusha, even though the photos were taken on Centre Island or at Niagara Falls and these children had died in another country. For a long while I only knew that they'd died young. I hugged this mystery to myself, half-shocked and half-enchanted: nobody else I knew possessed this kind of ghost, was singled out in such a distantly macabre way. And then, much later, information came without my asking. When I was pregnant my mother told me, for the first time, that Ivan had died only a few days after his birth: that Marusha had suffered all her short life, from epilepsy. They couldn't afford doctors, there was no hospital nearby, and so to keep the baby from harming herself they would put her into the trough used for kneading dough, holding her body straight until the fits had passed. And then my mother told me of the night her year-old sister died: the open coffin, no bigger than a cradle, being placed on a high shelf, and my mother, curious, not understanding, reaching up to where the baby lay. Finding something impossibly cold and small, something which she still cannot believe had been her sister's hand. Years later, my mother recounted a dream my grandmother had had, the night before Marusha's death. Something evil had come into the house—something long, snakelike, thick as felt in the mouth. She'd had to roll up this evil thing in her arms, roll it up like a carpet and then push it outdoors. When she woke she'd found herself standing outside, arms pressed against the fence, her feet and fingers stiff with snow.

I have in my possession a plain brown envelope stuffed with tissue-paper documents the colour of dead leaves. I have, too, a set of stories, memories of other people's memories. And an obsession with a vanished country, a landscape of differences and mirrors, prodding me to link scraps and pieces into something durable, before silence undoes all the strings. My grandparents' lives haunt their photographs and signatures on those dead passports stamped with heraldic eagles. The faces of my mother and my aunt reflect the faces in their Polish passport photos the way a gibbous moon reveals the new. Sometimes new stories are disclosed   things I can't imagine and don't know how to ask for. Not long ago I spoke on a radio program to do with Ukrainians and war crimes about the need to face and respond to, not just "transcend" the past. I spoke of how the children of immigrants had never been told the necessary things, how any history of complicity and guilt had been hidden from us. And received, some weeks later, a letter from my aunt, who'd happened, by pure chance, to have heard me speak. It was a very ordinary, affectionate letter, full of news of her children and questions about mine. But she began by speaking of the radio interview and by telling a story of what had happened to a cousin of hers, who'd been a young boy when she left Poland in 1936. During the war, Nazi sympathizers in his village had gouged out his eyes, cut out his tongue, while his mother was forced to watch. Relatives had written, after the war, recounting this. And now my aunt wrote to me, not in anger, but in perplexity: "We never wanted to burden you children with this—how could we have told you? Is this what you really want to know?"

Not want, but have to know, along with all the stories of lovers in a garden, memories of neon stars and epic journeys by boat and train and foot. The stuff that my particular obsession feeds on, threading images and words through ever larger silences.

Social Studies

BY TANIS MacDONALD

"Eventually I encountered the dilemma: where does a normal, healthy, dance-loving gal go to meet people?"

Multiculturalism is a big deal here in Toronto. This city is filled with people from every corner of the globe, and it definitely makes the "City by the Lake" an exciting place to carve out a life.

But, arriving here from Winnipeg eight years ago, one of my first thoughts was—where, oh, where are the Ukrainians? Sure, there are Ukrainian "theme" restaurants where the perogies taste like paper, and I've culled out a Mom-and-Pop store that satisfies my 'Peg-fed taste for honeycake. But it's nothing like the overall living, breathing, Rusalka-dancing flavour that is paprikaed the length and breadth of Manitoba.

Now, not too long ago, the nostalgia for Ukrainian rare air overtook me with a vengeance. I initially moved to Toronto for school, and classes were chock-full of opportunities to mingle. Eventually I graduated, snagged a job, and encountered *the* dilemma: where does a normal, healthy, dance-loving gal go to meet people? Bars bored me, my co-workers were all married or similarly attached, and displayed a scary inclination toward suggesting singles clubs to me. What was left?

Into the blankness strode the bold question, "How did you meet people back home? How is this done in Winnipeg? It can't be so different here." Ah, but it is. For in Winnipeg, there is that time-honoured tradition of Saturday nights in old Legion halls, replete with peeling wooden tables and cheap speakers blaring top-forty tunes mixed with an insouciant polka or three, that most erudite of events—the *social*.

"The social what?" my ethnically uncluttered Ontarian friends asked, mystified at my deification of this wondrous phenomenon.

"Just a social. That's it. That's the whole name. That's what these things are called." I was at a loss to explain to them the romantic appeal of a badly lit community-centre hall. I was truly moved when I thought of the hours that I had spent cutting a swath across those tile floors. My friends, however, insisted on comparing a Winnipeg social to something tangible in their world, something knowable, something... pedestrian. Well.

"O.K. Socials are usually held as fundraisers for a young couple who are about to tie the knot."

"Like a dance?"

"No, much more personal, less antiseptic."

"Like a wedding party?"

"No, it's usually held several weeks before the wedding—plus, you don't have to know the bride or the groom to go to a social. In fact, tickets are printed up and sold by the friends of the lucky couple to whoever will buy them."

My friends were open-mouthed in their horror. "You mean a bunch of strangers will just show up and start drinking to the impending nuptials? Western weirdness. O.K., who made this up?"

"Nobody *made it up*. It's Ukrainian tradition, or Polish... I think. All that tends to blend together in Winnipeg. The melting pot, you know. But I know it's an Eastern European wedding staple."

"And as for the people, they're not really strangers, because they all have tickets, and will all have been invited by someone the couple knows. Besides, a huge mix of people is part of the point. The more people who don't know each other, the better."

My friends laboured to understand. "So, you go to this party, and these Ukrainian people show up and dance mazurkas or something, right? Like Caribana for the Eastern bloc set?"

My eyes cast themselves heavenward. "No, you're missing the whole point. It's not a staged cultural event. It's not so much Ukrainian in execution as in *essence*. Let me draw you a picture. For example, you never know who will appear at a social. Old friends from elementary school, your neighbours, your best friend's parents, whoever! And listen, that's an important bit—if the older people didn't show up, nobody would ever learn how to polka properly."

"Polka?" The single musical word sat like a pigeon turd in my friend's urbane mouth.

"Well, of course. There must be polkas, or it's not a social. And *everybody* polkas. No question. There is simply no pretending you're too cool for it. Nobody thinks that hard about it—we just polka because we can. We were always outclassed by the older couples, though. Elderly folks who hobbled in at 8:30 would be slicing up the dance floor to 'Roll Out the Barrel' by 10:00.

"All those dances! The Butterfly, the Bird Dance, and always the cult faves. In the seventies, Rock Lobster and the Time Warp were big." My friends' eyes were growing steadily more convex in their heads. "In Rock Lobster, there's the part where the music winds down and everyone would get down on the floor and Worm, and in the Time Warp, there's the Jump to the Left, then the Little Step to Your Right; Put Your Hands on Your Hips... "

"Wait." Their eyes were glazing over.

But I was on a roll. I could not be stopped. I steamrolled full force into smoky reminiscences of my long-dormant Winnipegism. My lenses steamed over with details, a cultural memory whose taps had burst.

"Someone, I guess the best man, or any of the men in the wedding party, or on the groom's hockey team, or the bride's brothers, would get a special-events licence from the L.C. and stand behind the bar selling beer or liquor—I don't ever remember any wine—in plastic cups. But nobody cared, because it was so cheap. Then you would go back to your table and eat Old Dutch potato chips, or pretzels, or peanuts, and pick the slivers off the fraying wood table. It peeled off in big chunks—lots of women would run their stockings on the edges, so you had to be careful getting up out of your chair. But I only recall sitting down to glug back my drink, then get up to dance some more.

"And sweat! Those places were always overheated in the winter—too cold to start the evening but steam baths by the time 1:30 came around. All those people gyrating and leaping about in the small space really steamed it up. People would arrive perfectly coiffed and groomed, and leave looking like they had just been through the wringer and loved it. My boyfriend and I used to leave and sit in his Toyota with our coats open in 30-below weather, hair plastered to our heads, clothes limp, trying to release some of that human humidity."

My friends had left the room. They got on the subway and went down to the Dome to watch the Jays. I kept talking. It felt good.

"Then about midnight, food was served. Always the same food. Cold cuts and squares of cheese that somehow acquired a fine sheen of oil, and the same rye bread every time. The rye was never quite fresh, always pretty chewy. Once in a while, I remember, cabbage rolls served cold. But not often, because then you needed utensils. But always the cold cuts and cheese and rye. And everyone ate it. Without exception. Not because it was good, or because we wanted to, but because the food had been supplied specifically to absorb the liquor in our stomachs—most of which was sweated out anyway—and the older women had taken their valuable polka time to whip this repast together, and because that was what you did at socials. It also gave you a few minutes to talk to the guy that you had been dancing the Butterfly with all night. You knew how they sweated, now what part of the city were they from? Time to play a little Who-Do-You-Know.

"See, the Butterfly... mostly it would be two women with a man in the middle, and trust me, it's an icebreaker. All conventional mating rituals are declared null and void, after you've been flung around in ever-increasing circles by a guy who's running out of breath because he is also flinging about his second partner—usually your best friend—on alternate swings. After that, he's glad to sit and eat cold cuts and hear that he went to school with your cousin in the North End.

"When it was over, a whole bunch of us, including the Butterfly guy, would go to the Country Kitchen for coffee and breakfast and cigarettes and a general rehashing of who danced with whom, and who was drunk, and who was that tall guy in the blue shirt, or that girl with the hair who came with the group from Sturgeon Creek. All the important stuff. The guys had just as much to say as the women, maybe more. Who says men don't gossip? I'd roll back home by about three, and be awake the next morning in time to wash the smoke out of my hair, and be at the 11:00 service."

I took a breath, and found myself alone in my apartment. Feeling oddly content, I went to bed early, and fell asleep listening to the Jays' game. When my friends phoned me the next morning to tell me about Devon White's spectacular play in the seventh, they avoided any mention of Winnipeg and things Ukrainian. Finally, I broached the subject.

One of them sputtered, "I just don't get it. Your grandparents came from Scotland! You're about as Ukrainian as shortbread. The closest you could ever come to 'the Old Country' is the Selkirk Settlers! The whole thing exists in some Winnipeg-inspired vacuum. So, unless there's some Polish tartan that I haven't heard about, what cultural memories can this bizarre ritual possibly have for you?"

I can't explain to them why I find this sweaty, cheesy memory so sublime. I can't begin to tell them that when I was six, those whirling girls with the hair ribbons in Dauphin were princesses to me. I can't fill their tongues with the tart sensation of borscht. I can't forget growing up Waspy and pale and middle-class, and then the sheer giddy joy of being embraced into a loud and aromatic society which demanded that I dance and eat and gossip passionately into the cold winter night. I can't tell them that for years, this was my heart. I can't tell them that, because it makes no sense. And yet I know that it is so.

Bags of Golden Promises: Good Food, Family, Friends

BY VICTORIA CROSS

In difficult times, we appreciate basic values more than ever.

This winter, I gained a new appreciation for onions.

Onions are, of course, a commonplace cooking ingredient. Simple bulbs that reek of the earth and speak of soup. Onions, even at their most expensive, from Vidalia, Ga., U.S.A., packed in boxes and ordered from the back pages of *The New Yorker*—are cheap compared to other gourmet delights.

No home is without onions, or their kissing cousins: pungent garlic, sturdy leeks, tender shallots, sharp chives. By their very availability, onions remain an underrated commodity, stuffed in a dark kitchen vegetable drawer or kept, as they were in my family home, in a dark root cellar under the basement stairs. Where I come from, onions aren't valued highly.

In general, my family did not eat over-flavourful food. Any food that brought heavy cooking smells with it was suspect. For the worst offenders, fish, for example, there was a ceiling fan to circulate the air and an aerosol can of air freshener to eliminate any lingering smells that weren't lemon-fresh. My mother usually cut in half the amount of onion called for in a recipe. A two-kilo bag of onions lasted at least a month.

Not so in my husband's home; there, onions and their cousins are an absolute of life. A necessity. Raised by a Canadian-Ukrainian mother and a Russian father, my husband thrives on Eastern European cooking. Onions and garlic are central to almost every meal, even breakfast. My mother-in-law mixes chopped garlic with butter and spreads it on toast. She says it keeps colds away.

As I have grown and travelled, my formerly size-8, very white-bread self has succumbed to the exotic, odoriferous delights of perogies and stuffed cabbage, of country French *pot-au-feu*, Spanish *aioli*, chicken with 24 garlics. I thought I had a properly enlightened view of onions, having learned to cook and eat many varieties. When I walked into the Russian Orthodox Church's annual banquet, I was looking forward to the food.

There were about 100 people gathered there. Most were old, wrinkled as if they were apples left too long in a warm room. There were a few like my husband and me—"younger" people who came to keep their elderly parents company. There were several languages hovering in the air—Russian, Ukrainian, a smattering of Romanian. We were served heaping platters of turkey, gravy boats filled with wild mushrooms—hand-gathered by the old ones from secret places in the country—and home-baked treats. But it was the raffle that brought home the true importance of onions.

The bearded bishop announced there were to be 50 prizes. With just 100 people in the room and tickets priced at $2 each, my husband and I decided to throw caution to the winds and purchase five. Our money-wasting behaviour caused some concern at neighbouring tables. Would we win all the best prizes? Sure enough, one of our tickets was the second called.

My husband went to retrieve our prize and was granted a choice. Either a wrapped "mystery package" or a 10-pound bag of onions.

"Not just any onions," announced the priest, "Canada No. 1 Fancy Grade Onions donated specially to us by a very fine friend."

The crowd cheered. Sure enough, heaped in a corner were 20 bags of onions. Nearly half the possible prizes were these onions. A hush fell over the room. What would this man who chose to marry an English woman pick?

To a round of applause, my husband chose the onions. He presented them to me as if he were one of Robin Hood's merry men producing a heart for Maid Marian. I made proper cooing noises, and wondered, secretly, what I would do with 10 pounds of onions.

The others in the room begged for their chances at the onions. Whenever they were presented with the choice of a mystery package or the onions, the onions won hands down. Another of our tickets was pulled. "Iley," shouted a heavily accented voice. "They can't have two bags of onions." We were reminded we needed to share the onions, and given a mystery prize. It was a bottle of Heinz Chili Sauce and a small can of tomato juice.

As winners were selected, the bags of onions spread throughout the room, filling the hall with warm kitchen smells. The firm golden globes shone under the overhead lights. Upon winning her red net bagful, one woman danced an impromptu step before the bishop, proudly displaying the onions high above her head. Between the crowded tables, the new owners of Canada No. 1 Fancy Grade Onions compared their bags much as young mothers might compare their babies. Cooking secrets were swapped. Plans were made. Meals were described. "My sister couldn't come today because she is sick. I will give her the onions as a get-well gift," announced a well-dressed matron.

We won again, and again. Ultimately, all five of our tickets were winners. But we never were granted another bag of onions, which was probably just as well, since my mother-in-law and her sister had also won a bag each. Thirty pounds of onions were more than enough for our small family. My modern self took a long walk that day as I went to collect our fifth and final prize. It was a small package of scented soaps.

"What will you do with all your onions?" asked the smiling priest, quizzing me.

"Pickle them," I lied.

"Oh," said the priest to his wife, "she will pickle them."

"Yes," I volunteered. "I have a wonderful recipe."

"She requires a recipe," nodded the priest's wife, smiling. Clearly, a woman who must use a recipe for onions had much to learn about life. "Your mother-in-law will help you," she said, indulging me. "We are glad you have won so many prizes, so many onions. Perhaps you will come to visit us again."

As the banquet broke up, the old ones cradled their onions and made their way up the creaking stairs to waiting cars.

In ancient Egypt, onions represented life, and legend says the pharaohs gave wagons of gold in exchange for wagons of onions to feed the workers who built their pyramids. In Latin, their very name means "one." In Windsor, on that damp winter day, onions meant the promise of more good food to come, family spirit, and the prize of community. I will never think of onions in quite the same way again.

Bear Spirit in a Strange Land

BY RUDY WIEBE

In the 1970s, Rudy Wiebe wrote a major novel about Big Bear, chief of the Plains Cree in the late 1800s. Here he describes tracking down the last physical remains of Big Bear—the medicine bundle that was the symbol and seat of his personal power and that is now held in an American museum.

A bear is not a bear," said the prairie Cree who knew the giant plains grizzly, now extinct. "A bear is a four-legged Person, he is spirit. That spirit dwells in every bear you can see, but mostly it is on high. There are many bear spirit powers and over them all is the great one that can never be seen, the Great Parent of Bear."

On a New York subway a man is leaning over me, left hand hooked on the bar above, the right gesturing down the car. With each lateral lunge of the train his mouth swings almost against my ear. He is an official trying to explain how I must get off to find the American Museum of Natural History, but there seem to be too many trains at too many levels steel-screaming beside and over and under us through the Manhattan rock; no matter how close he swings he cannot quite bellow loud enough for me to understand him. But he keeps on repeating the same words, I understand that, and gradually something emerges in the unbelievable noise that is so shrill and unending it already seems to be no sound at all except my head breaking: "… this express, catch the local… back… " When the train finally stops he gets me through the hissing doors, pointing, a friendly uniformed man whose face smiles between the large pads clamped like earphones to his head. Somewhere under there he may be wired for Mozart. The train shrieks away, taking most of the oily air with it, but above me, or perhaps below, another is coming. Up the moving stairs I run, wait in another grimed green tunnel where for an instant nothing moves. The father of a Cree girl I know has, she thinks, a power thing with worms; there may be one in his bundle which her mother no longer puts up with in the house. If I told him about these immense steel worms, I believe he would never again catch so much as an accidental gopher in his traps.

So what am I doing here? I'm on the trail of a man buried on a cold January in Saskatchewan in 1888, but who for me is far from dead. His name is Big Bear. For several years I have tried to follow him where he lived: from his birthplace near the North Saskatchewan River to Frog Lake, Alberta, in the north, to the Missouri River, Montana, in the south: to find traces of him, to see what is left of what he saw in that long lifetime before 1885 when he and the Plains Cree who followed him rode over the prairie wherever the spirit moved them.

On March 24, 1879, the *Saskatchewan Herald* explained who Big Bear was: "All the tribes—that is the Sioux (of Sitting Bull), Blackfoot (of Crowfoot), Bloods, Sarcees, Assiniboines, Stoneys, Cree and Saulteaux—now form but one party, having the same mind. Big Bear, up to this time, cannot be accused of uttering a single objectionable word, but the fact of his being the head and soul of all our Canadian plain Indians leaves room for conjecture." The *Herald* was quoting a man who knew: Father Lestanc, O.M.I., veteran priest of the Saskatchewan Métis, who were out on the plains that dreadful winter of 1878–79 because the buffalo no longer came within five hundred kilometres of Batoche. The Métis, led by Gabriel Dumont, were wintering with Big Bear's People at The Forks of the Red Deer and South Saskatchewan Rivers.

For by the spring of 1879 it was finally becoming clear even to government officials that the buffalo was on the brink of annihilation; that the 15,000 prairie Indians, already decimated by smallpox, were actually dying of malnutrition. Several thousand had wintered with Big Bear at The Forks because there were still some buffalo there and because he alone of all the ancient and traditional chiefs (in contrast to Hudson's Bay and government sanctioned chiefs) had never yet signed any treaty, surrendered anything to the white man. Clearly, if the prairie Indians were to get a better treaty than the present one which was, as Governor Morris explained so carefully in

1876, "offered as a gift since they had still their old mode of living," Big Bear was the leader to get it. Without the buffalo there was no "mode of living" on the plains—they needed far more than "gifts."

Big Bear in New York? Not voluntarily, of course, but the tunnels around me here don't actually seem that much different from the limestone-and-steel corridors of Stony Mountain Penitentiary high above the Manitoba plain where I followed him a year ago. Except for the noise and dirt. White men are very resourceful; once they have forced you to give up the land, there isn't very much they cannot legally arrange to do with you, one way or another. And this new violence must be the approaching local.

When I emerge from underground, the first-of-June air along Central Park West smells almost of leafy trees, of grass; but immediately more of diesel, and sausages roasting on a brazier wheeled against the iron fence. A man turns them occasionally as I pass. Inside the Theodore Roosevelt Memorial Entrance the air is cleaner—cleaned, I guess—a probably-steel statue of the Rough Rider President presiding. The stone hall is immense, people echo there like whispers moving in caves, and then at the information booth I discover that I have come across the continent and somewhere mislaid the letter I need to get myself beyond the public display to the guardians of the museum vaults. I search myself again: there's a list of numbers I want, but no letter. I must have a name to call, I ask for the museum directory—I'll probably recognize the name—and am handed a fifty-page book in double columns. Confound it, if I can find an arrowhead in a six-centuries-old buffalo kill I can find a woman in a New York building! Or was it a man? Eventually I soothe the boothed lady into letting me within arm's length of a telephone, I discover "Department of Anthropology," dial again, and again, talking fast. Yes, there are people there; yes, I can get a pass. The man controlling the barrier points: "Voluntary Admission Fee." I hand him a bill and push at the turnstile.

"What's this?" the man says.

"Huh? It's—five dollars!"

"This don't mean nothing here," he says, and I stare in disbelief. New York is New York, O.K., but don't they even recognize anything under—and then I recognize the Queen's face.

"Sorry!" I give him two colourless American dollars and get through.

The Plains Indians artifacts are not underground, and I'm happy about that following Dr. Philip Gifford up stone steps and iron steps, through fire doors and up to a small door which, unlocked, breathes asthmatically of air conditioning. There can be no window here and when the light clicks on it is as if out of the darkness an entire culture had exploded: the tiny room is crammed, stuffed tight. Gifford is working his way in but I stop in the doorway; mostly what I see is buffalo robes folded hide out in heaps on the floor and on the metal shelves, and then gradually there are beaded buckskin suits and drums and stone axes and rattles and incredible bladed clubs and horse bridles and black copper kettles and whips and beaded saddles and saddlebags and parfleches and bowl-shaped shields and buckskin gun cases crusted with unbelievable porcupine-quill embroidery.

Gifford is opening drawers. "The Mandelbaum smaller stuff is here, somewhere," he says. "It's all numbered very simply and in order." The tanned side of the buffalo skin seems tensile as nylon and on the other side the curly hair is almost coarse, but in deeper your fingers can feel—what is it?—delicacy, softness opening, warmth as if the animal were still alive beneath you there, breathing. "Yeah, this must be it. This what you wanted to see? Mr. Wiebe?"

I hear him then. He is holding a small grey stick towards me, grey canvas I see, weathered and pitted with holes very much like the binder canvas I remember from our bush farm in Saskatchewan. I stare so long he says, "It's the numbers all right, here," and he's about to pull out what's inside the sack and I step forward and take it from him quickly.

Just holding it I should— well, I'm no primitive; I can't defy classification. I've come over 4,000 miles by jet and bus and subway and only about half a mile on my own feet and not one step actually on ground, so I check the numbers on the little tags dangling from the open end of the sack. 50.2-3739 A–M. Yes. I am holding in my hands the sacred bundle of Big Bear. In the centre of this bundle is that spirit gift which gave Big Bear his name and his wisdom and his power, which hung around his neck when he rode on a raid or danced his vow to the Thunderbird in the Thirst Dance.

The vision for the bundle was given him at The Forks of the Red Deer and the South Saskatchewan Rivers. It was fitting that his Cree should be wintering there in 1878–79, the last winter the buffalo would ever come north into Canada, because all his life that place had been the centre of the world for Big Bear. Whenever he mentioned it he would rotate the stem of a smoking pipe to the four directions and then point it toward The Forks because sometime before 1840 the Great Parent of Bear came to him there and gave him the vision that shaped his life.

Big Bear spent two years at the Stony Mountain Penitentiary.
He was released on March 4, 1887.

Perhaps very early one morning his father walked with the lad (no one knows what his name was, then) to the top of Bull's Forehead Hill. Together they erected the stick frameworks and hung cloth offerings on them, they placed the buffalo skull under their shelter, spread the bearskin. Then his father offered up a pipe, and left him. He saw Sun come over the knobbly line of the Sand Hills and he kept his face facing Him all day, praying for vision, crying out and raising his arms in agony when it seemed he could no longer stand upright in the terrible light of the endless summer day. Stripped to his breechcloth, his feet on the bear fur, he looked into the sun over the plains and the straight deep valley of the South Saskatchewan and the hills folded down to the point like old blankets until Sun finally vanished black into the wide bloody loops of the Red Deer and he could collapse.

On the second day he did not stand, or move. He was not hungry: it was thirst that wanted to break his concentration. He did not look even at the point where the rivers imperceptibly joined grey water and bent north and then east together. He wept and prayed, and at night the spirits began to come. Not one, many, but he refused; bear spirits came but he would not listen to them either. He fasted and prayed until finally out of his accepted suffering the overlord of all bear spirits came: the Great Parent of Bear. On that cactus-studded hill Bear scooped up wet clay and clawed it over his face, taught him his song and the words of it—

My teeth are my knives
My claws are my knives

—and told him how to make "That which is kept in a clean place": his sacred bundle. All of his life it would be his sign that he was chosen; that, under the Creator, the most powerful spirit known to his people had come, and would come again, to him.

More than a hundred and thirty years later in a small room on the sixth floor of the American Museum of Natural History in New York City, I hold this sacred bundle. I tell anthropologist Gifford that this is it, yes, and he tells me I'm welcome to look around and take any pictures I want and finally he leaves. Even up in the centre of the building the walls and floor shiver with a kind of roar; perhaps the subway burrows directly below here. I pull the bundle out of its battered sack.

It is a soft rectangle of greyed-mauve plaid cotton about half a metre long, twenty-five centimetres wide and ten thick; at one end the cloth is folded in but the other hangs free. The whole is tied together, not with leather thongs, but with binder twine. I guess that, like everything else, is symbolic too.

There are proper ceremonies for opening this bundle, I know, and there are enough pipes here (carefully labelled in drawers) and the ransacked riches of prairie People undoubtedly already provide the proper circle of belief, but I am no proper person. The bundle was to be opened only when its core was to be worn either in battle or in ceremonial dance, but here there is no wet clay to claw over my face even if I had the faintest notion in which direction to turn toward The Forks, even if I knew one single word, had either song or prayer. Though I do intend to go into battle: against all the variegated and clotted ignorance of myself and my people about our past. Having held this story in my hand.

At each opening a new cloth was added inside as a thank offering, so the oldest is outside and the ten layers of printed cotton gradually brighten through shades and patterns of trader cloth to an innermost wrapping of red, yellow and blue stylized flowers on cream background crisp with newness. As I touch that I should feel something: something for this having been dragged across a continent to an up-and-down world that cannot be oriented in the cardinal directions because here there is no sun or earth or believable air; something for my own apprehension of wanting to see this, to somehow *have* this like any white who never has enough, of anything, as if it were even possible to actually have enough of anything except within your self; something of a prayer to the Great Spirit who Big Bear, and I also, believe shaped the universe as He did for no other reason than that apparently He wanted to; some prayer. So then I unfolded the newest cloth.

The core of the bundle is "Chief's Son's Hand." It is a bear paw skinned out but with claws still attached, tanned and supple, sewn onto red flannel shaped like a bib. The Cree believe that a person's soul comes to him at birth and resides along the back of the neck, and so wearing this Big Bear felt the weight of the Hand against his soul: he was in the assured, perfect relationship with the Great Bear Spirit.

The soul lives in the base of the neck: on September 13, 1876, Big Bear refuses the treaty by asking the Governor "to save me from what I most dread—hanging; it is not given to us to have the rope about our necks." And Morris interprets that to mean Big Bear is a criminal and afraid of literal hanging! A logical enough thought, I guess, for a white man to whom language is always only proposition, and never parable.

In the nest of cloth with Chief's Son's Hand there is a short twist of tobacco and about fifteen centimetres of braided sweetgrass. The tobacco is dead but when I lift the sweetgrass I smell prairie. "When the sun rises on this land," Big Bear once said, "the shadow I cast is longer than any river."

I stayed in New York two days, and when the museum was open I was up in that small room. Gifford was helpful and sympathetic. David Mandelbaum was simply a good anthropologist: he found a group of natives no one in Canada had any interest in, got himself sponsored by the American Museum and spent several summers after 1933 living on the Battle River reserves, writing his doctoral thesis and collecting whatever Plains Cree artifacts he could. The thesis was published (available in any good library), and it certainly did preserve much invaluable information on early plains life. Gifford understood that, to a Canadian now, the bundle was a priceless historical item, but a museum is great because it becomes an impersonal repository and never gives up anything it has once ransacked the world to get. Even if it really needed money badly, as the American Museum did; even if, by keeping this bundle locked in vaults, never displayed, it deprived a people of some historical and spiritual heritage they wanted badly to recover. All perfectly reasonable and of course unchangeable.

It was only two days, and it's hard to say what I did when the museum was closed. I certainly saw no Broadway play, nor was I lifted to the top of the Empire State Building. One night I know I walked around Times Square where, as John Mills wrote in *Life*, "every week are reported 15 robberies, 20 felonious assaults, 20 burglaries, 320 larcenies, 2 rapes, and more acts of prostitution, perversion and extortion than anyone has ever tried to count." Beyond the lights was violet sky, but everything on more or less the concrete level seemed like a machine set on "destruct," hammering me into pavement. I found an empty phone booth under a marquee spastic with *The Godfather* and in about a minute I was talking to Tena in British Columbia. She said the kids were all sleeping.

Mostly I think I lay on the saggy bed in a room on West 45th Street. Thinking about the unchanged panorama of The Forks. About the riverbank cemetery on the Poundmaker Reserve, where Big Bear is buried on the spot where he gave his last Thirst Dance, June 16 to 19, 1884. His last free summer as chief of the River People. When he felt the weight of Chief's Son's Hand against his soul for the last time.

Ancestors—The Genetic Source

BY DAVID SUZUKI

David Suzuki shares some of the forces that have made him a Canadian.

My grandparents emigrated from Japan to this country at the turn of the century. Like so many immigrants, they left their homeland reluctantly. But they came from a poverty so profound that they were prepared to take the risk and deal with the terrifying unknown of a totally alien culture and language. Their children, my parents, were born in Vancouver over seventy-five years ago. They were Canadians by birth. By culture, they were genuine hybrids, fluently bilingual but fiercely loyal to the only country they had ever known—Canada.

On December 7, 1941, an event took place that had nothing to do with me or my family and yet which had devastating consequences for all of us—Japan bombed Pearl Harbor in a surprise attack. With that event began one of the shoddiest chapters in the tortuous history of democracy in North America. More than twenty thousand people, mostly Canadians by birth, were uprooted, their tenuous foothold on the West Coast destroyed, and their lives shattered to an extent still far from fully assessed. Their only crime was the possession of a common genetic heritage with the enemy.

Although I have little recollection of that time, Pearl Harbor was the single most important event shaping my life; years later in reassessing my life during a personal trauma, I realized that virtually every one of my emotional problems went right back to it.

Throughout the entire ordeal of those war years, my parents acted with a dignity, courage and loyalty that this young country did not deserve. Today, my mother is dead, never having known the symbolic acknowledgment that a wrong was committed against her. But if there is anything worthwhile to be salvaged from those years, it is that her story and my father's, through me, will not be forgotten and will serve as a legacy to all Canadians, a reminder of the difficulty of living up to the ideals of democracy. The stories of how my parents and their parents fared in Canada are both a tribute to their strength of character and a record of the enormous changes that have occurred in this country. Whatever I am has been profoundly shaped by these two facts.

My genes can be traced in a direct line to Japan. I am a pure-blooded member of the Japanese race. And whenever I go there, I am always astonished to see the power of that biological connection. In subways in Tokyo, I catch familiar glimpses of the eyes, hairline or smile of my Japanese relatives. Yet when those same people open their mouths to communicate, the vast cultural gulf that separates them from me becomes obvious: English is my language, Shakespeare is my literature, British history is what I learned and Beethoven is my music.

For those who believe that in people, just as in animals, genes are the primary determinant of behaviour, a look at second- and third-generation immigrants to Canada gives powerful evidence to the contrary. The over-riding influence is environmental. We make a great mistake by associating the inheritance of physical characteristics with far more complex traits of human personality and behaviour.

Each time I visit Japan, I am reminded of how Canadian I am and how little the racial connection matters. I first visited Japan in 1968 to attend the International Congress of Genetics in Tokyo. For the first time in my life, I was surrounded by people who all looked like me. While sitting in a train and looking at the reflections in the window, I found that it was hard to pick out my own image in the crowd. I had grown up in a Caucasian society in which I was a minority member. My whole sense of self had developed with that perspective of looking different. All my life I had wanted large eyes and brown hair so I could be like everyone else. Yet on that train, where I did fit in, I didn't like it.

On this first visit to Japan I had asked my grandparents to contact relatives and let them know I was coming. I was the first in the Suzuki clan in

Canada to visit them. The closest relative on my father's side was my grand-mother's younger brother, and we arranged to meet in a seaside resort near his home. He came to my hotel room with two of his daughters. None of them spoke any English, while my Japanese was so primitive as to be use-less. In typical Japanese fashion, they showered me with gifts, the most important being a package of what looked like wood carved in the shape of bananas! I had no idea what it was. (Later I learned the package contained dried tuna fish from which slivers are shaved off to flavour soup. This is considered a highly prized gift.) We sat in stiff silence and embarrassment, each of us struggling to dredge up a common word or two to break the quiet. It was excruciating! My great uncle later wrote my grandmother to tell her how painful it had been to sit with her grandson and yet be unable to communicate a word.

To people in Japan, all non-Japanese—black, white or yellow—are *gaijin* or foreigners. While *gaijin* is not derogatory, I find that its use is harsh because I sense doors clanging shut on me when I'm called one. The Japanese do have a hell of a time with me because I look like them and can say in perfect Japanese, "I'm a foreigner and I can't speak Japanese." Their reactions are usually complete incomprehension followed by a sputtering, "What do you mean? You're speaking Japanese." And finally a pejorative, "Oh, a *gaijin!*"

Once when my wife, Tara, who is English, and I went to Japan, we asked a man at the travel bureau at the airport to book a *ryokan*—a tradi-tional Japanese inn—for us in Tokyo. He found one and booked it for "*Suzuki-san*" and off we went. When we arrived at the inn and I entered the foyer, the owner was confused by my terrible Japanese. When Tara entered, the shock was obvious in his face. Because of my name, they had expected a "real" Japanese. Instead, I was a *gaijin* and the owner told us he wouldn't take us. I was furious and we stomped off to a phone booth where I called the agent at the airport. He was astonished and came all the way into town to plead our case with the innkeeper. But the innkeeper stood firm and denied us a room. Apparently he had accepted *gaijin* in the past with terrible consequences.

As an example of the problem, Japanese always take their shoes off when entering a *ryokan* because the straw mats (*tatami*) are quickly frayed. To a Japanese, clomping into a room with shoes on would be comparable to someone entering our homes and spitting on the floor. Similarly, the *ofuro*, or traditional tub, has hot clean water that all bathers use. So one must first enter the bathroom, wash carefully and rinse off *before* entering the tub. Time in the *ofuro* is for relaxing and soaking. Again, Westerners who lather up in the tub are committing a terrible desecration.

To many Canadians today, the word "Jap" seems like a natural abbreviation for Japanese. Certainly for newspaper headlines it would seem to make sense. So people are often shocked to see me bristle when they have used the word Jap innocently. To Japanese-Canadians, Jap or Nip (from "Nippon") were epithets used generously during the pre-war and war years. They conjure up all of the hatred and bigotry of those times. While a person using the term today may be unaware of its past use, every Japanese-Canadian remembers.

The thin thread of Japanese culture that does link me to Japan was spun out of the poverty and desperation of my ancestors. My grandparents came to a Canadian province openly hostile to their strange appearance and different ways. There were severe restrictions on how much and where they could buy property. Their children, who were born and raised in Canada, couldn't vote until 1948 and encountered many barriers to professional training and property ownership. Asians, regardless of birthplace, were third-class citizens. That is the reality of the Japanese-Canadian experience and the historical cultural legacy that came down to the third and fourth generations—to me and my children.

The first Japanese immigrants came to Canada to make their fortunes so they could return to Japan as people of wealth. The vast majority was uneducated and impoverished. But in the century spanning my grandparents' births and the present, Japan has leapt from an agrarian society to a technological and economic giant.

Now, the Japanese I meet in Japan or as recent immigrants to Canada come with far different cultural roots. Present-day Japanese are highly educated, upper-middle class and proud of their heritage. In Canada they encounter respect, envy and curiosity in sharp contrast to the hostility and bigotry met by my grandparents.

Japanese immigrants to North America have names that signify the number of generations in the new land (or just as significantly, that count the generational distance *away* from Japan). My grandparents are *Issei*, meaning the first generation in Canada. Most *Issei* never learned more than a rudimentary knowledge of English. *Nisei*, like my parents, are the second generation here and the first native-born group. While growing up they first spoke Japanese in the home and then learned English from playmates and teachers. Before the Second World War, many *Issei* sent their children to be educated in Japan. When they returned to Canada, they were called *Kika-nisei* (or *Kibei* in the United States). Most have remained bilingual, but many of the younger *Nisei* now speak Japanese with difficulty because English is their native tongue. My sisters and I are *Sansei* (third generation); our children are *Yonsei*. These generations, and especially *Yonsei*, are growing up in homes where English is the only spoken language, so they are far more likely to speak school-taught French as their second language than Japanese.

Most *Sansei*, like me, do not speak Japanese. To us, the *Issei* are mysteries. They came from a cultural tradition that is a hundred years old. Unlike people in present-day Japan, the *Issei* clung tightly to the culture they remembered and froze that culture into a static museum piece like a relic of the past. Not being able to speak each other's language, *Issei* and *Sansei* were cut off from each other. My parents dutifully visited my grandparents and we children would be trotted out to be lectured at or displayed. These visits were excruciating, because we children didn't understand the old culture, and didn't have the slightest interest—we were Canadians.

My father's mother died in 1978 at the age of ninety-one. She was the last of the *Issei* in our family. The final months of her life, after a left-hemisphere stroke, were spent in that terrible twilight—crippled, still aware, but unable to communicate. She lived the terminal months of her life, comprehending but mute, in a ward with Caucasian strangers. For over thirty years I had listened to her psychologically blackmailing my father by warning him of her imminent death. Yet in the end, she hung on long after there was reason to. When she died, I was astonished at my own reaction, a great sense of sadness and regret at the cleavage of my last link with the source of my genes. I had never been able to ask what made her and others of her generation come to Canada, what they felt when they arrived, what their hopes and dreams had been, and whether it was worth it. And I wanted to thank her, to show her that I was grateful that, through them, I was born a Canadian.

Describing Circles

BY ROHINTON MISTRY

"As a child, it always struck me with wonderment and incredulity that I should have an uncle who lived in Dharmsala.... To me, a thousand miles away in Bombay, this land of mountains and snow had seemed miraculously foreign."

It was still raining when we stopped outside Hotel Bhagsu. I took my socks off the taxi's corroded chrome door handles, where they had hung to dry for almost four hours, and pulled them over my clammy feet. The socks were still soggy. Little rivulets ran out of my shoulder bag as I squelched into the lobby. The desk clerk watched with interest while I fastidiously avoided a trail of water that ran from the leaky umbrella stand to the door. Why, with the shoes already sopping wet? he must have wondered. I was not sure myself—perhaps to emphasize that I did not generally go about dripping water.

As I signed the register, shaking raindrops from my hands, the desk clerk said that candles would be sent to my room before dark. "Candles?" I asked.

He had assumed I would know: "There is a small problem. Electricity workers are on strike." Worse, the strikers were sabotaging the power lines. No electricity anywhere, he emphasized, in case I was considering another hotel: not in Upper Dharmsala, not in Lower Dharmsala, nowhere in Kangra District.

I nodded, putting out my hand for the room key. But he held on to it. With that circular motion of the head which can mean almost anything, he said, "There is one more problem." He continued after a suitable pause: "There is also no water. Because of heavy rains. Rocks fell from the mountains and broke all of the water pipes."

He seemed surprised by the lack of emotion with which I greeted his news. But I had already glimpsed the handiwork of the pipe-breaking avalanches during my four-hour taxi ride. The car had laboured hard to reach McLeod Gunj, up the winding, rock-strewn mountain roads, grinding gears painfully, screeching and wheezing, negotiating segments that had become all but impassable.

Perhaps a bit disappointed by my stolidity, once again the desk clerk assured me it was the same in Upper and Lower Dharmsala, and in all of Kangra District; but management would supply two buckets of water a day.

So there was no choice, the hotel would have to do. I requested the day's quota hot, as soon as possible, for a bath. He relinquished my room key at last. Its brass tag had Hotel Bhagsu engraved on one side. "What is Bhagsu?" I asked him, picking up my bag.

"In local language, means Running Water," he said.

The room had an enormous picture window. The curtains, when thrown open, revealed a spectacular view of Kangra Valley. But I could not linger long over it, urgent matters were at hand. I unzipped the bag and wrung out my clothes, spreading them everywhere: over the bed, the chair, the desk, the doorknob. Wet and wretched, I sat shivering on the edge of the bed, waiting for the hot water and remembering the warnings to stay away from Dharmsala while it was in the clutches of the dreaded monsoon.

When the Dalai Lama fled Tibet in 1959, just hours before the Chinese conducted a murderous raid on his palace in Lhasa and occupied the country, he found refuge in India. For months afterward, other Tibetans followed him, anxious to be with their beloved spiritual leader. The pathetic bands of refugees arrived, starving and frostbitten—the ones lucky enough to survive the gauntlet of treacherous mountain passes, the killing cold, and, of course, Chou En-lai's soldiers. Each arriving group narrated events more horrific than the previous one: how the Chinese had pillaged the monasteries, crucified the Buddhist monks, forced nuns to publicly copulate with monks before executing them, and were now systematically engaged in wiping out all traces of Tibetan culture.

The Dalai Lama (whose many wonderfully lyrical, euphonious names include Precious Protector, Gentle Glory, and Ocean of Wisdom) spent his first months of exile in anguish and uncertainty. Faced with unabating news of the endless atrocities upon the body and soul of Tibet, he eventually decided that Dharmsala was where he would establish a government-in-exile. Perhaps this quiet mountain hamlet in the Himalayas reminded him of his own land of ice and snow. Soon, a Tibetan colony evolved in Dharmsala, a virtual country-within-a-country. Visitors began arriving from all over the world to see Namgyal Monastery, Tibetan Children's Village, and the Dalai Lama's new temple, or to study at the Library of Tibetan Works and Archives.

As a child, it always struck me with wonderment and incredulity that I should have an uncle who lived in Dharmsala. In this remote mountain hamlet he ran the business which has been in the Nowrojee family for five generations. To me, a thousand miles away in Bombay, this land of mountains and snow had seemed miraculously foreign. Photographs would arrive, from time to time, of uncle and aunt and cousins wrapped in heavy woollens, standing beside three-foot-deep snowdrifts outside their home, the snow on the roof like thick icing on a cake, and the tree branches delicately lined with more of the glorious white substance. And in my hot and sticky coastal city, gazing with longing and fascination at the photographs, I would find it difficult to believe that such a magical place could exist in this torrid country. Now there, somewhere in the mountains, was a place of escape from heat and dust and grime. So, to visit Dharmsala became the dream.

But for one reason or another, the trip was never taken. Those old photographs: snow-covered mountains and mountain trails; my cousins playing with their huge black Labrador; uncle and aunt posing in the *gaddi* dress of native hill people, a large hookah between them—those old black-and-white photographs curled and faded to brown and yellow. Years passed, the dog died, my cousins got married and settled elsewhere, and my uncle and aunt grew old. Somehow, the thousand miles between Bombay and Dharmsala were never covered. There was always some logistical or financial problem, and travelling third class on Indian trains was only for the foolish or the desperate.

Then, by a quirk of fate I undertook a different journey, a journey ten thousand miles long, to Canada, and I often thought about the irony of it. So this time, back in Bombay to visit family and friends, not monsoon rain or ticket queues or diarrhea or avalanches could keep me away from Dharmsala.

Thus twenty-eight hours by train (first class) brought me to Chakki Bank, in Punjab. It was pouring relentlessly as the first leg of the long journey ended. "Rickshaw, *seth*, rickshaw?" said a voice as I stepped off the train. I quickly calculated: there could be a big demand for transportation in this weather, it might be prudent to say yes. "Yes," I said, and settled the price to Pathankot bus station.

Outside, auto rickshaws—three-wheelers—were parked along the station building in a long line. Enough for everyone, I thought. They had black vinyl tops, and plastic flaps at the side which could be fastened shut, I noted approvingly. I followed my man.

And we came to the end of the line. There, he placed my bag in a pitiful cycle rickshaw, the only one amidst that reassuringly formidable squadron of auto rickshaws. The cycle rickshaw had open sides, and old gunny sacks tied to the top of the frame formed a feeble canopy. I watched in disbelief, appalled by my bad luck. No, stupidity, I corrected myself, for it was clear now why he had come inside the station to solicit a fare. That should have made me suspicious. Once upon a time it would have.

The cycle rickshawalla saw my reaction. He pointed pleadingly at the seat, and I looked him in the face, something I never should have done. I am trusting you, his eyes said, not to break our contract. The auto rickshaws taunted me with their waterproof interiors as I stared longingly at them. Their owners were watching, amused, certain I would cave in. And that settled it for me.

Within seconds of setting off, I was ruing my pride. The gunny sacks were as effective as a broken sieve in keeping out the rain, and despite my raincoat I was soon drenched. The downpour saturated my bag and its contents—I could almost feel its weight increasing, minute by minute. The cycle rickshawalla struggled to pedal as fast as he could through streets ankle-deep in water. His calf muscles contracted and rippled, knotting with the strain, and a mixture of pity and anger confused my feelings. I wished the ride would end quickly.

In Pathankot, he convinced me that a taxi was better than a bus in this weather. Afterward, I was glad I took his advice: on the mountains, buses had pulled over because the avalanches, the pipe-breaking avalanches, had made the roads far too narrow. Meanwhile, I waited as the rickshawalla and the taxi driver haggled over the former's commission.

And four hours later I was draping my underwear, socks, shirts, and pants over the doorknob, armchair, lamp shade, and window. There was a knock. The houseboy (who doubled as waiter, I discovered later in the restaurant) staggered in with two steaming plastic buckets, one red and the other blue. He looked around disbelievingly at my impromptu haberdashery. "All wet," I explained. He smiled and nodded to humour the eccentric occupant.

I wondered briefly where the water in the buckets came from if the pipes were broken. My guess was a well. In the bathroom, I splashed the hot water over me with a mug.

Dharmsala is a collection of settlements perched across the lower ridges of the Dhauladur range. The Dhauladur range itself is a southern spur of the Himalayas, and surrounds the Kangra Valley like a snow-capped fence. McLeod Gunj, at seven thousand feet, is one of the highest settlements. I had passed others on my way up by taxi: Lower Dharmsala and Kotwali Bazaar, the main commercial centre crowded with hotels, shops, and restaurants; Forsyth Gunj, a one-street village; and, of course, the huge military cantonment, which was the beginning of everything, back in the British days.

Early in this century, the British were considering making Dharmsala their summer capital; they found the plains unbearable in the hot season. But an earthquake badly damaged the place in 1905, and they chose another hill station, Simla, a bit farther south. (Later, my uncle would describe it differently: the official in charge of selecting the capital was travelling from Dalhousie to Dharmsala when he caught dysentery on the way, reached Dharmsala, and died. The idea of Dharmsala as summer capital was promptly abandoned.)

I wanted to see more of McLeod Gunj and Upper Dharmsala. But first I was anxious to meet my aunt and uncle. Next morning, I telephoned them at their general store, and they were delighted to hear my voice. The line was so bad, they thought I was calling from Bombay. No, I said, Hotel Bhagsu, and they insisted I come immediately, their place was only a five-minute walk away.

It was still drizzling. Along the side of the hotel, under every rain spout was a plastic bucket. My red and blue were there as well. The houseboy was standing guard over them, watching them fill with the run-off from the roof. He looked away guiltily at first when he saw me. Then he must have decided to put the best face on things, for he acknowledged me by smiling and waving. He seemed like a child caught red-handed at mischief.

My uncle and aunt were sorry for the way my visit had begun. "But didn't anyone tell you? This is not a good season for Dharmsala," they said. I had been warned, I admitted, but had decided to come anyway. They found this touching, and also confusing. Never mind, uncle said, perhaps half our troubles would soon be over: the military cantonment had dispatched its men to find and repair the sabotaged power lines. The only snag was, as soon as they mended one, the strikers snipped through some more.

As for water, said my aunt, not to worry, their supply had not been affected, I could shower here.

Not affected? How? Just then, customers arrived, asking for candles. My aunt went to serve them and my uncle told the story.

During the devastation of the 1905 earthquake, the Nowrojee Store was practically the only structure that survived. Uncle's grandfather had handed out food and clothing and blankets from store supplies till proper relief was organized by the British District Commissioner. When McLeod Gunj was back on its feet, the District Commissioner wanted to show his gratitude to the family. He gifted a mountain spring to them, and arranged for a direct water supply from the spring to their house. That private pipeline was still operating after eighty-odd years, and had survived the present avalanches.

I promised I would use their shower in the evening. Then more customers entered, and he had to assist my aunt. Local people were inquiring if the newspaper delivery was expected to get through to Dharmsala. Foreign tourists in designer raincoats were seeking out the sturdy black umbrella which, locally, was the staple defence against the rains. The tourists were also laying in a stock of Bisleri mineral water.

There was a lull in business after this surge. My aunt suggested that uncle take me around Dharmsala for a bit, she could hold the fort alone. So we set out for a walk.

At first the going was slow. Almost every person we passed stopped to exchange a few words, mainly about the weather, and which roads were closed and which were still passable. But it was heartening to see the Tibetan monks, in their crimson robes, always smiling joyfully. For a people who had suffered such hardships and upheavals, struggling to start a life over again in a strange land, they were remarkably cheerful and happy. Perhaps this, and their Buddhist faith, is what sustained them. They had the most wonderful beaming, smiling faces. Just like their spiritual leader, whom I had watched some time ago on "60 Minutes," whose countenance seems to radiate an inner well-being.

Exchanging *namaskaars* with everyone we met (the folded-hands greeting, which translates into "I greet the God in you," common to Hindus and Buddhists), we arrived at a tall gold-crowned structure at the centre of a group of buildings. It was a *chorten*, a religious monument, dedicated to the memory of all those suffering under Chinese occupation in Tibet. The faithful were circling round it, spinning two rows of prayer-wheels and reciting mantras.

We left the little square and the buildings which housed Tibetan handicraft shops, restaurants, and hotels. Farther down were the Tibetan homes: shacks and shanties of tin and stone, and every window was adorned with flowers in rusty tin cans. Faded prayer-flags fluttered in the trees overhead.

The road climbed steeply. Before I knew it, the buildings and the *chorten* were below us. My uncle turned and pointed. There used to be a beautiful park there, he said, at the centre of McLeod Gunj, but it had to go when the refugees came.

During our walk I had gathered he loved the Tibetan people, and had done much to aid them. I could hear the respect and admiration in his voice when he talked about the Dalai Lama, whom he had helped, back in 1959, to acquire suitable houses and properties where the Tibetans could start rebuilding their lives. But now, as my uncle told the story of Dharmsala and the arrival of refugees, I could not help feeling that there was also some resentment toward these people who had so radically changed and remade in their own image the place where he was born, the place he loved so dearly. My aunt, who likes the hustle and bustle of big cities and gets her share of it by visiting relatives periodically, said he would pine away if she ever insisted they leave Dharmsala.

We continued to climb, and on the mountain spur that dominates the valley rose the golden pinnacles of Thekchen Choeling, the Island of Mahayana Teaching, the complex which was the new residence of the Dalai Lama. His cottage had a green corrugated roof, and the temple was a three-storey lemon-yellow hall topped by gold spires. On a low veranda surrounding the temple, a woman was performing repeated prostrations.

She was making a circuit of the temple, measuring her progress with her height.

We removed our shoes and went inside. The main hall had a high throne at one end: the Dalai Lama's throne, on which he sat when he gave audiences and preached. There would be no audiences for the next few days, though, because he was away in Ladakh to deliver the Kalachakra—Wheel of Time—Initiation. Behind the throne was a larger-than-life statue of the Buddha in the lotus position. The Buddha was locked in a huge glass case. Myriads of precious and semiprecious stones formed a halo around the Buddha's solid-gold head, and hence the locked glass: things had changed in Dharmsala; the increase in population and the tourist traffic forced the monks to take precautions.

The changes were having other effects, too. The mountain slopes were being rapidly deforested by the poverty-stricken population's hunger for firewood. And, as elsewhere in the world, the disappearance of trees was followed by soil erosion. My uncle had pointed out the gashed and scarred hills on our climb up. He said that so many mud-slides and rock-falls were unheard of in the old days; and there was less and less snow each year.

I thought of those photographs from my childhood. Their memory suddenly seemed more precious than ever. The pristine place they had once captured was disappearing.

Inside the temple, at the throne's right, more statues were displayed. One of them had multiple heads and arms: Chenrezi, the awareness-being who symbolizes compassion in the Tibetan pantheon. The legend went that Chenrezi was contemplating how best to work for the happiness of all living things when his head burst into a thousand pieces as he realized the awesome nature of the task. The Buddha of Limitless Light restored him to life, giving him a thousand heads to represent the all-seeing nature of his compassion, and a thousand arms to symbolize the omnipresence of his help. But now Chenrezi, along with other statues bedecked with gold and jewels, was locked behind a floor-to-ceiling collapsible steel gate.

The rain finally ceased. My uncle wished the mist would clear so he could show me Pong Lake in the distance. When the moon shone upon the water, he said, it took one's breath away. But the mist sat over the valley, unmoving.

Descending the temple road, we saw several monks, prayer beads in hand, walking a circular path around the complex. They were simulating the Lingkhor, the Holy Walk circumscribing the Potala, the Dalai Lama's palace in Tibet. Round and round they walked, praying, perhaps, for a time when he would be back in his palace, and they treading the original Lingkhor.

Inside: the woman, making a mandala of her prostrations around the temple. Outside: the monks, creating circles of prayer around their beloved leader's residence. Circles within circles. The Wheel of Time.

Back at the general store, bad news awaited: the taps were dry. The Tibetan refugees (everyone, Tibetans included, used that word, despite their having lived here thirty years; perhaps clinging to this word kept alive the hope of returning to their Land of Snows) had discovered that the Nowrojee pipeline still held water. They had cut it open to fill their buckets. Strangely, my uncle and aunt were not too upset. It had happened before. They just wished the people would come to the house and fill their buckets from the taps instead of cutting the pipe.

Later that night, I found my way back to Hotel Bhagsu with a borrowed flashlight. My uncle accompanied me part of the way. Near the incline that led to the hotel, where the road forked, there was a little lamp in an earthen pot, sitting at the very point of divergence. How quaint, I thought. A friendly light to guide the traveller through the pitch-black night. But my uncle grabbed my arm and pulled me away. He said to tread carefully to the right of the lamp, by no means to step over it.

What was it? Something to do with Tibetan exorcism rites, he answered. Did he believe in such things? He had lived here too long, he said, and seen too much, to be able to disbelieve it completely. Despite my skepticism, he succeeded in sending a shiver down my spine. It was only the setting, I explained to myself: a pitch-dark mountain road, the rustling of leaves, swirling mists.

Back at the hotel, the desk clerk apologetically handed me the stubs of two candles. Dharmsala was out of candles, what remained had to be strictly rationed. I asked for water.

One more day, I decided, then I would leave. There was not much to do. The avalanches had closed the roads farther north, and the side trips I had planned to Dalhousie, Kulu, and Manali were not feasible. The houseboy knocked.

He was carrying the red bucket. "Where is the blue?" He shook his head: "Sorry, not enough rain. Today only one bucket."

* * *

The electricity was back next morning, I discovered thankfully. Around nine, I went to the empty restaurant and ordered tea and toast. Afflicted with a bad stomach, I had been virtually living on toast for the past three days. The houseboy in the persona of waiter took my order cheerfully and left.

Thirty minutes later I was still waiting. The door marked Employees Only was ajar, and I peered into the kitchen. It was empty. The backyard beyond the kitchen window was deserted too. I went to the front desk. No one. Finally, I ran into the night watchman, who had just awoken. "What is going on?" I asked him with manufactured testiness, remembering long-forgotten roles and poses. "Waiter has disappeared, no one in the kitchen, no one on duty. What has happened? Is this a hotel or a joke?"

He studied his watch and thought for a moment: "Sunday today? Oh yes. Everyone is watching 'Ramayan.' But they will come back. Only five minutes left."

The *Ramayana* is one of the two greatest Sanskrit epics of ancient India. The other is the *Mahabharata*, which recently found its way in translation onto Western stages in Peter Brook's production. But when the *Ramayana*, the story of the god Rama, was made into a Hindi TV serial, sixty million homes began tuning in every Sunday morning, and those who did not own TVs went to friends who did. In the countryside, entire villages gathered around the community set. Before the program started, people would garland the TV with fresh flowers and burn incense beside it. Classified ads in newspapers would read: Car For Sale—But Call After "Ramayan." Interstate buses would make unscheduled stops when the auspicious time neared, and woe betide the bus driver who refused. Ministerial swearing-in ceremonies were also known to be postponed.

The series ended after seventy-eight episodes, which, however, were not sufficient to cover the entire epic. In protest, street sweepers went on strike and there were demonstrations in several cities. The Ministry of Information and Broadcasting then sanctioned a further twenty-six episodes in order to bring "Ramayan" and the strike to their proper conclusions.

But the story does not end there. Not satisfied with burning incense and garlanding their television sets on Sunday mornings, people began mobbing the actor who played the role of Rama, genuflecting wherever he appeared in public, touching his feet, asking for his blessing. To capitalize on the phenomenon, Rajiv Gandhi's Congress Party enlisted the actor-god to campaign for their candidate in an upcoming election. The actor-god went around telling people that Rama would give them blessings if they voted for the Congress Party, and how it was the one sure way to usher in the golden age of Rama's mythical kingdom of Ayodhya.

At this point, the intellectuals and political pundits sadly shook their sage heads, lamenting the ill-prepared state of the masses for democracy. Suspension of disbelief was all very well when watching television. But to extend it to real life? It showed, they said, the need for education as a prerequisite if democracy was to work successfully.

When it was time to vote, however, the masses, despite the actor-god and the shaking heads of the intellectuals, knew exactly what to do. The Congress candidate went down in a resounding defeat, and the actor-god became sadly human again.

My waiter returned, promising immediate delivery of my tea and toast. I threw my hands in the air and pretended to be upset: How long was a person supposed to wait? Was this a hotel or a joke? In response to my spurious annoyance, he affected a contrite look. But, like me, his heart was not in it. Like the voters and the actor-god, we played out our roles, and we both knew what was what.

In Bombay, at the beginning of the trip, I had listened amusedly when told about the power of the serial. Intriguing me was the fact that what was, by all accounts, a barely passable production lacking any kind of depth, with embarrassingly wooden acting, could, for seventy-eight weeks, hold a captive audience made up not only of Hindus but also of Muslims, Sikhs, Parsis, and Christians—cutting right across the religious spectrum. Could it be that under the pernicious currents of communalism and prejudice there were traces of something more significant, a yearning, perhaps, which transcended these nasty things, so that the great Sanskrit epic of ancient India, a national heritage, could belong to all Indians?

I had not expected to receive a personal demonstration of the Sunday-morning power that "Ramayan" wielded. Least of all in this faraway mountain hamlet. In a way, though, it was fitting. Everywhere, "Ramayan" brought diverse communities together for a short while, to share an experience. But in Dharmsala, the native population and the refugees have been sharing and living together for many years. Even the electricity saboteurs cooperated with the show. Of course, shortly after "Ramayan" the region was once again powerless.

*   *   *

Halfway between McLeod Gunj and Forsyth Gunj was an old English church my uncle had told me about. The pure scent of pine was in the air as I walked to it. The rock face of the mountain appeared to have burst into fresh green overnight. The rains had given birth to countless little streams and rivulets that gurgled their descent. Sometimes, at a bend in the road, the noise of water was so loud, it seemed that a huge waterfall was waiting round the corner. But it was only the wind and the mountains playing tricks, orchestrating, weaving, and blending the music of the newborn runnels and brooks into one mighty symphony of a cataract.

The church of the beautiful name came into view: the Church of Saint John in the Wilderness, a lonely reminder of the British Raj. It looked very much like any English parish church. The grounds were in grave neglect. A tall pine had fallen across the walk-way, brought down by the rains, no doubt. Sunday-morning service was in progress. Tourists and local residents made up the scanty congregation.

I walked around to the back and found myself in the churchyard. A ten- or twelve-foot monument dominated the cemetery. Intrigued, I went closer. James Bruce, 8th Earl of Elgin and 12th Earl of Kincardine (1811–1863) read the inscription, barely legible. And then, the positions he had held in the far-flung corners of the Empire: Governor of Jamaica; Governor General of Canada; Viceroy and Governor General of India.

I examined other gravestones. But weather and time had successfully effaced most of the words. A date here, a first name there: Dear Wife... , or Faithful Husband... , and then Final Rest... , and Heavenly Peace—these fragments were all I could read.

I went back to Lord Elgin's grave and sat before it on a stone ledge. The churchyard was deserted. I read again the words carved in stone, thinking about this Viceroy who had died in Dharmsala, so far from his own country. I imagined the long journeys he had undertaken for Queen and Country: what had he thought about this ancient country? Had he enjoyed his stay here? How might he have felt at having to live out his life in distant lands, none of them his home? Sitting on the moss-grown ledge, I thought about this man buried here, who, a hundred and twenty-five years ago and more, had governed them both, my old country and my new; I thought about the final things.

The weather-beaten gravestones, the vanished epitaphs, the disappearing inscriptions, somehow brought back to me the fading, indistinct photographs of uncle and aunt, cousins and dog, snow on the rooftops and trees. How far away was it—that Dharmsala of my imagination and of my uncle's youth—how far from what I had seen? As far away, perhaps, as the world of empire in whose cause Lord Elgin had undertaken his travels.

I thought about my own journey: from the Dharmsala of childhood fantasies to the peaceful churchyard of Saint John in the Wilderness; and then, amidst the gentle ruins of weather-worn, crumbling gravestones, back to the fading, curling photographs. To have made this journey, I felt, was to have described a circle of my own. And this understanding increased the serenity of the moment.

It started to drizzle. I put on my raincoat and opened the umbrella. As it gathered strength, the rain streamed down the sides of Lord Elgin's monument and blurred the words I had been reading. Thoughts of departure, of descending from the tranquillity of the mountains into the dusty, frenetic plains, began gnawing at the edges of the moment. But I pushed them away. I sat there a little longer, listening to the soothing patter as the rain fell upon the leaves and upon the gravestones all around.

Canada Is a Grand Dream

BY ROCH CARRIER

"I am still thrilled by the immensity of our country.... How great it is to enter so many regions without having to show a passport!"

My father attended school for a short time. I own a photograph of him at 13. He is smoking his pipe. He is standing in a group of tough and mustached men in front of a loggers' camp. Like them, he is holding a big axe.

Years later, he had become a small businessman and I, his son, was going to school. He made it clear to me that I would go to school for a long time. There was no doubt in his mind that his son had no choice but to become prime minister of Canada. Is it not a great country you live in when a lumberjack may dream of his son becoming prime minister?

My first feeling about Canada was that it was a difficult place for French Canadians. My father's and mother's families were poor. Many uncles and cousins had to emigrate to the United States because there was no work here for them. Some cousins had also left for a big city such as Montreal. Their bosses were always rich and *anglais*, according to what they said.

In order to prepare myself to become the prime minister of Canada, I religiously listened to political discussions at the general store in my village. I accompanied my father to the municipal council meetings, and other grown-ups to political rallies. I was 10. It was time to be sent to boarding school, where, very soon, I abandoned adventure novels to read history books. Since the conquest of Canada by the *anglais* in 1759 on the Plains of Abraham, I was told, our people, our culture, our language and even our religion (the only right and true one) had been threatened. French Canadians were surviving only through a miracle of God.

I also read that, in 1839, a government document called the Durham Report made a complete inventory of our ignorance, our lack of history and our lack of culture. According to the report, the only way to solve the misery of French Canadians was for us to accept English values and let ourselves be assimilated. That's what I read. That's what I was taught.

My father did not want that to happen. As a prime minister, I would protect French Canadians. My father was a man with hope. I read more history books. I learned to recite by heart some great speeches by famous politicians. I felt in my heart that my fellow French Canadians were waiting for me. At the same time, I discovered English literature: the Venerable Bede, *Beowulf*, Chaucer, Shakespeare. With my teacher, I deciphered those texts word by word. Our masters, though, were keeping an eye on us: they were teaching us ancient English literature so we'd know what English people think, but they did not want us to learn too much of the modern language. They were protecting us from assimilation.

At 16 or 17, as a true patriot, and as a future prime minister, I took part in an election rally. At the microphone, I addressed the crowd. The loudspeakers carried my words all over the small town. A cabinet minister and some MPs encouraged me: "Give them hell, kid!" The scene was dramatic. The rally took place in a factory that had been closed some months earlier. It was full of people. Most of them were now out of a job. Suddenly, just because everyone was listening to me, just because they were applauding the shouting kid that I was, and just because I was intoxicated by their attention, I promised them that *we* would reopen the factory if *we* were elected. There was applause, shouts, tears. To get more of that, I announced that *we* would order a huge quantity of the buses they would produce again. None of the politicians told me that I was wrong. Instead I was congratulated for my good speech.

It was my last political appearance. My feeling of guilt for having lied to people was so intense that ever since, I have run away when I hear the word *politics*.

At the beginning of the sixties, I went to study in France, the land of my ancestors. I satisfied my endless curiosity about history and people. I travelled. I made friends with students from many countries. Among my friends were a shepherd's son from Sardinia and a young prince who was enjoying a harem in his desert. I discovered the diversity and complexity of the world; I discovered its richness.

At the same time, French Canadian students were already discussing Quebec separation. The idea of a separate Quebec put sparkles into my friends' eyes.

Their dream of an independent Quebec, where everybody would be cemented by the same culture, did not attract me. To me, separation was uninteresting compared with the world of human richness. Their dream of liberating the French Canadians from oppression was not convincing to me. Freedom is no magic. Proclaiming your independence does not necessarily make you independent or free. To me, they were rejecting the most challenging opportunity: to be partners in a big country in North America, a country that would be the future of the world.

On the other hand, my separatist friends were not all wrong. No doubt, my fellow French Canadians were, in those days, second-class citizens. They were undereducated. They had low self-esteem. They had no vision for the future. By the time I returned to Quebec in 1964, I discovered that a Quiet Revolution had already started. The Roman Catholic Church had lost its grasp on people's consciousness, on the education system, on clergy and politicians. Education for everyone had become a top priority. The government was promoting the idea that Quebecers must become masters of their economy.

I also knew I would not become a prime minister. I had taken another path. I would not realize my father's dream. Too early, perhaps, I had learned that politics uses language to disguise the truth. I was convinced that literature makes a better use of language. And, in the electric atmosphere of the Quiet Revolution, I expressed in my first books my frustration, my despair, my anger, my hope as a young French Canadian. I was labelled a separatist. But I was not one. I never believed that Quebec had to jump out of Canada to solve its problems. When you live in a land of such opportunities, you don't emigrate elsewhere! I strongly wished for change. My books were tools that would help this revolution to come alive.

Demonstrators in the streets clamoured to restrict the use of English. According to them, English signs were masking the "French face" of Montreal. I was living in a quiet all-French-Canadian suburb with trees, birds, squirrels. One evening, I was strolling in downtown Montreal with my daughter. Suddenly, she asked me, "How come I can read at home and I cannot in Montreal?" It took me a few moments to understand that she was unable to read the signs written in English. I decided then that she would learn it. Today, she is travelling the world and communicating with people in many countries, thanks to the 10 or more languages she has mastered while some so-called patriots are still busy counting stop signs, which, according to them, threaten our culture.

Twenty years later, my fellow Quebecers are in control of themselves. Their education level is high, they're successful in world business. Their cultural life is rich and highly innovative. They have a powerful political strength. I believe that if the Quiet Revolution was able to change a medieval Quebec society into a modern one and servants into entrepreneurs, Quebec can accomplish anything it wants within the Canadian federation frame.

When speaking about Canada, am I too idyllic? I'm not ready to fall into our national depression. I'm a Canadian who feels good about this country. I feel this way after spending 30 years here and abroad promoting my French-Canadian culture. Sure, we are encountering some problems. Canada is so huge that Canadians don't know one another. Canada is covered by ignorance about itself. Canadians don't know their country. We don't travel it. We don't know our history, we don't read our literature. Having two languages cuts the reality of the country into parts that sometimes are impermeable.

Too many jurisdictions, services or functions overlap at different levels of government, but that's a structural problem that can be fixed. We also suffer from an intolerable rate of poverty and unemployment. I firmly believe that when we stop comparing the weight of commas in the Constitution, we will be able to create new ways to be successful in the world market and to overcome poverty and unemployment. Although Canada's problems are painful to those who suffer from them, to travellers coming from anywhere abroad, they seem very small.

Last fall, some friends from Israel visited Canada. For some days, they stayed at our place. We kept them rather busy. At the end of the trip, while waiting to leave for the airport, we had a few extra minutes. What to do? We turned on the news channel. There was a hot discussion between farmers from British Columbia, Ontario, Quebec and Nova Scotia. It was a manly discussion. The topic was, Where in Canada is the best apple produced? My friends returned to troubled Israel, where their 17-year-old son was on military duty in a place he was not permitted to name. When they think about Canada, they remember a peaceful country, with hills, lakes and big cities, where the important debate is about who produces the best apples. Since their visit, the debate has moved on a bit. Now it seems that the big question is, Which piece of the apple pie will I get?

Some oppose the fact that Canada has two official languages. They should know that six million people will not stop speaking their own mother tongue. The greatest privilege I have experienced was to become a father. The second one was certainly to learn a second language. For a developed country, having two official languages should be considered a blessing! What a fertile condition. What an advantageous position, to be at a crossroad where two great world cultures meet and dialogue with their varying knowledge, heritage and connections in business, culture and politics. If universities were living in the real world, they would refuse to grant a diploma without the knowledge of at least two languages. What a gift it would be for our kids and for the country!

Like my ancestors, who arrived here in 1657, like my grandfather, like my father, I'm a Canadian. I come from a village where land was important—it's the only thing you really own and that's what you'll leave to your children. From a hill in that village, I would watch the train that I knew had been crossing the country for many days. The small local factory sold products to Vancouver. I was fascinated reading that name on the boxes. I knew Vancouver was incredibly far away. When I'd hear the manager talking to "them" in Vancouver, speaking in a language I did not know, it was magical. I was amazed to live in one of the biggest countries in the world, spread between three seas.

I am still thrilled by the immensity of our country. I hate frontiers, customs, fences, barriers. How great it is to enter so many regions without having to show a passport! My separatist friends show a fascination for small countries—Sweden, Lithuania, Holland, Costa Rica. Deep in their hearts, I'm sure they share with me the special relationship that other Canadians entertain with vastness. This giant country might be too big for small minds.

I belong to Quebec, as I belong to my family. But I believe that the future of Quebec lies in being a dynamic part of a large, powerful, productive and caring Canada. I also believe that the future of Canada is to have a part in the destiny of Quebec. With all our differences, and because of them, Canadians can make such a dream come true.

This place must be attractive: half of the world wants to immigrate here. The bottom line is that we are all immigrants—Inuit, Indians, French, English, German, Pakistanis—we all share a common experience. All of us have gone through a failure. The French failed in their project of a New France. The English failed in their business of assimilating the French. The Indians failed in getting rid of all of us. The Inuit probably failed somewhere in their continent of origin before moving here. All the immigrants that came afterward probably failed somehow and wished to start all over. On the basis of failure, would it not be a great idea if we all decided to make Canada work better?

I was a very young playwright when Jean Gascon, then the artistic director of the Stratford Festival, shared this advice with me: "If you bring many different people together, give them a goal and help them work together, some marvellous result will come out." It was quite a privilege to be educated that way.

I'm writing these notes along the Richelieu River, in Quebec. Below my room, more than 300 years ago, was a fort that was built by the French. On this same spot, in 1775, Roman Catholic French Canadians, Protestant Loyalists, businessmen, farmers, soldiers, Mohawks, Germans and Swiss fought together against the American invaders. Later, Canadians of all origins lost their lives during the First and Second World Wars. Thus was woven the fabric of Canada, whose invisible threads are still between us—very strong.

Sometimes Canadians complain that our politicians are weak. Thank God they are! I congratulate them for being so. Canadians are wise to select them that way. Too many countries suffer with strong politicians. Having elected weak politicians, Canadians know they must not rely on them. Canadians must take care of their own business. They must get involved. They themselves must be responsible. To be responsible is to be free.

The Canadian external policy is a subject often discussed in intellectual circles. I hear that it is inconsistent, low profile, uncommitted, ambivalent—in a word, bleak. Again I say, Thank God! Our external policy has made Canada a friend of all. Everybody knows that a Canadian passport opens most doors. Even the separatist Quebeckers want it!

Canada is a dream in the making. In most other countries, people have a common origin, the same history, a single religion, one language.

Canadians don't have many things in common. That's why we have a lot to share. Sharing: that's what a confederation is about. We are still in the process of inventing our country. Canada is able to become the country the whole planet will look up to when it is time to move away from tribalism and embrace the 21st century. Canada can be the country where the future will find the favourable conditions to materialize.

I'm more comfortable in a grand dream like Canada than in a narrow park where everybody speaks like me, eats like me, has a pale face like mine, reads the same books and where everybody feels threatened by anybody who is not like me.

Canada is a dream. Not many politicians have the gift of dreaming any more, but I want to live that dream and make it real. The future of Canadians lies in pursuing that dream. The future of Quebec is to be part of that dream.

Jamaican Dreams

"I vowed then I would visit my family frequently. And I meant it. But once again the demands of my own life got in the way, and I forgot my vow."

I have lived in this country for half of my life. I came here a Jamaican. But with each passing year I have become more and more Canadian, less and less Jamaican. If you were to ask me, I would probably say I am now mostly Canadian. That is how I see myself, most of the time. But my past has a way of tripping me up. One night about four years ago, I had a worrisome dream. I dreamed that all my teeth had fallen out.

My friend, born and raised in Canada, blamed my dream on indigestion. "Upset stomach," she declared. "Gives you nightmares." My husband, also raised in Canada, had another explanation: "You forgot to brush your teeth before going to bed. That's what your subconscious was trying to tell you." I laughed out loud, not bothering to remind him that I never forget to brush my teeth before going to bed.

A feeling of unease gnawed at me.

I called Pat, my older sister, who also lives in Toronto. My sister has managed to become a Canadian without rejecting Jamaican traditions, cures and dream interpretations. "I dreamed that my teeth fell out," I told her.

"Uh-oh," she said. "You know that means death."

"Well, I know it means death if you live in Jamaica. But does it mean the same if you live in Canada?" I made a feeble attempt at laughter. My sister didn't laugh back. I hung up and reminded myself that the last time my sister dreamed about fish, no one she knew became pregnant. It's a Jamaican belief that if you dream of fish, someone you know will get pregnant.

I tried to keep my thoughts away from the dream, but my mind kept shifting gears on its own. I called my sister again: "You heard from home?"

"Not since Momma phoned," she replied. "That was three weeks ago. She sounded great, and said everyone was fine. Try not to worry yourself."

If I were as Canadian as I claimed, if I had really dismissed those Jamaican beliefs, I would have dropped the whole thing right then. But I didn't. As I folded the laundry, another thought popped into my head. Why had our mother phoned? She had only phoned me once in all the time I'd been in Canada. That was right after she received my letter telling her I was pregnant with my first child. My mother didn't even have a telephone in her house. She lived on top of a hill outside the town, and the telephone company had said it was "not economically feasible" for them to run a line that far. So why had my mother walked all the way to town to call us? She told Pat she had tried to reach me first, but I was out. Just to say everything was fine? Or had she also been dreaming of death?

Maybe it's time to go home, I thought. But then, the automatic reply: you can't afford to. They need you at work. It's just cost a thousand dollars to fix the car. Now the insurance is due.

It didn't occur to me to pay for the trip with my credit card. Mounting debts have the same effect on me as a cross reputedly has on a vampire. This problem had once been diagnosed by a friend as an immigrant condition. "You don't feel secure enough to go heavily into debt," she said knowingly.

"Nonsense," I replied. "I took out a mortgage. I bought a car. Now that's a lot of debt."

But it just didn't feel right to leave for Jamaica then. For one thing, you can't show up in your hometown with your "two empty hands"—when you go home you feel compelled to bring gifts for every relative, friend, and kindly neighbour. Going home is not as simple as it sounds. Every logical bone in my body said there was no reason to visit Jamaica. But, like the atheist who half-believes in God at night, I was unable to shake the dream of my teeth falling out: What if the Jamaican interpretation of my dream was a warning from up above?

An unbidden memory kept creeping to the edges of my mind. Another time, another dream, another justification for not going home. Something terrible had happened.

The person at the heart of that memory was Ken, my mother's younger cousin. He was tall, handsome and stylish. He was also a bright, well-read man who challenged me with provocative arguments. Ken told me wonderful stories about our multiracial, multiclass, multireligious family. With a hint of pride and great relish, he would divulge the details of ancient family scandals. He would give a hilarious twist to tales our family elders had tried so hard to keep secret.

There was no question that of all the people in our huge family conglomerate, Ken and I were each other's favourite. One anecdote said Ken had fallen in love with me when I was barely 2 and he was 21. It happened the night he accidentally got me drunk by leaving his wineglass within my reach. Ken loved to tell the story of the drunken 2-year-old who staggered around repeating something that sounded suspiciously like a Jamaican cussword.

As I grew older, there seemed another reason why Ken and I got along so well. We were both oddities in our family. Ken belonged to the mostly Chinese branch of the family, but unlike his parents and many of his siblings, he had light-brown hair streaked with blond. I too differed from my parents and siblings. I had brown hair streaked with a coppery red. Our looks were easily explained as a product of our extended family's racial confusion. But we stood out nonetheless.

Ken and I shared something else. We dared to dream of things way beyond the scope of our small-town upbringing. We dared to ask questions of things that current wisdom deemed unquestionable. Together we would debate politics, the authenticity of the Bible, even the existence of God. Together we dreamed of travelling the unknown of foreign lands, of writing the great family chronicle.

Birthdays always brought a special gift from Ken. My first camera. My first set of dangling gold earrings. My first pair of sling-back shoes with a matching handbag, both in yellow patent leather.

But on my fifteenth birthday, Ken showed up mysteriously empty-handed. "Get dressed," he said. "We're going into town." And so we did. He pulled up in front of the local branch of the Royal Bank of Canada in nearby Mandeville. Once inside the doors, Ken stopped and turned to me. "In a couple of months you will be graduating from high school," he said. "Every young lady should have a bank account." Then he entered the bank manager's office and started an account in my name. Initial deposit: $1,000. It was a small fortune, as the Jamaican dollar in the late sixties was worth about $1.25 (U.S.). Around Ken I had always been a chatterbox, but now I was silent. My gratitude choked me up.

"Use your money wisely," was all Ken said as we left the bank.

Suddenly, the day seemed shiny and bright with promise. To a 15-year-old girl feeling trapped in a small town, a thousand dollars buys a lot of hope. And now my dreams of going abroad to study didn't seem so impossible.

I brought that money, plus interest, with me when I left for Canada in 1974. It would help send me to journalism school at Ryerson.

I left Ken behind in Jamaica with a promise that I would "do something meaningful" with my life. I made another solemn promise: that I would return to help him write that book about "our crazy family."

I would, to some extent, keep the first promise to Ken. I got my degree and became a television news reporter with the CBC. I did voluntary work on behalf of immigrant and minority children. But the second promise lay in the recesses of my mind, almost forgotten. I had originally planned to go home and work on the book with Ken right after graduation. But schooling expenses had worn me out. The CBC job offer came just in time.

It seemed there was always a commitment, always an expense preventing me from going home to keep my second promise. And, to tell the truth, I was getting caught up in my own obligations. I had already started a family. I thought less and less about Ken.

Then, one day while I was preparing a story for the late news, the phone rang. It was my husband.

"Call your sister in Jamaica," he said. "Something about Ken."

I called right away. "What about Ken?"

"He's sick. All of a sudden, he lost the use of his legs. The doctors say they've never seen anything like it."

I was in Jamaica within two days. The trip took all my savings, but that didn't matter at all. By the time I got there, Ken had been moved to the University Hospital in Kingston. He squinted at me as I approached his bed in the intensive care ward. I rushed to hug him. He didn't hug back. Within minutes I realized he had lost the use of his arms too. "Scratch the top of my head for me," he asked in a weak voice. I scratched his head and dampened his soft hair with my tears. Huge, unstoppable tears that burned my eyes and cheeks.

Ken had never been sick in all the time I'd known him. Or perhaps he had, but he'd never let me see him when he was ill. He was the most fiercely independent person I had ever met. I knew without being told that Ken would sooner die than not be able to care for himself. These thoughts went around and around, even as I held Ken's useless hand between my own hands.

The doctors had still not diagnosed his illness. But whatever it was, this disease moved swiftly, mercilessly.

Then, one week later, Ken started to improve. He was still in bed, but he could sit up. His colour came back. He spoke clearly now. His sisters and brothers who had flown home from other countries were delighted with the improvement. There were so many other relatives around that I felt sure Ken wouldn't miss me if I returned to Toronto.

As I said goodbye, I promised Ken I'd return. But this time I put a deadline on it: six months, a year at most.

I told Ken I was sorry I couldn't afford to stay. He remarked, without bitterness, that "now would have been perfect. I'm not going anywhere in this condition."

But he did. Ken did not last a year. He didn't even last six months.

On a Sunday morning in the spring, the phone rang. It was Ken's sister Glenna, who had stood with me beside Ken's hospital bed.

"Hya?" she called me by my Jamaican pet name in her unmistakably Jamaican lilt.

"Don't say anything, Glenna," I whispered. "I don't want to hear."

"I'm really sorry," was all she said.

"I promised to go back, Glenna. I thought we had time." I was babbling on, but unable to cry.

I had a lot of time for memories on that four-hour flight to Kingston. Sweet memories of Ken. But one memory belonged to a much more recent past. A memory of a dream I'd had just one week earlier. In that dream, I was in my mother's garden. I was picking green fruit from my mother's orange tree and digging up yams from the ground. Jamaicans will tell you that such a dream warns of great disappointment and death. My sophisticated Canadian self had told me to ignore it.

The funeral went the way of Jamaican funerals. People wore their most dignified black or purple clothes. Everywhere you looked, there were somber, tear-stained faces. A priest stood at the altar and said wonderful things about the "dearly departed," in this case a man he barely knew, since Ken never went to church.

At a get-together after the funeral, people swapped warm memories of Ken's life, and shared dreams that had foretold Ken's death. I could hardly bear to share my memories, and I didn't share my dreams. I returned to Toronto racked with guilt.

Then, one day, a chat with a neighbour turned into a discussion about what it means to live so far from your family. My neighbour had come to Canada from Italy many years before. Year after year, she saved a bit of money toward her planned trip home. Finally, she had saved enough. She could hardly wait to see her parents. But just two weeks before her planned visit, the phone rang. Her mother was dead.

"It is the curse of being an immigrant," said a Scottish-born neighbour who had joined us. "You never have enough money to go home. Then someone dies and somehow you find the money. I have been home only twice. Each time it was to bury somebody."

I vowed then I would visit my family frequently. And I meant it. But once again the demands of my own life got in the way, and I forgot my vow.

Then, several years later, came the dream about losing teeth.

I told myself I didn't really believe in dreams. I told myself the dream had only served to remind me of my promise to return home. Still, I took some overdue vacation, booked a flight, and started packing. Whatever was scarce in Jamaica could be found in my bulging suitcases: rice, soap powder, garlic, running shoes, money.

Once there, I scrutinized everyone with a worried eye. My mother seemed a little shorter, a little older, her hair a little more grey. But her smooth brown skin was radiant, and she seemed strong and healthy. My stepfather looked exactly the way I had left him. His dark-brown face seemed to glow with good health. No one seemed ill or in danger of imminent death. It was wonderful to be home.

By the time I returned to Toronto, the bad dream was forgotten. I was so broke I didn't even have enough money to buy gas for my car. But going home had recharged me. My mother, as usual, had loved and inspired me.

They say superstition is born from people's deepest fears. Bad dreams, I think, must come from the same place. My deepest fear about my loved ones in Jamaica is that they will die suddenly, giving me no opportunity to say goodbye, no opportunity to fully repay debts of kindness. Perhaps that is why today, even while I shrug off many of the beliefs with which I was raised, there are some dreams that have the power to shake up my new life and remind me of the life I left behind.

These days, I have started to see the dreams in a different light. I see now they give me an occasion to linger awhile in memories of the life I left behind. They remind me to cherish the people and places in my younger life who helped make me what I am. And they remind me to write home more often.

ABOUT THE AUTHORS

Margaret ATWOOD (1939–) spent much of her childhood in the north. Apart from her writing, she is active as a spokesperson for human rights and the environment.

Janice McCurdy BANIGAN (1942–) is a writer specializing in social, civil-rights, and health-related issues. She is working on a memoir about growing up black in Ontario.

Arthur BLACK (1943–) is host of the CBC Radio show *Basic Black* and has published several books—*That Old Black Magic, Back to Black*, and *Arthur! Arthur!*

Rose BORRIS (1932–) grew up in rural New Brunswick and moved to Toronto in the 1950s to run a rooming house. Her son featured her in his films *Rose's House* and *Alligator Shoes*.

Born in Toronto, **Harry BRUCE** (1934–) fulfilled his parents' dreams of returning to Nova Scotia. His essays have appeared in *Each Minute As It Flies* and *Movin' East*.

Born and raised in Quebec, **Roch CARRIER** (1937–) recently won the Leacock Medal for Humour for *Prayers of a Very Wise Child*.

Victoria CROSS is a writer from Windsor, Ontario.

Moira FARR (1958–) has worked as editor of *This Magazine* and is now an editor of *Equinox*.

Timothy FINDLEY (1930–) lives in the village of Cannington, Ontario. His novels include *The Wars, Famous Last Words, Headhunter*, and *Not Wanted on the Voyage*.

Adrian FORSYTH (1951–) has done extensive field work around the world, particularly on tropical ecosystems. His books include *The Nature of Birds, Journey through a Tropical Jungle*, and *A Natural History of Sex*.

Ursula FRANKLIN (1921–) was born in Munich, Germany, and gained her Ph.D. in experimental physics in 1948. The author of many articles and books on the social history of technology, she is a committed feminist and peace activist.

Josh FREED (1949–) writes a column for the *Montreal Gazette*, in addition to making documentary films for CBC TV and PBS. His books include *Moonwebs*, the *Anglo Guide to Survival in Québec*, and *Sign Language and Other Tales of Montreal Wildlife*.

Robert FULFORD (1932–) was editor of *Saturday Night* for almost 20 years. Self-educated, he started his career as a copy boy in 1949.

Carol GEDDES is a member of the Tlingit Nation, from the Yukon. She has made several films, including *Doctor, Lawyer, Indian Chief*, a National Film Board production about native women.

Jacinta GOVEAS (1957–) grew up in Pakistan and now works in Toronto's immigrant and refugee community.

Hugh GRAHAM (1951–) is a Toronto writer who is currently working on a collection of essays.

Ray GUY (1939–) is a writer, humorist (as such, a winner of the Leacock Medal), and political commentator from St. John's, Newfoundland.

Michael IGNATIEFF (1947–) works in Britain as a television commentator and columnist for *The Observer*. His books include *Asya*, *Scar Tissue*, and *Blood and Belonging: Journeys into the New Nationalism*.

Jay INGRAM (1945–), the winner of several Canadian Science Writers' Awards, is the author of a number of books, including *Twins: An Amazing Investigation*, *Real Live Science*, and *Talk Talk Talk*.

Best known as a poet, **Paulette JILES** (1943–) came to Canada in 1969. Her book *Celestial Navigation* won the Governor General's Award in 1985.

Janice Kulyk KEEFER (1952–) is a novelist, teacher, and short-story writer who lives in Eden Mills, Ontario. Her books include *Travelling Ladies*, *Rest Harrow*, and *Constellations*.

Alan S. KESSELHEIM (1952–) has taken two 14-month canoe trips through northern Canada, and after each trip he wrote a book. The most recent is *Water and Sky*.

Deborah LEE (1950–) was born in Victoria, B.C., but has lived in various parts of Canada, the U.S., and Japan. Her work has appeared in *Golf*, the *Ellery Queen Mystery Magazine*, and *Barbed Lyres*.

A.R.M. LOWER (1889–1988) was a historian whose *Colony to Nation*, published in 1946, explores a sense of national community in Canada.

Born in Winnipeg, **Tanis MacDONALD** (1962–) works as a teacher, poet, and AIDS activist.

Jil McINTOSH (1959–) is a freelance writer who contributes to several antique-car publications in Canada and the U.S. She also writes romance novels under a pseudonym.

Catherine MECKES (1942–) is a graduate of the journalism program at Ryerson Polytechnic University in Toronto. She now works as a freelance writer.

Rohinton MISTRY (1952–) grew up in Bombay and moved to Canada in 1975. His *Tales from Firozsha Baag* and the novel *Such a Long Journey* garnered him a significant reputation.

Born in Weyburn, Saskatchewan, **William Ormond MITCHELL** (1914–) is best known for the novel *Who Has Seen the Wind*. He has also written plays, including *Jake and the Kid*.

Alice MUNRO (1931–) is famous for her short stories, which demonstrate a rare ability to capture character and situation. Her most recent collection is *Friend of My Youth*.

Susan MUSGRAVE (1951–) is a confirmed Vancouver Islander whose books include the poetry collections *Forcing the Narcissus* and *The Embalmer's Art* and the journalism collections *Great Musgrave* and *Musgrave Landing*.

Naheed MUSTAFA (1970–) studied journalism at Ryerson Polytechnic University in Toronto and is currently working as a freelance writer in Pakistan.

Anna NIELSEN is a freelance writer from Burlington, Ontario.

Cynthia REYES is a CBC television reporter living in Toronto.

Raised on Montreal's St. Urbain Street, **Mordecai RICHLER** (1931–) is well known for his journalism as well as his fiction. His most recent novel is *Solomon Gursky Was Here*.

Pat STEPHENS (1950–) is a Toronto freelance artist who says she "derives only a precarious income from her chosen career."

The *Royal Bank Letter* appears every month with an anonymous essay in the classic style. It has been edited since 1979 by **Robert STEWART** (1938–), who lives in Montreal.

Dan STRICKLAND (1942–) is chief park naturalist in Ontario's Algonquin Park. For 20 years he has written a monthly essay in the park newsletter, "The Raven."

David SUZUKI (1936–) is the host of CBC's *The Nature of Things*. His autobiography, *Metamorphosis: Stages in a Life*, appeared in 1987.

Drew Hayden TAYLOR (1962–) grew up on the Curve Lake Ojibway Reserve near Peterborough, Ontario. His plays include *Toronto at Dreamer's Rock*, *Education Is Our Right*, and *The Bootlegger Blues*.

Sydell WAXMAN (1944–) is a teacher, author, and speaker who specializes in women of the last century. She is currently writing a biography of Canada's first female doctor, Emily Stowe.

Tom WAYMAN (1945–) is a teacher of creative writing at the Kootenay School of Writing in British Columbia. His essays are collected in the book *Inside Job*.

Rudy WIEBE (1934–) was born in Saskatchewan and teaches at the University of Alberta. His novels include *The Temptations of Big Bear*, which won the Governor General's Award in 1973, *The Scorched-Wood People, and A Discovery of Strangers*.

ACKNOWLEDGMENTS

Permission to reprint copyrighted material is gratefully acknowledged. Every reasonable effort has been made to contact the people who hold copyright on material that appears in this volume. Any information that enables the publisher to rectify any error or omission will be welcomed.

The epigraph is from *Colony to Nation* by A.R.M. Lower. Used by permission of the Canadian Publishers, McClelland & Stewart, Toronto. **Pretty like a White Boy** by Drew Hayden Taylor appeared originally in *This Magazine*, August 1991. Reprinted, by permission of the author, from *An Anthology of Canadian Native Literature in English*, edited by Daniel David Moses and Terry Goldie (Oxford University Press, 1992). Copyright © Drew Hayden Taylor. **Prairie Summer** by W.O. Mitchell: Reprinted from the *Imperial Oil Review*, summer 1993, by permission of the author. **All Quiet on the Northern Front** by Josh Freed: Reprinted, by permission of the author, from *Sign Language and Other Tales of Montreal Wildlife* by Josh Freed, Vehicule Press, Montreal. **When Jannies Visited** by Ray Guy first appeared in *Canadian Geographic*, November–December 1993. Reprinted by permission of the author. **The Mothers of Confederation** by Sydell Waxman: Reprinted from *The Beaver* magazine, October–November 1992, by permission of the author. **Life and Death in Ontario County** by Hugh Graham: Reprinted from *The Idler*, November 1990, by permission of the author. **The Misery Index** by Arthur Black: Copyright © Basic Black Inc. Reprinted from *Back to Black*, by Arthur Black: by permission of the author. **The Lesson of Canadian Geography** originally appeared in *Canada: A Landscape Portrait* by Janis Kraulis (Hurtig). Reprinted by permission of the author, Robert Fulford. **Shoot That Puck, Grab That Briefcase** by Harry Bruce: Copyright © Harry Bruce, from *Movin' East*, reprinted by arrangement with Bella Pomer Agency Inc. **Hi-Tech Conception Ignores Kids' Rights** by Jil McIntosh: Reprinted from *The Toronto Star*, January 6, 1994, by permission of the author. **Our Home and Racist Land** by Janice McCurdy Banigan: Reprinted from *This Magazine*, June–July 1993, by permission of the author. **Hoard Money and Food, but Never Joy** by Anna Nielsen: Reprinted from *The Globe and Mail*, February 9, 1993. **On Being Creatively Homeless** by Pat Stephens: Reprinted from *The Toronto Star*, January 31, 1994, by permission of the author. **The Poverty of Affluence** by Jacinta Goveas: Reprinted, by permission of the author, from *The Toronto Star*, February 14, 1993. **My Body Is My Own Business** by Naheed Mustafa: Reprinted from *The Globe and Mail*, June 29, 1993, by permission of the author. **Wearing a Uniform of Oppression** by Catherine Meckes: Reprinted from *The Globe and Mail*, July 5, 1993, by permission of the author. **What Kind of Men Are These?** by Michael Ignatieff: Reprinted from *The Globe and Mail*, May 1, 1993, by permission of *The Observer* (London). **The Evolution of the Teddy Bear** by Jay Ingram: From *The Science of Everyday Life*. Copyright © Jay Ingram, 1989. Reprinted by permission of Penguin Books Canada Limited. **A Walk on the Wild Side** by Alice Munro: Copyright © 1989 by Alice Munro. Reprinted by arrangement with Virginia Barber Agency, Inc. **No New Worlds** by Adrian Forsyth: Reprinted from *Equinox* no. 64 (July–August 1992) by permission of the author. **Hardball** by Margaret Atwood © 1992 O.W. Toad Ltd. Reprinted from *Good Bones* by permission of Coach House Press. **The Real World of Technology** by Ursula Franklin: Massey Lectures text reprinted in revised form by permission of the author. **The Moosehide Gloves** by Alan S. Kesselheim: Reprinted from *Up Here*, September–October 1989, by permission of the author and of *Up Here/Life in Canada's North*. **It's Yer Genuwine High-Tech** by Dan Strickland appeared originally in "The Raven," the newsletter of Algonquin Park, vol. 33, no. 7 (August 6, 1992). Reprinted from *The Best of The Raven*, 1994, by permission of the author and of the Friends of Algonquin Park, Box 248, Whitney, Ontario K0J 2M0. **Twenty-five Dollars and a T-4 Slip** by Susan Musgrave: Reprinted from *Great Musgrave*, published by Prentice-Hall Canada. **Cosmo Girls** by Moira Farr: Reprinted from *What!* no. 25 (November–December 1990), by permission of the author. **Absent-Minded People** by Deborah Lee: Reprinted from the Vancouver *Sun*, April 23, 1993, by permission of the author. **At a Loss for Words** by Rose Borris with Paulette Jiles: Reprinted from *Saturday Night* magazine, June 1988, by permission of Paulette Jiles. **Margaret Laurence: In Memory** by Timothy Findley: Reprinted from *The New Morningside Papers* by permission of the author. Copyright © 1987 Pebble Productions Inc. **The Importance of Teaching** by Robert Stewart: Reprinted from the *Royal Bank Letter* 70, no. 5 (September–October 1989) by permission of the author. **A House without Books** by Tom Wayman: Reprinted from *A Country Not Considered* by Tom Wayman, published by the House of Anansi in association with Stoddart Publishing Co. Limited. Reprinted by permission of the author and of Stoddart Publishing Co., Don Mills, Ontario. **From Batman, through G.A. Henty, to *All Quiet on the Western Front*** by Mordecai Richler: Reprinted from *Broadsides: Reviews and Opinions*. Copyright © Mordecai Richler, 1990. Reprinted by permission of Penguin Books Canada Limited. **Growing Up Native** by Carol Geddes: Reprinted from *Homemaker's Magazine*, October 1990, by permission of the author and of *Homemaker's Magazine*. **Another Country** by Janice Kulyk Keefer was originally broadcast on CBC Radio. Reprinted from *Canadian Literature* no. 120 (spring 1989) by permission of the author. **Social Studies** by Tanis MacDonald first appeared in *Prairie Fire*, August 1992, and was a finalist for a Western Magazine Award. Reprinted by permission of the author. **Bags of Golden Promises: Good Food, Family, Friends** by Victoria Cross: Reprinted from *The Globe and Mail*, February 10, 1994. **Bear Spirit in a Strange Land** by Rudy Wiebe: Reprinted from *A Voice in the Land*, NeWest Publishers, 1981, by permission of the author. **Describing Circles** by Rohinton Mistry: Copyright © 1990 Rohinton Mistry. Reprinted by permission of the author. **Canada Is a Grand Dream** by Roch Carrier: Reprinted from *Canadian Living*, September 1992, by permission of the author. **Jamaican Dreams** by Cynthia Reyes: Reprinted from *Toronto Life*, December 1992.

ℓ ART AND PHOTOGRAPHS

P. 11 Norman Piluke/Tony Stone Images. **P. 37** Glenbow Archives, Calgary, Alberta (NC-43-13). **P. 61** A.Y. Jackson (1882–1974), *Hills, Killarney, Ontario (Nellie Lake)*, ca. 1933, oil on canvas, 77.3 x 81.7 cm; McMichael Canadian Art Collection, gift of Mr. S. Walter Stewart, 1968.8.28. **P. 65** Canapress Photo Service (Fred Chartrand). **P. 97** © Michael Melford/The Image Bank Canada. **P. 130** Beadwork by Julie Lacorne; photo by Tessa Macintosh, Government of the Northwest Territories. **P. 137** Andrew Sacks/Tony Stone Images. **P. 146** By permission of *Cosmopolitan* Magazine. **P. 191** © Toby Molenaar/The Image Bank Canada. **P. 216** O.B. Buell/National Archives of Canada/C-0001873.